WILLIAM BLAKE

LONGMAN CRITICAL READERS

General Editor:
STAN SMITH, Professor of English, University of Dundee

WILLIAM BLAKE

Edited and Introduced by

JOHN LUCAS

LONGMAN
LONDON AND NEW YORK

Addison Wesley Longman Limited
Edinburgh Gate
Harlow
Essex CM20 2JE
United Kingdom
and Associated Companies throughout the world.

Published in the United States of America
by Addison Wesley Longman, New York.

First published 1998

ISBN   0 582–23711–4 CSD
       0 582–23710–6 PPR

British Library Cataloguing-in-Publication Data

A catalogue record for this book is available from the British Library

Library of Congress Cataloging-in-Publication Data

Lucas, John, 1937–
    William Blake / edited and introduced by John Lucas.
       p.   cm. — (Longman critical readers)
    Includes bibliographical references and index.
    ISBN 0–582–23711–4 (ppr). — ISBN 0–582–23710–6 (csd)
    1. Blake, William, 1757–1827—Criticism and interpretation.
    I. Title.   II. Series.
    PR4147.L83   1998   97–42999
    821'.7—dc21   CIP

Set by 35 in $9\frac{1}{2}/11\frac{1}{2}$ pt Palatino
Produced by Addison Wesley Longman Singapore (Pte) Ltd.,
Printed in Singapore

Contents

General Editors' Preface

The outlines of contemporary critical theory are now often taught as a standard feature of a degree in literary studies. The development of particular theories has seen a thorough transformation of literary criticism. For example, Marxist and Foucauldian theories have revolutionised Shakespeare studies, and 'deconstruction' has led to a complete reassessment of Romantic poetry. Feminist criticism has left scarcely any period of literature unaffected by its searching critiques. Teachers of literary studies can no longer fall back on a standardised, received methodology.

Lecturers and teachers are now urgently looking for guidance in a rapidly changing critical environment. They need help in understanding the latest revisions in literary theory, and especially in grasping the practical effects of the new theories in the form of theoretically sensitised new readings. A number of volumes in the series anthologise important essays on particular theories. However, in order to grasp the full implications and possible uses of particular theories it is essential to see them put to work. This series provides substantial volumes of new readings, presented in an accessible form and with a significant amount of editorial guidance.

Each volume includes a substantial introduction which explores the theoretical issues and conflicts embodied in the essays selected and locates areas of disagreement between positions. The pluralism of theories has to be put on the agenda of literary studies. We can no longer pretend that we all tacitly accept the same practices in literary studies. Neither is a *laissez-faire* attitude any longer tenable. Literature departments need to go beyond the mere toleration of theoretical differences: it is not enough merely to agree to differ; they need actually to 'stage' the differences openly. The volumes in this series all attempt to dramatise the differences, not necessarily with a view to resolving them but in order to foreground the choices presented by different theories or to argue for a particular route through the impasses the differences present.

The theory 'revolution' has had real effects. It has loosened the grip of traditional empiricist and romantic assumptions about language and literature. It is not always clear what is being proposed as the new agenda for literary studies, and indeed the very notion of 'literature' is questioned by the post-structuralist strain in theory. However, the uncertainties and obscurities of contemporary theories appear much less worrying when we see what the best critics have been able to do with them in practice. This series aims to disseminate the best of recent criticism and to show that it is possible to re-read the canonical texts of literature in new and challenging ways.

RAMAN SELDEN AND STAN SMITH

The Publishers and fellow Series Editor regret to record that Raman Selden died after a short illness in May 1991 at the age of fifty-three. Ray Selden was a fine scholar and a lovely man. All those he has worked with will remember him with much affection and respect.

Acknowledgements

The Publishers are grateful to the following for permission to reproduce copyright material:

The Trustees of Boston University for the article 'Female Subjectivity and the Desire of Reading In(to) Blake's *Book of Thel*' by Gerda S. Norvig from *Studies in Romanticism*, vol. 34, no. 2, 1995; Cambridge University Press and Mrs Dorothy Thompson for the essay 'The Divine Image' from *Witness against the beast: William Blake and the Moral Law* by E. P. Thompson (1993); Duke University Press for 'Blake, Women and Sexuality' by Brenda Webster in *Blake and the Argument of Method* (ed) Miller et al. Copyright © 1987, Duke University Press; Gill & Macmillan Ltd, Dublin for the extract 'Producers and Devourers' from *Blake in Context* by Stewart Crehan; Oxford University Press for an extract from *Dangerous Enthusiasm: William Blake and the Culture of Radicalism in the 1790's* by John Mee (1992), 3–11. © John Mee 1992; Princeton University Press for the essay 'Infinite London' from *Blake, Prophet Against Empire* by David Erdman. Copyright © 1977 by PUP; Routledge and the author, Susan Matthews for '*Jerusalem* and Nationalism' from *Beyond Romanticism* (ed.) Stephen Copley and John Whale (Routledge, 1992); the Editor of *Style* for the article 'Who Didn't Kill Blake's Fly: Moral Law and the Rule of Grammar in "Songs of Experience"' by Michael Simpson (originally appeared in *Style*, vol. 30, no. 2 (Summer 1996), 220–40; Thames & Hudson Ltd for the essay 'A New Mode of Printing' from *William Blake* by Kathleen Raine (1970); Yale University Press for extracts from Ch. 3 'A Blake Dictionary' from *The Political Theory of Painting From Reynolds To Hazlitt* by John Barrell (London, 1986).

We are also grateful to the British Museum for reproduction photographs of *Songs of Innocence*, 1789, Title-page; *Songs of Innocence*, 1789, Frontispiece; *Songs of Experience*, 1789–94, Title-page.

For Lyndy Abraham and Michael Wilding

1 Introduction

'Mad' Blake

When William Blake died in 1827, he was a largely unknown figure. As an artist and engraver he had some younger admirers, but few cared for, or were even aware of, his poetry. The diarist and friend of writers, Henry Crabb Robinson, paid Blake several visits in the poet's last years and thought him a 'remarkable man. Shall I call him artist or genius – or mystic – or madman?'[1] These questions continue to haunt students of Blake. For some, he is best thought of as a mystic-cum-genius whose preoccupations with religious matters place him in the tradition of the inspired prophet or seer, his visions transmitted through poems and visual images which, he told Crabb Robinson, had been granted him by 'The Spirit'. He also told Crabb Robinson that the Spirit had commanded him ' "Blake, be an artist and nothing else. In this there is felicity." His eye,' Crabb Robinson recalls, 'glistened when he spoke of the joy of devoting himself solely to divine art. . . . Blake said: "I should be sorry if I had any earthly fame, for whatever natural glory a man has is so much detracted from his spiritual glory. I wish to do nothing for profit. I wish to live for art. I want nothing whatever. I am quite happy." '

This claim to happiness is addressed by Yeats, in an essay of 1900, where he contrasts Blake with that other great Romantic visionary, Shelley. Yeats writes:

> In ancient times, it seems to me that Blake, who for all his protest was glad to be alive, and ever spoke of his gladness, would have worshipped in some chapel of the Sun, but that Shelley, who hated life because he sought 'more in life than any understood,' would have wandered, lost in a ceaseless reverie, in some chapel of the Star of infinite desire.[2]

By the time Yeats wrote that essay, Shelley's reputation, previously so high, had dipped far down. Blake's by contrast was on the rise.

1

The process of recovery, even of rediscovery, was most importantly signalled by the publication in 1863 of Alexander Gilchrist's *Life*, although the early championing of Blake by Carlyle and later by the Rossetti brothers undoubtedly helped. Then in the 1890s Yeats undertook with a young painter poet Edwin J. Ellis an edition of *The Works of Blake, Poetic, Symbolic and Critical*, published in three volumes in 1893. Blake is here credited with Irish ancestry and Yeats undoubtedly saw in the English poet a spiritual predecessor. Blake was, he said, 'a symbolist who had to invent his symbols. . . . He was a man crying out for a mythology, and trying to make one because he could not find one to his hand.' This sounds very like W. B. Yeats.

But then it could be said that Blake has endlessly been made over into the image of those who write about him. He becomes his admirers. This is no doubt true of all great writers and artists, but it is especially true of Blake because his work – allegorical, symbolic, visionary, call it what you will – is capable of bearing a host of different interpretations. Such work can be made to mean whatever you want it to mean, the more so as much of it is not merely symbolic but also difficult to the point of opacity. Interpreting Blake has been for some a lifetime's effort. For others, the study of Blake is as demanding and perhaps obsessive an exercise as 'proving' that Marlowe (or Bacon or whoever) wrote Shakespeare's plays or that the key to all mythologies can be disinterred from the accretions of history. And, of course, there are those for whom Blake is himself a case study, a 'madman', to use Crabb Robinson's term, someone who can best be understood in terms made available by twentieth-century psychology or, even, psychiatry. Many years ago now Allan Rodway argued that Blake can only be adequately accounted for if we assume 'him to be – or to have imagined himself into the world of – a rare psychological type, the intuitive introvert *to whom the inner world of the imagination is more vivid and actual than the outer world*' [Rodway's italics].[3] In an essay included in the present collection, Brenda S. Webster replaces Rodway's Jungian model by a more familiar Freudian one, when she claims that 'Of all the available psychologies, Freudian psychoanalysis is most productive for studying Blake. The psychoanalytic emphasis on Oedipal conflict and motives of "Love & Jealousy" is in many ways similar to Blake's own. . . . Blake's manifest emphasis begs to be described as Freudian' (p. 132).

There is no doubt that Blake's 'wildness' has caused some of his commentators to doubt his sanity. On one occasion when Crabb Robinson called at Fountain Court, where Blake and his wife lived in considerable poverty, Blake told him that 'he had committed many murders . . .', a remark he followed up by claiming that 'careless gay people are better than those who think.'[4] Which may remind us that Yeats once told Robert Graves that a poet-friend of Graves was 'too reasonable, too truthful. We poets should be good liars, remembering always that the Muses are women and prefer the embrace of gay, warty lads'.[5] That Blake was capable of mischief I have no doubt, and at one time this led some critics to caution against taking him seriously. More importantly, his disrespect for certain traditional values, whether in art, religion, politics or sexual relations, meant that other critics saw in him a dangerous rebel against social norms. The Catholic D. G. James regarded Blake's mind as 'extremely confused; and . . . the huge difficulty and obscurity of his work arises from an intellectual and imaginative disorder'.[6] T. S. Eliot both registered what he, too, took to be confusion and more suavely dismissed it and by implication Blake himself when he remarked that

We have the same respect for Blake's philosophy . . . that we have for an ingenious piece of home-made furniture: we admire the man who has put it together out of the odds and ends about the house. England has produced a fair number of these resourceful Robinson Crusoes; but we are not really so remote from the Continent, or from our own past, as to be deprived of the advantages of culture if we wish them.[7]

Eliot of course writes from a position which might be defined as basically catholic. The knee must be bowed to the Church, for the Church bears a whole weight of tradition on which its unopposable authority rests. In absolute contrast to this conservatism, which is as much political and cultural as it is religious, Blake came out of the traditions of non-conformity, and though he was undoubtedly alert to, and informed in, the ways and beliefs of different sects which abounded in London during his lifetime, including the teachings of Swedenborg and Boehme, that is not what either Eliot or James would have thought of as forming either tradition or culture. In what follows I shall have little to say about critical and scholarly disagreements as to the exact nature of Blake's beliefs, not so much because I do not think they can be resolved as that their bearing on the present state of Blake studies is comparatively unimportant.[8]

With one crucial exception. The various non-conformist groupings which had emerged at the time of the previous century's Civil War had gone underground after the Restoration. But that does not mean that they had died, any more than had their variously radical or re-volutionary convictions. These were based on interpretations of the Bible. The Bible, not the Church, was the ungainsayable authority on which non-conformity depended, including the authority of a social vision. The God of non-conformity, properly understood, offers his followers a new Jerusalem, a utopia to be achieved by struggle against false authority. Hence non-conformity's contempt for priest and Church, who claim sole authority as interpreters of God's truths in order to justify self-interest, and whose 'sanctioned' interpretation of holy writ is therefore a way of protecting that self-interest, usually at the expense of the poor and disadvantaged. It is probably too loose to say that the energies of the different non-conformist sects, long hidden after the disaster of 1660, burst into the light of day in July, 1789, with the opening up of the Bastille. It is, however, proper to note that in the closing years of the eighteenth century political and religious radicalism was once more becoming a powerful agency in the lives of many. This was especially so for those in the growing industrial-urban areas who were conscious of themselves as oppressed by new social arrangements which they needed to oppose and who, as a result, were developing a growing self-consciousness which would show itself, in E. P. Thompson's classic formulation, as 'the making of the English working-class'. Blake was very conscious of his artisanal status and in this connection we need to recognise that his religious convictions cannot be prised away from his politics. Until the last years of his life, when he seems to have accepted a more orthodox form of Christianity, he was as radical in his religious as in his political thinking. It is, then, scarcely surprising that he appeals to critics and commentators on the political left, nor that in recent years there has been much enquiry into the non-conformist groupings of late eighteenth-century London.

Marxist Criticism

Expressions of Blake's appeal to left-wing writers first began to show themselves in the 1930s. This is to be expected. During the decade between the Wall Street Crash and the start of the Second World War, socialist and Marxist ideas came to influence many young writers and intellectuals. History had to be rewritten, especially the history of key moments in what was often called 'the people's struggle against their oppressors', and, as a result, the period that roughly coincides with the years 1770–1825 became crucial as 'A Revolutionary Era'. The phrase was coined by Jack Lindsay and Edgell Rickword for their anthology, *A Handbook for Freedom*, first published in 1939. (It was republished two years later as *Spokesmen for Liberty: A Record of English Democracy Through Twelve Centuries*.)[9] A two-page selection from Blake's *Songs* and his *Prophetic Books* appears under the running title 'Against the Satanic Mills', although neither 'Jerusalem' nor 'The Tyger' is included. More importantly, Lindsay and Rickword follow their selection from Blake with a number of petitions. One of these, which comes from Northamptonshire and is dated 1797, tells of the privations caused by enclosure. Other petitions include one by sailors complaining of wretched conditions on board ship, which gave rise to the 1797 naval mutinies, first at Spithead, then at Nore. Lindsay and Rickword provide as a running title for these petitions 'The Dispossessed Speak'.

Blake was not dispossessed, but in placing his poems in *A Handbook for Freedom* where they do, Lindsay and Rickword remind us that unlike nearly all the other great writers of the time, who were university educated, he came from the artisanal class, and all his life had had to work for a living. So, too, did John Clare, born to the life of agricultural day labourer, his circumstances far less fortunate than Blake's. For Blake had more coherent and keenly articulated traditions of radical as well as artistic thought to draw on than did Clare, the Northamptonshire 'peasant poet', born four years before the petition protesting against enclosure which Lindsay and Rickword print in their anthology. And the enclosure of the common lands round Helpston, the village where Clare was born, was the single greatest grievance of his life. As the petition makes evident, there were undoubtedly traditions of rural protest on which Clare could draw – including oral transmission of ballad, of tale, of rural radicalism – but urban, artisanal experience made for a complex skein of intertwined radical ideas which Marxist critics in particular have set themselves to distinguish in order to recognise which threads run through Blake's writing.

Here, the work of the Marxist historian, A. L. Morton, has been of great influence on all subsequent left-wing commentators on Blake. In 1958 Morton published *The Everlasting Gospel: A Study in the Sources of William Blake*, in the introduction to which he remarked that his book had its inception when, several years previously

> I was reading . . . a good deal of the pamphlet literature dealing with the religious sects of the seventeeth century. I found myself saying, from time to time, 'Blake might have written that': presently I said, 'and why not – these men were only three or four generations earlier. London in his boyhood must have contained many old men who had seen and perhaps talked with Cromwell and Coppe, to say nothing of Muggleton and Kiffin.'[10]

Given that Cromwell died in 1658 and that Blake was born virtually a hundred years later, this is best thought of as a pardonable exaggeration. It enables Morton to recognise the importance of placing Blake's writings in the context of what he calls 'a revolutionary tradition, tenaciously held by the descendants of the small tradesmen and artisans who had formed the extreme left of the Commonwealthsmen'.[11] And Morton emphasises the importance of two facts about Blake which cannot, he says, be overstressed. One, he was born into the world of London dissenting radicalism, and apart from one disastrous episode he lived his entire life in the city. Two:

> he was and remained all his life, a manual worker, one of the highly skilled craftsmen who formed a substantial part of the population of London in his time. . . . It was from the craftsman's special standpoint that Blake regarded the rapid development of industrial capitalism in England.[12]

Put these matters together and we have three separate although inevitably interlocked issues of the greatest significance for socialist critics: the precise, or it may be problematic, nature of Blake's involvement with the English radical tradition, the fact that he was a Londoner, and the equally important fact that he came of, and remained within, the artisan class. It is worth dealing with these matters in turn.

Blake and the Radical Tradition

In *Witness Against the Beast: William Blake and the Moral Law*, E. P. Thompson spends some time tracing Blake's thought back to its sources in antinomianism, especially as that emerged in the later years of the eighteenth century and took its stand on 'carrying to an extreme the advocacy of grace, and bringing the gospel of Christ into direct *antagonism* to "the covenant of deeds" or the "moral law"'. (Thompson's italics.)[13] This entails reading the Bible in a manner which challenges the authority of Mosaic Law and, in particular, in recognising that the 'gospel is eternal because it exists within man's faith every day'. The gospel, Blake says, enables 'every man [to] converse with God & be a King & Priest in his own house'. In which case, 'It appears to me Now that Tom Paine is a better Christian than the Bishop'.[14] The Bishop referred to here is the Bishop of Llandaff, who had published an *Address to the People of Great Britain*, the overriding purpose of which was to urge submission to both Church and state. However, the words Thompson quotes are not Blake's own. They were uttered by another radical dissenter, Gilbert Wakefield. But this is Thompson's point. Blake was not alone. The work of Blake the antinomian, Thompson says, has a confidence, an assured reference, very different from an eccentric or a solitary. It also assumes something like a radical constituency, an 'us' of 'the People' or of 'every man' as against 'them' of the State, or the Bishops or the servitors of 'the Beast and the Whore'. The antinomian argument does not drift off into transcendental essays on 'faith' versus 'works' but is pressed, always, to a political conclusion.[15]

With this in mind we can understand the importance to Thompson of Blake's poem 'The Divine Image', and its display of what Thompson calls Blake's 'egalitarian humanism' (p. 33). For when, in harmony with the meaning of his poem, Blake wrote 'Every thing has as much right to Eternal Life as God who is the Servant of Man' he was all but echoing a remark of Colonel Rainborough's, that 'the poorest he that is in England hath a life to live as the greatest he.' Christopher Hill has shown that Rainborough's claim, made during the famous Putney debates of 1647, when, after the defeat of the king, the General Council of Cromwell's army, together with elected representatives of the rank and file and 'some London Levellers, was discussing what should be the future constitution of England', provided what Hill calls 'a unique occasion'.[16]

Unique or not, Hill's essay on 'The Poor and the People' does much to show that the terms in which the victorious commonwealthers argued for a republican, democratic England survived the disaster of the Restoration. True, the language of radicalism went underground. It would have been dangerous, not to say disastrous, to have spoken openly of the ideal of a democratic, republican England in the years after 1660. But historians of the left, such as Morton, Thompson and Hill himself, have been able to show that when, at the end of the eighteenth century, voices once again asserted the desirability and propriety of what Thompson calls democratic humanism, the words those voices uttered were not so much new-minted as the recovered coinage of an earlier generation.

This is why Milton meant so much to Blake, as he did of course to that ardent revolutionary, king-and-priest hater, Shelley. For Milton as epic poet set out to write a book of the people and Blake shares the earlier poet's ambition. Nor is such ambition confined to Blake's Prophetic Books. It is fully present in *Songs of Innocence* and *Songs of Experience*. As I have noted elsewhere, both these collections 'speak out of – and for – a passionately non-conformist and in all senses radical rejection of those Anglican pieties whose politics are deferential, hierarchical, monarchical, and which then are inevitably to be identified with "duty", with submission, and with warning against the follies and dangers of the explosive exuberance which characterise the innocent children of Albion'.[17]

London and Artisanal Culture

Songs of Innocence was published in London in 1789. This was at a moment when the city was alive with radical energies, animated by debates at all social levels on such matters as the questionable status of the established Church; the undesirability of the monarchy; the need for universal suffrage; the rights of men and, less frequently, women, to live their lives to the full; the need to return the land to the people; and much else besides. There is no space here to provide an account of these debates, but the accounts exist and between them they give an overwhelming impression that the moment was one of great gaiety for radical enterprise.[18] Perhaps inevitably this could not last. By the time *Songs of Experience* saw the light of day in 1794, London was no longer a city safe for those who expressed radical sympathies. Britain was at war with republican France and those whom Authority could identify as not wholly at one with the war effort might expect a hard time of it. Treason was a capital offence and those who published what could be officially regarded as seditious material were threatened with prison, loss of livelihood, transportation, or worse. The government had its spies out and they regularly infiltrated meetings of those thought to be hostile to the crown. By 1794 the capital was, as Blake unforgettably put it in his poem 'London', a city of 'mind-forg'd manacles'. *Songs of Experience* was in fact issued together with the reprinted *Songs of Innocence*, – the two volumes were bound together and continued to be so – and while this has led most commentators to argue that Blake means them to be read against each other, we might also sense that he would have thought it dangerous to publish the later collection on its own, given that some of the songs are deeply critical of Church, monarchy, and the apparatus of state power.

We can sense something of the fall from the high optimism of 1789 if we note that in 'Holy Thursday', one of the *Songs of Innocence*, the orphan children marching into St Paul's 'with radiance all their own', are described as 'a hum of multitudes . . . raising their innocent hands'. As always, Blake here makes use of the Bible as justification for the radical tradition. The Bible is the book of the people and read aright it will be found to contain the revelation of God's purpose for man. Blake's readers would have known that the 'hum of multitudes' had its source in Isaiah. 'The noise of a multitude in the mountains, like as of a great people; a tumultuous noise of the kingdoms of nations gathered together: the Lord of hosts mustereth the host of the battle' (13: 4). The children compose an army waiting to enter their promised land, a redeemed England. Moreover, the image of their raised hands alerts us to an exuberant energy which is also one of defiance, of a breaking of the shackles. The gesture is close to, may be identical with, the extended arms of the nude male youth Blake had depicted in 'Glad Day' in 1780 as stepping out of his picture frame. This image is more properly known as 'Albion Rose' or 'The Dance of Albion'. Visual and poetic images are thus linked together in an imagined continuum of revolutionary energy.

But as the historian Linda Colley points out in her book *Britain: Forging the Nation, 1707–1837*, (1992), in the early 1790s parliament decided 'to employ state revenues to place statues of military and naval officer heroes in St Paul's cathedral in London – something which had never been done before'.[19] Elite heroism replaces the collective energies of Blake's vision of the children, that 'multitude of lambs'. 'Holy Thursday' of *Songs of Experience* grieves over a lost paradise:

> Is that trembling cry a song?
> Can it be a song of joy?
> And so many children poor?
> It is a land of poverty!

The poverty is not merely literal, of course, although Blake's poem certainly takes account of the real hardships many had to endure. The 'trembling song' is evoked in the poem's hesitant cadences, the four-stress quatrains at huge odds with the uninhibitedly joyous, often anapestic septennaries of *Songs of Innocence*'s 'Holy Thursday'. With this in mind we can better understand E. P. Thompson's remark that Blake's writing is, in its antinomian commitment, 'as always, combative, even if, at the last moment, Blake shrinks from the combat'. The reason for what might be called a tactical withdrawal is that, as I have noted, London in the mid-1790s was a dangerous place for anyone with radical sympathies.

This is a matter addressed throughout John Mee's *Dangerous Enthusiasm: William Blake and the Culture of Radicalism in the 1790s*. It is why Mee calls his manner of interpreting Blake's poetry 'an archaeology of reading: it includes an effort to seek out the encoded politics of Blake's rhetoric' (p. 45). Like Thompson, Mee places Blake firmly within the radical tradition whose various strands include the antinomian habit of thought so engrained among small tradespeople of the eighteenth century, but which for Mee also presupposes a kind of grab-all readiness to make use of ideas in a manner he defines as 'bricolage'. He also suggests, as does Thompson, that previous commentators have misunderstood Blake in so far as they have seen him as a lonely genius, at odds with all around – and thus, it goes without saying, providing an example of the 'Romantic' poet, isolated, misunderstood. For Mee, as for Thompson, Blake is part of a lively, participatory radical city culture, which, as we have seen, Thompson identifies as 'writing which comes out of a tradition . . .'.[20] And Mee remarks that while the processes out of which Blake makes his art 'might seem to be spectacular examples of [his] "Poetic Genius", they are also typical of the strategies and priorities of a range of radical texts of the 1790s' (p. 48).

'History From The Bottom Up': The New Historicism versus Romantic Idealism

When in 1963 E. P. Thompson published his classic *The Making of the English Working Class*, he noted that one of his ambitions was to rescue hitherto unremarked people, like the poor stockinger, 'from the enormous condescension of posterity'. What lay behind this ambition was not merely Rainborough's affirmation of the life to be lived by the poorest he that is in England, but a recognition that those who offered no more than condescension were incapable of recognising, still less of evaluating, the rich cultural and political inheritance of those to whom they condescended. What has become known as 'History From The Bottom Up' has had an important part to play in demonstrating Blake's complex allegiances, religious, political, cultural, and, as we have seen, in placing them within the context of late eighteenth-century radicalism. The wholly beneficent result of such work is that no future commentator on Blake will be able to treat him as a maverick or wild exotic, in the manner begun by Crabb Robinson, who seems to have been quite unaware of the roots of Blake's radicalism, although until comparatively recently this view was still being peddled as a legitimate approach to his art.

There is, however, a corresponding danger. It is that Blake will be seen as merely 'representative'. Raymond Williams made regular use of this term in order to suggest that the still-persistent Romantic notion of 'creative genius' dangerously mystified the actual circumstances out of which art was made. A poem did not descend like the holy ghost from the clouds, nor was it an instance of divine afflatus. On the contrary, a poem was made out of material circumstances: nationality, gender, class, the historical moment, and so forth. This connects with an aspect of recent critical theory in which literature's 'privileged' status, as the term is, becomes denied. Writing is writing. That is all. Hence, literature itself is usually fenced off by quotation marks, to show that its status is problematic, may even be illusory: it isn't literature that ought to concern us but 'literature'. This position is one closely associated with what is called The New Historicism, a movement which, while it owes much to Marxist historians and critics of a previous generation, rejects any idea of the propriety of the aesthetic. That is merely an outmoded and discredited form of idealism. Thus George Montrose, one of the leading New Historicists, has argued that we need to reject the very concept of literature, at all events insofar as it is thought of 'as an autonomous aesthetic order that transcends the shifting pressure and particularity of material needs and interests'.

In saying this, Montrose may at first seem to be doing no more than recommending a return to 'contextualising literary texts'. Why, for example, should a contextual critic of the old school find anything to worry about in Montrose's contention that we need 'to resituate canonical literary texts among the multiple forms of writing, and in relation to the non-discursive practices and institutions of the social formation in which those texts have been produced'? The answer is that for Montrose and the New Historicists, the gap between text and context, which the contextualist critic took for granted, cannot exist. One person's text is another's context. In which case neither can claim a 'privileged' status and writers are at best representative of the moment in which their writings are produced and consumed.[21] (The terms imply that 'literature' is as much commodity as anything else brought to market.)

As far as I know, Raymond Williams, who is in close sympathy with the New Historicist position, did not apply the term 'representative' to Blake. But then he hardly needed to. As we have seen, the work of Thompson and others had made clear in what ways Blake was indeed representative of late-eighteenth century radicalism. But as one of those ways was in his use of the word 'genius', which he often invoked, he himself can look vulnerable to the charge of romantic idealism. In a sense this is obviously the case. Blake was, after all, part of that historical moment we choose to call Romantic, and one of the distinguishing features of Romanticism was its belief in a poet's 'calling'. This was often enough identified as 'genius', and there was customarily an unstated belief that those called had been summoned by an unopposable authority. In short, there was a religious dimension to belief in genius.

There always had been. But in the late-eighteenth century a newly important emotion emerged as the evidence for the propriety of such belief. Poets of genius were also poets of joy. For Wordsworth and Coleridge every bit as much as for Blake, joy was the presiding emotion of the poet *as* poet, and joy was god-given. When Wesley turned the unfaithful, the doubters and the ungodly to the true religion, he always referred to their moment of conversion as one of an accession of joy, the discovery of god within. And when, in 'Dejection: An Ode', Coleridge felt himself no longer able to trust his poetic worth, he mourned the loss of 'Joy that ne'er was given,/Save to the pure'. Never mind the psycho-pathology of Coleridge's guilt feelings. What matters is his sense that in having joy withdrawn from him he cannot function as a poet. The presence of joy declared the active genius of the poet. To put it this way runs the risk of reducing complex ideas and habits of thought to parody, yet if we do not register the importance to Blake of the word genius we shall not fully understand him as a great, *radical* poet.[22]

For when Blake spoke of genius he meant to make plain that poetic worth was not a function of what we would call class. *Anyone* could be a genius, could, that is, have been chosen to be a true poet. In this connection we need to recall that in the later years of the eighteenth century the noun was often preceded by the adjective 'natural', and the 'natural genius' was not dependent on school learning nor the acquisition of classical education for his or her poetry. Hence, Burns's declaration in the preface to the Kilmarnock edition of his poems that

> The following trifles are not the production of the Poet, who, with all the advantages of learned art, and perhaps amid the elegancies and idlenesses of upper life, looks down for a rural theme, with an eye to Theocritus or Virgil. . . . Unacquainted with the necessary requisites for commencing Poet by rule, he sings the sentiments and manners, he felt and saw in himself and his rustic compeers around him, in his and their native language.[23]

And hence one of the many contemptuous and angry marginal comments Blake made to the *Discourses* of Sir Joshua Reynolds, the eighteenth century's most famous portrait painter, first president of the Royal Academy, and a man who, according to Blake, was 'hired to depress genius'. I shall return in due course to reasons for Blake's intense dislike of Reynolds. Here, I want merely to note that when he came to 'Discourse III', Blake wrote:

> A work of Genius is a Work 'Not to be obtain'd by the Invocation of Memory & her Syren Daughters, but by Devout prayer to that Eternal Spirit, who can enrich with all utterance & knowledge & sends out his Seraphim with the hallowed fire of his Altar to touch & purify the lips of whom he pleases.' MILTON[24]

The key phrase comes at the end. If the eternal spirit visits genius upon 'whom he pleases', then the poorest he is as likely a subject

as the richest. In other words, the late-eighteenth-century concern
with natural genius, which Blake's marginal comment here acknowledges, is an intensely radical one, as is his marginal comment on
Swedenborg's *Wisdom of Angels Concerning Divine Love and Divine
Wisdom*, that 'if he has wisdom may perceive it is from the Poetic
Genius, which is the Lord'.[25] We badly misunderstand Blake if we
fail to register that his concern with poetic genius is part of his
radical antinomianism.

In this as in other senses Blake is undoubtedly representative. But
I had better make my own position plain by saying that I believe he
is also a great poet and visionary artist and that it is nonsense to
think of him as working at the same level as, say, decent, humdrum
artisanal writers such as John Freeth and Joseph Mather.[26] And in this
sense he *isn't* representative. David Erdman's work, *Blake: Prophet
Against Empire*, which Erdman has gone on revising since its first
appearance over forty years ago, is invaluable not merely because
it so fully documents Blake's involvement in political issues and
concerns of the late-eighteenth century, but because Erdman recog-
nises that the intensity of Blake's response to, his engagement with,
these matters is that of a great artist. Others no doubt felt as keenly,
thought as deeply about them, but Blake alone created *Songs of
Experience*, at its heart 'London', which Erdman, echoing a phrase
of Oliver Elton's, rightly calls Blake's 'mightiest brief poem'. Later
commentators, among them Heather Glen and E. P. Thompson, have
developed Erdman's arguments, and in so doing have helped to
deepen our understanding of this almost inexhaustibly rich poem.
But all would acknowledge the importance of Erdman's work.[27]

So would Stewart Crehan. His essay 'Producers and Devourers'
makes use of Erdman's pioneering scholarship, as it does of A. L.
Morton and Christopher Hill. Crehan also draws on Marx himself.
Like other left-wing critics, Crehan is keen to stress Blake's
allegiances with the political and social ethos of the eighteenth-
century urban craftsman or, as Morton called him, 'skilled artisan'.
And like others he traces these allegiances back to various radical
groupings which emerged at the time of the seventeenth-century
commonwealth, although he volunteers a different source for the
ideas that fed through to Blake's particular form of radicalism. For
Crehan, Gerrard Winstanley's *The True Levellers' Standard Advanced*
(1649), which Crehan offers as a work by the man 'who has a prime
claim to the title of the first English socialist' (p. 65) provides an
'unambiguous and lucid account of how mankind came to be
divided into classes. . . . A spokesman for the dispossessed landless
laborers of the seventeenth century, Winstanley anticipates the
method of modern historical materialism. His "contraries" compare

interestingly with Blake's . . .' (p. 65). Blake's contraries are Heaven and Hell, and Crehan is surely correct in arguing that to tear his *Marriage of Heaven and Hell* from its social and political context is to empty it of 'its living, revolutionary significance' (p. 61).

But Blake is not a reborn leveller. Crehan argues that where Winstanley celebrated the agricultural labourer, Blake's heroic 'producer' is the 'prolifically creative, Radical artist-craftsman or artisan who as an "active citizen" (at least in Westminster), struggles to free himself, his fellow-producers, and hence society as a whole, from the economic, political, moral and aesthetic constraints of the old aristocratic, monarchical system' (p. 66). Blake, in other words, derives more from the revolutionary thinking of the Ranters than from the peasant collectivism of the Diggers.

What prompts Crehan's argument is his wish to claim that 'with astonishing far-sightedness, anticipating Marx, Blake is able to perceive . . . an *irreconcilable* enmity between "two classes of men"' (p. 72). Perhaps so, but I am not sure that the distinction Crehan wishes to force, between ideas and convictions inherited from Diggers on the one hand, and those descending from Ranters on the other, can be made to work. It is certainly true that even in the smoky ferment of the commonwealth years Ranters and Diggers were as markedly different from each other as they were from other contending sects. It is, however, far less easy to argue that by the end of the eighteenth century an essentially rural, peasant, collectivism can be distinguished from more advanced radical-revolutionary thought, situated in the city and common among craftsmen, even though this is a commonplace assumption of Marxist thought. For Marx, true working-class consciousness develops on the shop floor. The factory worker is revolutionary, the peasant reactionary. To put the issue this way runs the risk of stark reductiveness, but is not at bottom unfair to the classic Marxist position; and it goes without saying that communist governments have always treated peasant life as inherently backward.

Yet if there was Ned Ludd there was also Captain Swing. Militant protest against the de-skilling of craftsmen in the English north and midland counties during 1812–13 was echoed by militant protest – including cattle-maiming and rick-burning – which spread across the southern and middle shires of England nearly twenty years later. Moreover, the urban radicalism which Blake found congenial was shared by Thomas Spence, whose own thinking, as David Worrall has shown, was deeply marked by his belief that there should be common ownership of the land. In 1800 there were food riots in London, specifically over the price of bread. Worrall remarks that in this context we should understand that

Blake's *The Four Zoas* [written and revised between 1975–1804]
hints at the radical stance, well articulated in later Spencean circles,
that the toil of the agricultural labouring poor was the national
repository of wealth entitling them to the shared ownership of the
land's productivity: 'The poor smite their oppressors they awake
up to the harvest', 'The Kings & Princes of the Earth cry with a
feeble cry/Driven on the unproducing sands & on the hardend
rocks'.

(The Four Zoas IX 117:119 and IX 125:9–10)

And Worrall further notes that Spence's remedy for what he called
the 'artificial famine' was, in his own words, the 'total destruction
of the power of these Samsons' of landed property. 'The People have
only to say "Let the Land be Ours" and it will be so.'[28] Worrall shows
that much of this thinking comes from Irish radicalism as that developed during the eighteenth century; and in this context the belief that
land should be held in common is inseparable from the desire for
land nationalisation, a belief which finds its way into the thinking
of many of those in England who opposed the enclosing of the
common land.

We should also note that when the primitive methodists parted
company from the main body of the methodist church in the early
years of the nineteenth century, they became known as Ranters. In
the mid-1820s John Clare thought of becoming a Ranter, and Ebenezer
Elliott wrote a poem called 'The Ranter', about a Sheffield preacher,
Miles Gordon, who goes out into the fields to preach the cause of
'The slander'd Calvinists of Charles's time', who 'fought (and they
won it) freedom's holy fight'. Gordon ends his sermon by promising
his listeners that 'the hour/Cometh when all shall fall before thee
– gone/Their splendour, fall'n their trophies, lost their power'.[29]
Admittedly, Elliott's poem was written in 1832, five years after
Blake's death, and the year in which the Great Reform Act disap-
pointed as many hopes as its promise had raised, and as a result
of which those still disenfranchised threatened and often carried
out violent measures against their continued exclusion from official
politics. (Nottingham Castle was burnt down.) But Elliot's poem
testifies to the fact that radical ideas of the late-eighteenth century,
no matter how historians try to keep them to what they perceive to
be separate channels, insist on feeding into a larger stream of radical
energy. The work of Thompson, Mee, Erdman, Crehan, and others
not represented here shows, whether by intention or otherwise, that
Blake cannot be claimed for a narrowly sectarian radicalism, not
anyway without an understanding that such sectarianism can never
be 'pure.' On the other hand, there can be no doubt of the significance

of Blake's identity as a skilled craftsman in the shaping of that
radicalism. This is a matter on which all the commentators so far
discussed properly agree. And in this sense they are right to regard
Blake's radicalism as representative, even if this is emphatically *not*
true of his poetry.

Blake and Art Criticism

Nor is it true of his art. 'Every body does not see alike,' Blake
famously told the Rev. Dr Trusler. 'As a man is, so he sees.' Blake
is here making a proud claim for his visionary powers. 'I know
that This World is a World of Imagination and Vision,' he further
remarked to Trusler. Yet as artist, and specifically as engraver and
illustrator, he had also to be involved in the daily minutiae of making. We would therefore expect any discussion of Blake as an artist
to take account of his status as craftsman. After all, he made a living
– often not much of a one – from his trade as engraver and designer.
Susan Matthews is plainly aware of this, although she has other
matters to attend to in her essay on '*Jerusalem* and Nationalism'.
There is, indeed, a hint of revisionism in her argument that Blake's
radicalism is not so far-reaching as to abandon a masculinist tend-
ency. Nor is he willing to surrender nationalist, patriotic impulses to
universalism. 'The Eternal Man will seem to be male and . . . Albion
will be read as a figure of the nation. Whilst *Jerusalem* works towards
a point at which national identities merge, it nevertheless does so
through the form of a national epic poem' (p. 99). Matthews's work
is here in harmony with a number of recent developments in literary
and historical studies. Her feminist scepticism about the 'universalist'
implications of Blake's radicalism is, as we shall see, shared by
Brenda Webster. And like Linda Colley, whose *Britons* makes fascinating use of Hogarth as an important iconographer of 'Britishness',
Matthews well understands Hogarth's importance to Blake in the
'concept of English character, typical of the emergent nationalism
in its emphasis on the blunt, honest, sincere man' (p. 84). Moreover,
in noting that ancient Greece 'provides Blake in the 1790s with an
image of a society in which art, the artist and the imagination are
rightly honoured' (p. 82), Matthews very interestingly identifies him
with late-eighteenth century classicism, even though earlier generations
of commentators would have been quick to reject the identification.
For them, Blake was quintessentially Romantic in his rejection of
such classicism – especially as the classic spirit was identified with
imitation. Blake was the true original: Gothic, northern, Ossianic.
This requires some explication.

16

In the early years of the eighteenth century what might be called English classicism provided a cultural orthodoxy for the new nation state. In architecture, in art and in poetry, the models to be followed were those supplied by ancient Greece and Rome or by Renaissance Italy. But then a reaction to this begins to show itself. One of the key documents of this reaction is Edward Young's *Conjectures on Original Composition*. In this essay, published in 1759, Young, a poet and man of letters, compares what he calls 'the scholar poet' unfavourably to the 'true genius'. The former

> makes one of a group, and thinks in wretched uniformity with the throng; incumbered with the notions of others, and impoverished by their abundance, he conceives not the least embryo of new thought; opens not the least vista through the gloom of ordinary writers, into the bright walks of rare imagination, and singular design; while the true genius is crossing all public roads into fresh untrodden ground . . .[30]

'Fresh untrodden ground': the language invites us to consider that true genius lurks in out-of-the-way places, is not to be thought of as at home in the city state nor to be looked for among the 'throng' of conventionally educated and cultured people to whom scholar poetry will appeal. The rejection of all that was meant by 'Augustanism' could hardly be more absolute.

The time was now propitious for a new kind of poetry to make its appearance. A year after Young published his essay a 'true genius' of the kind he had described actually turned up. Or so it seemed. 'I am gone mad about my old Scotch (or rather Irish) poetry,' the poet Thomas Gray wrote to his friend Thomas Wharton in 1760.[31] He was referring to the poems of 'an ancient bard' which had been sent to him by the Rev. James Macpherson, who claimed to have translated them from the original Gaelic. *Fragments of Ancient Poetry Collected in the Highlands of Scotland* caused something of a sensation in mid-eighteenth century London, and this was intensified when, in 1761, Macpherson brought out *Fingal, an Ancient Epic Poem in Six books, together with Several Other Poems composed by Ossian, the son of Fingal, translated from the Gaelic language*. Here was true genius. Unfortunately, most of this 'ancient' work was in fact fake. Macpherson had found only scraps of Ossianic verse and had woven these into a romance of his own making. But this matters less than the enormous impact which the Ossianic poems made. They very evidently 'proved', as Gray said, that 'The imagination dwelt many hundreds of years ago in all her pomp on the cold and barren mountains of Scotland. The truth (I believe) is that without any respect of climates she reigns in all nascent societies of men . . .'[32]

Blake admired Gray. More relevant to this discussion is the fact that he gives decidedly 'Ossianic' names to the characters of his Prophetic Books. More relevant still, some of the marginalia to his copy of Reynold's *Discourses* look as though they might have been dictated by Young or Gray. This applies to one of the most famous.

Reynolds's Opinion was that Genius May be Taught & that all Pretence to Inspiration is a Lie & a Deceit, to say the least of it. For if it is a Deceit, the whole Bible is madness. This Opinion originates in the Greeks' calling the Muses Daughters of memory.
The enquiry in England is not whether a Man has talents & Genius, But whether he is Passive & Polite & a Virtuous Ass & obedient to Noblemen's Opinions in Art & Science. If he is, he is a good man. If Not, he must be Starved.[33]

Given this, it is not hard to see why in the 1960s Blake should have been thought of as the law-giver for those 'children of Albion' who raged against forms of education and art which they wished to discredit, and, as a result of which, any number of walls at art school and university were spray-gunned with Blake's famous Proverb of Hell, 'The tygers of wrath are wiser than the horses of instruction.'
But while Blake certainly believed in 'original genius' he also valued careful craft. Hence, his marginal comment in the *Discourses* that 'Invention depends Altogether upon Execution or Organization; as that is right or wrong so is the Invention perfect or imperfect.'[34] Moreover, he wanted proper recognition for his art.

Liberality! We want not Liberality. We want a Fair Price & Proportionate Value & a General Demand for Art.
Let not that Nation where Less than Nobility is the Reward, Pretend that Art is Encouraged by that Nation. Art is first in Intellectuals & Ought to be First in Nations.[35]

Put these marginal comments together and what emerges is a sense of Blake as a proud, professional craftsman/artist whose radical energies are devoted to championing an art that is not subservient to or aligned with 'Noblemen's Opinions', even though it may well align itself with classical or Renaissance models.
Indeed, the claim that Art ought to be first in Nations is one that Dryden and Pope would have been quick to endorse, engaged as they were in keeping open a conduit to the Graeco-Roman past. This is one of the important strands of John Barrell's argument for Blake the artist. He notes that even Blake's insistence on 'original' art doesn't mean that he is against 'copying *per se*. It is essential to the

education of an artist that he should learn "the Language of Art by making many Finish'd Copies both of Nature & Art"; and even an original artist must be a copyist, must indeed be a more perfect copyist than an uninspired artist could ever be' (p. 102). He further remarks that, with Reynolds no doubt chiefly in mind, Blake made clear that he was himself opposed to the implicit subservence of the portrait painter to patronage. Portrait painters were employed for 'sordid drudgery', their task amounted to no more than making 'facsimile representations of merely mortal and perishing substances' (p. 112). This was not what the true artist was for, nor was it what Blake meant by the 'individual'.

What he *did* mean is touched on by Kathleen Raine, in the chapter of her book *William Blake*, 'A New Mode of Printing'. In discussing Blake's *Tiriel*, a work which 'denounced the current view of childhood . . . as a passive state to be "formed" by "instruction",' Raine notes that Blake's 'realization, "Every man's genius is peculiar to his individuality," is one he shared with Rousseau and Mary Wollstonecraft' (p. 122). The great 'realisation' of this, literally and visually, is to be found in the combination of poem and engraving out of which Blake made *Songs of Innocence* and *Songs of Experience*. This *is* to make a copy of individuality. Raine's account of these books is especially important for the detailed attention she pays to Blake's method of 'illuminated printing'. She refers us to Gilchrist's information that Blake 'ground and mixed his watercolours himself' and although this was and remains common practice among artists, it is interesting to know that Blake added diluted carpenter's glue to the mixture, because 'as the early Italians had found out before him', such glue proved a good binder (pp. 120–1). This is a perfect example of how secrets of the trade are passed from craftsman to craftsman down the centuries, irrespective of national boundaries. And it is therefore good to know that Ruthven Todd, a man-of-letters and now-dead contemporary of Kathleen Raine's, should have had the . assistance of the great Spanish surrealist artist, Joan Miró, in trying to repeat the method Blake developed for printing off his illustrated songs. Reading of how Todd found this to be 'a very delicate process' increases our respect for Blake as a meticulous and technically re-sourceful artist, forever immersed in the practicalities of his trade.

Feminism and Psychoanalytic Criticism

In her discussion of *Songs of Experience*, Raine suggests that Blake shows life impeded and denied 'by unrequited love, as in "The Angel" or "Ah! Sunflower"; by childhood oppressed, as in "Nurse's

Song" and "The Chimney Sweeper"; by moral oppression as in "The
Garden of Love" and "A Little Girl Lost"...' (pp. 127–8). I do not
wish to comment on this beyond saying that 'NURSES Song' (as
Blake prints it) is about adolescence rather than childhood. The
illustration to the poem makes plain beyond doubt that this is so.
It shows an adolescent youth sulkily allowing the nurse to comb his
hair while behind him his pubescent sister sits droopily at an open
doorway beyond which she is evidently scared to look, let alone
venture. Both adolescents are, we understand, oppressed by sexual
fear. Hence the importance of the capitalised NURSE. She is the
instrument of oppression.

> When the voices of children are heard on the green,
> And whisperings in the dale,
> The days of my youth rise fresh in my mind,
> My face turns green and pale.

In the 'Nurse's Song' of *Songs of Innocence* the Nurse's warning
voice is answered by the vitality of her charges' song. In *Songs
of Experience*, on the other hand, the NURSE is given unopposable
authority. The second, concluding stanza runs:

> Then come home my children, the sun is gone down,
> The dews of night arise,
> Your spring & your day, are wasted in play
> And your winter and night in disguise.

There is a terrible sadness about this. If the Nurse is an oppressor
she is also one of the oppressed. At the last she unconsciously
admits that her life of self-repression is a wasted one, as will be
those of the youth and his sister. The nurse had in her youth disguised from herself her true desire for play, and now in age she
lives a life of self-disguise, of denial.

So at least I read the stanza. Geoffrey Keynes, however, in his
commentary on the Oxford Illustrated *Songs of Innocence and
Experience* sees the matter very differently. I do not disagree with
Keynes when he remarks that 'The nurse's face turns "green and
pale" because that is traditionally the colour of the sex-starved
spinster, sick with longings for experience which will never be hers.'
But I part company from him when he goes on to say that 'The evil
of female domination, so destructive of the male personality, already
explicit in this poem, was often in Blake's mind, as we know from
passages in other writings. The cottage door from which the boy has
come is conspicuously wreathed with vines, symbol of the pleasure

he will find in life'.[36] But the youth, not 'boy' as Keynes would have it, can expect to find no such pleasure if he remains in fear of the NURSE, as both poem and illustration suggest he will.

To say this is not, however, to say that I think Blake is guilty of the near-misogynistic attitude to women which Keynes imputes to him, albeit without intending any criticism. It is rather that in desiring equality between the sexes Blake passionately rejects the orthodox Christian assumption of women as embodiments of restraint, of self-denial, which afflicts the Nurse. We should remember that Blake, the friend of Mary Wollstonecraft, wrote

> What is it men in women do require? –
> The lineaments of gratified desire.
> What is it women do in men require? –
> The lineaments of gratified desire.[37]

This quatrain, which was committed to a Notebook of 1791–2, at about the time he was writing *Songs of Experience*, is not mentioned in Brenda Webster's 'Blake, Women, and Sexuality', although Webster accepts that 'Liberated sexuality seems a source of high value for Blake'. On the other hand, 'sexuality also elicits his most hostile, negative, and regressive images' (p. 130). Having posited this dichotomy in Blake's thinking, Webster chooses to submit him to Freudian pyschoanalysis, arguing that 'The psychoanalytic emphasis on Oedipal conflict and motives of "Love & Jealousy" is in many ways similar to Blake's own. Freudianism is unique in its emphasis on the the problems caused by man's long dependency and the psychic cost involved in the taming of his sexual and aggressive impulses. . . . Particularly in his late work, Blake's manifest emphasis begs to be described as Freudian' (pp. 132–3). It is not entirely clear whether Webster is using 'man' as the universal – to mean 'humankind' – or whether she means to indicate male as opposed to female. Freud undoubtedly meant the former; Webster seems sometimes to mean that, sometimes the latter. For hers is a combative essay. She argues that in his earlier work Blake is liberationist, seeing women as 'a source of salvation', and that he 'continually imagines his heroes liberating females from paternal tyrants'. However, as he grows older, and especially in the rewriting and Christianising of *Vala*, 'he comes to see woman as responsible for the Fall' (p. 141).

But the story is yet more complicated. Even in the early work there is, Webster argues, 'a strong undercurrent of hostility and fear', and to demonstrate this she focuses on *Thel*, which Blake was working on at the very end of the 1780s. Her argument therefore makes an interesting contrast with that of Gerda S. Norvig, in

21

'Female Subjectivity and the Desire of Reading In (to) Blake's *Book of Thel'*. Unlike Webster, and like most feminists, Norvig is unimpressed by Freudian psychoanalysis. Feminist theory commonly takes its cue from Juliet Mitchell's classic argument that Freudianism is deeply compromised by its author's unexamined assumptions about masculinity and femininity. Norvig therefore tells us that her essay 'includes an implicit plea for the revision of our knee-jerk response toward the unpalatable sexism often inscribed in Blake's text. . . . I aim to uncover those elements lurking within Blake's portrait of Thel that make her an icon of resistance to sexist indoctrination' (p. 149).

Language Games and Deconstruction

In pursuing her argument, Norvig makes use of several elements in current critical theory. Reader-response is evoked on p. 150, as is intertextuality. She very persuasively draws attention to the fact that the text of *Thel* 'not only beckons across thresholds but also inscribes the liminal [and so] mimics its heroine's posture by standing, sitting, lying between a vast number of intertexts, seductively drawing on them even while it simultaneously refuses adequate dialogue with them. I made a personal list of 25 such texts – texts which bear on yet fail to penetrate *Thel*, producing readings that titillate without satisfying interpretive desire' (p. 151). Norvig's language here draws attention to the text as a site for pleasure, even if the pleasure is ultimately frustrated, in a manner that owes much to the work of Roland Barthes and his follower Jacques Derrida. For Barthes, *écriture*, the written text, permits multiple readings and cannot be pinned down to any one sufficient meaning. Hence the 'play' of meanings. The text 'pleasures' us and one way in which it does so is through its teasing elusiveness, its refusal to be trapped in a single, fixed meaning. In this sense, Norvig argues, Blake makes *Thel* a work which enacts a resistance to being incorporated into, or captured by, any one reading, just as the heroine herself, in her liminal position between innocence and experience, refuses to step into a world which will objectify her sexuality. Feminism conscripts both Barthes and Derrida at this point, for if the former encouraged the reading of texts as denying fixed meaning, the latter has done more than anyone to suggest that an adequate reading of any text, just because it is a linguistic construct, will not merely bear but positively require 'active' readings which report on how parts play against each other, in ways which 'produce' meaning that doesn't have to be referred back to the writer's presumed intention and which also allows for other readings. For deconstructionist theory argues that all readings are, in Paul de Man's term, 'misreadings', and no one reading can claim a privileged status for itself as indubitably 'correct'. Nevertheless, some readings are better than others. Norvig draws attention to the unselfconscious and therefore unguarded ways in which commentators (mis)read *Thel* in terms of their own preoccupations. Having suggested that Blake represents his heroine as desiring a 'real female subjectivity' able to resist the various images of womanhood which other characters in the poem attempt to force on her, and which between them 'embrace a philosophy of repetitive and uncreative self-sacrifice', Norvig goes on to remark that she has been amazed

> to discover how so many commentators on *Thel* are drawn by some activation of their own identifications and desire to make strong moral judgements on the character Thel. Often their critical comments are vicious, vituperative, debasing – all in the name of lamenting Thel's so-called retreat from experience. (p. 161)

Norvig's *Thel* is thus a poem whose feminism cannot be unmasked, as Webster claims, in order to reveal underlying masculinist fears and hostilities. Quite the reverse. *Thel* is best read as a truly liberationist, feminist poem.

Reader-Response Theory

Norvig's criticism of inadequate readings points us towards another element in recent developments of critical theory. While some theorists have concerned themselves with the problematic nature of texts, others have swivelled their attention onto the readers of those texts, who are sometimes, although not I think happily, called 'consumers'. Such theorists have as a result created what are usually called 'Reader-Orientated Theories'. Michael Simpson's essay offers what he calls a 'version of reader-response criticism' in order to throw open questions about who Blake may be imagining as the 'implied reader' of his *Songs*, and about the agency of such a reader as well as other, 'actual', readers Blake might not have imagined. The terms 'implied reader' and 'actual reader' were coined by Wolfgang Iser in his book *The Act of Reading: A Theory of Aesthetic Response* (1978). The 'implied reader' is one the writer, or perhaps it is more accurate to say the text, self-consciously creates or appeals to – in the case of *Songs of Innocence* the child or childlike person, in that of *Songs of Experience* the adult. But as 'actual' readers we may stand at some distance from those to whom the *Songs* make their conscious appeal. Simpson notes that behind the *Songs* stands the genre of the chapbook with its emphasis on homiletic lessons in morality aimed at both children and adults. 'By identifying itself as a version of the chapbook Blake's *Songs* structurally projects these reading positions' (p. 170). Simpson gives some examples of these chapbooks and then interestingly suggests that 'Since many of these works incorporate a preface evidently addressed to adult readers, along with a text that seems specifically targeted on children, the eventuality of co-reading seems to be structurally implied by this form'. And so, even if Blake's *Songs* parody the chapbook genre, 'this parody nonetheless employs the device of team reading that is a feature of the form being satirized'.

Although Simpson does not say so, 'team reading' – or rather team-singing – is surely implied not merely by the title *Songs* but by the fact that most of the poems which make up the two collections employ ballad measures, especially 'common measure' (four line rhyming stanzas of alternate four and three stresses). These measures were widely used by eighteenth-century hymn writers, Watt, the Wesleys, William Cowper. There is then in the forms Blake chooses for his *Songs* a deliberate desire to make them poems of the people. In his essay on 'Blake's *Songs of Innocence and Experience*' Matt Simpson implicitly acknowledges this when he argues that Blake demands that 'we experience [the Songs] in a three-dimensional way and know them . . . as something, not just intellectually challenging, but rich and strange, vigorously alive at the point of reading – in a word, as visionary' (p. 189). Reading here includes, as Matt Simpson remarks, looking. He is quick to emphasise the importance of the pictures Blake provided for the poems. He also, very importantly, reminds us that Blake is reported to have made musical settings for his songs. 'In other words they belong to the voice as well as to the page' (p. 190). Lacking these settings, 'we are condemned to partial readings'. What is heartening about Matt Simpson's essay is its untroubled taking for granted of that universal 'we'. Not that he is unaware that 'we' are to some extent affected by gender, time, place, and so forth. But he also knows that partiality is often an effect of fashion, and that nothing is more fashionable – and therefore quicker to become *démodé* – than the critical orthodoxies of the age, of any age. Matt Simpson would, I think, agree with Samuel Johnson's famous claim that 'by the common sense of readers uncorrupted with literary prejudices, after all the refinements of subtilty and the dogmatism of learning, must finally be decided all claim to poetical honours'. Yet as a fine poet himself, Matt Simpson is all too aware that the act of reading, as of writing, is never as uncomplicated, commonsensical, as Johnson makes it appear. The major justification for any critical theory is that it should alert us to what is involved in the act of reading and, perhaps, the act of writing. Becoming better readers of Blake won't help Blake, but it will do us a great deal of good.

Notes

1. *Henry Crabb Robinson on Books and Writers* ed. EDITH J. MORLEY 3 vols (London: Dent, 1935), vol. 1, p. 325.

2. W. B. YEATS, 'The Philosophy of Shelley's Poetry' in *Essays and Introductions* (New York: Collier Books, 1968), p. 94.

3. ALLAN RODWAY, *The Romantic Conflict* (London: Chatto & Windus, 1963), p. 126.

4. *Henry Crabb Robinson*, op. cit., p. 337.

5. ROBERT GRAVES, *The Crowning Privilege* (Harmondsworth: Penguin, 1959), p. 138.

6. D. G. JAMES, *The Romantic Comedy* (London: Oxford University Press, 1963), p. 4.

7. T. S. ELIOT, 'William Blake' in *Selected Essays* (London: Faber, 1953), p. 321. The essay was written in 1920.

8. For those wanting to further their awareness of the issues surrounding Blake's religion, the writings of KATHLEEN RAINE and NORTHROP FRYE are of especial help.

9. *A Handbook for Freedom*, chosen by JACK LINDSAY and EDGELL RICKWORD (London: Lawrence and Wishart, 1939). The same publishers brought out *Spokesmen For Liberty* (1941).

10. A. L. MORTON, *The Everlasting Gospel: A Study in the Sources of William Blake* (London: Lawrence and Wishart, 1958), p. 11. Morton notes that Muggleton had died in 1698 at the age of 89. The last 'Muggletonian' died as recently as 1971 and left his library to E. P. THOMPSON.

11. *The Everlasting Gospel*, p. 12.

12. *The Everlasting Gospel*, p. 14.

13. E. P. THOMPSON, *Witness Against The Beast: William Blake And The Moral Law* (London: Merlin Press, 1993), p. 13.

14. *Witness Against The Beast*, p. 62.

15. *Witness Against The Beast*, p. 62.

16. CHRISTOPHER HILL, 'The Poor and the People' in *Collected Essays, vol. 3, People and Ideas in 17th Century England* (Brighton: Harvester Press, 1986) p. 250.

17. JOHN LUCAS, *England and Englishness: Ideas of Nationhood in Poetry, 1688–1900* (London: Chatto and Windus, 1900), pp. 78–9.

18. In addition to *England and Englishness* work by MARILYN BUTLER and DAVID WORRALL should be consulted. See Further Reading.

19. LINDA COLLEY, *Britons: Forging the Nation 1707–1837* (London: Pimlico, 1992), p. 182.

20. *Witness Against The Beast*, p. 62.

21. LOUIS MONTROSE, 'Renaissance Literary Studies and the Subject of History', *English Literary Renaissance*, no. 16, (1986) pp. 6–9.

22. For a fuller explanation of these terms see my essay 'The Poet in his Joy,' in JOHN LUCAS, *Romantic to Modern, Essays and Ideas of Culture, 1750–1900* (Hassocks: Harvester Press, 1982).

23. For more on this see *England and Englishness*, pp. 52–3.

24. *Poetry and Prose of William Blake*, ed. GEOFFREY KEYNES (London: Nonesuch Press, 1961), p. 785.

25. *Poetry and Prose of William Blake*, p. 737.

26. For a good essay on these two poets, see CHARLES HOBDAY, 'Two Sansculotte Poets: John Freeth and Jospeh Mather,' in *Writing and Radicalism*, ed. JOHN LUCAS (London: Longman, 1996), pp. 61–83.

27. See especially the discussion in *Witness Against the Beast*, pp. 174–94 and the relevant pages in Heather Glen's *Vision and Disenchantment* (Cambridge: Cambridge University Press, 1983).

28. See DAVID WORRALL, *Radical Culture: Discourse, Resistance and Surveillance, 1790–1820* (Hassocks: Harvester Press, 1992), pp. 46–7. See also, M. P. ASRAF, *The Life and Times of Thomas Spence* (Newcastle: Frank Graham, 1983). Asraf notes that 'the most radical land policy of the Chartist phase was nationalization . . .' and that this has its roots in Spence's argument for 'the People's farm', p. 124.

29. For this, see my essay 'Clare's Politics' in *Clare in Context*, eds HUGH HAUGHTON and ADAM PHILIPS (Cambridge: Cambridge University Press, 1994) esp., pp. 161–6.

30. See *English Critical Essays, XVI–XVIII Centuries*, ed. E. J. JONES (London: Oxford University Press, 1963), p. 289.

31. *Letters of Thomas Gray*, ed. J. BERESFORD (London: Oxford University Press, 1951), p. 250.

32. *Letters of Thomas Gray*, p. 250.

33. *Poetry and Prose of William Blake*, p. 779.

34. *Poetry and Prose of William Blake*, p. 772.

35. *Poetry and Prose of William Blake*, p. 772.

36. GEOFFREY KEYNES, *Blake's Songs of Innocence and of Experience*, with introduction and commentary, (London: Oxford University Press, 1970). Unpaginated. The quotation refers to plate 38.

37. *The Poems of William Blake*, ed. W. H. STEVENSON, text by DAVID V. ERDMAN (London: Longman, 1971), p. 167.

2 'The Divine Image'

E. P. Thompson

'The Divine Image', in my view, is the axle upon which the *Songs of Innocence* turn, just as 'The Human Abstract' is the axle for the *Songs of Experience*. It is often supposed to be a profoundly Swedenborgian song, and this is what we must examine. It is certainly true that the 'Divine Human' was at the centre of Swedenborgian discourse at that time; indeed, it might be said to be the signature of the New Jerusalem church. When Robert Southey visited a congregation, he found that

> Christ in his *divine*, or in his *glorified human*, was repeatedly addressed as the only God; and the preacher laboured to show that the profane were those who worshipped three Gods . . .[1]

In shorthand the doctrine was CHRIST IS GOD, and Robert Hindmarsh was astounded to find these words chalked by unknown hands on walls in and for miles round London in the early 1780s.[2]

The doctrine of Swedenborgian receivers was set forth as the first to be recorded in a 'Compendious View of the principal Doctrines of the New Church':

> Contrary to Unitarians who deny, and to Trinitarians who hold, a Trinity of persons in the Godhead, they maintain, that there is a Divine Trinity in the person of Jesus Christ, consisting of Father, Son, and Holy Ghost, just like the human Trinity in every individual man, of soul, body, and operation . . .

> That Jehovah God himself came down from heaven, and assumed human nature for the purpose of removing hell from man, of restoring the heavens to order, and of preparing the way for a new church upon earth; and that herein consists the true nature of redemption, which was effected solely by the omnipotence of the Lord's Divine Humanity.[3]

The Liturgy of the Church required that the Minister announce to the assembly that they were gathered to 'glorify his DIVINE HUMANITY'.[4]

The 'divine humanity' lay in the assumption by an omnipotent God of human nature in Christ's person. This was done, not by splitting into a Trinity, but by God infusing His own life into Christ, through the 'divine influx'. The doctrine created difficulties for early receivers. The Reverend Joseph Proud, a General Baptist minister in Norwich who was converted to the New Church, later recalled his troubles when a Swedenborgian introduced him to 'the doctrine of the LORD as the only God in His divine Humanity':

> I could very well agree to the Lord as being the *only God*, but when he mentioned a *divine humanity* I warmly opposed him and reply'd, 'what is divine cannot be *human*, nor what is *Human*, be *divine*'.[5]

Correspondents returned to the theme in the New Church magazines. Correspondents from Keighley affirmed

> That there is a Trinity in the Lord, namely, the Divinity, the Divine Humanity, and the Divine Proceeding . . . [but] a divine Trinity may be considered to exist in one person, and so to be one God; but not in three persons.[6]

The Reverend Proud, fully converted, explained the doctrine in a discourse in a newly opened New Jerusalem temple in Birmingham to which he ministered. God was *'in one person only'*:

> As to his essential divinity, he is the Father – as to his divine humanity, he is the Son – and as to his divine operation, he is the Holy Spirit . . .

He took on

> *our nature*; in that nature subdued the powers of hell, redeemed mankind, and made salvation possible to all; . . . he glorified that humanity, made it divine, united it with his own essential divinity, and is therefore *God and man in one divine person*.[7]

With the bringing of the divine together in one person, it is not surprising that the Unitarians viewed the Swedenborgians as competitors. Joseph Priestley addressed letters to members of the New Church, urging them to adopt the Unitarian solution and to acknowledge Christ as a man 'but that God was with him, and acted by him'. A ding-dong exchange ensued.[8] In the course of this some apologetics turned upon the contrasting sexual derivation of the divine human. Swedenborg affirmed that 'human nature cannot be transmuted into the Divine Essence, neither commixed therewith'. Therefore a distinction must be maintained in Christ's genesis between the 'human nature from the mother' and the Divine Essence from the divine influx, or from the Father (i.e. the male principle which infused his soul).[9] What Mary supplied was 'a covering, called the maternal human, or a body like our own, so that the divine human (which was eternal and infinite) dwells in the maternal human, which was finite . . .'. At the resurrection Christ cast off all materiality, the maternal human. 'Hence the God we worship, is not the material human of this world, but he that ever was, is, and ever will be, the invisible *I am* . . .'[10]

Correspondents in the *New Magazine* joined the same discussion, and it is difficult not to feel that the Virgin Mary was subjected to some male animosity. A distinction is laboured between the divine principle (always male) and the *humanum maternum* or in Swedenborg's phrase the *humanum infirmum*, 'the unfixed, unsteady, infirm humanity' (from the mother).[11] Ignoramus explained that 'by putting off the humanity from the mother, is evidently meant the conquering and expelling the evil, and by putting on the humanity from the father, is bringing the first principles of human nature, or the divine human, into the ultimates . . .'[12] Another correspondent concluded that Christ's conception (or infusion) was 'manifested in the lowest parts of human nature, and the infirm body derived from the Virgin was tainted with hereditary evil . . .'[13] Hence it must be decisively put off. Chastanier returned to the columns with yet another passage from Swedenborg from his store of manuscripts. From this it appeared that on the cross 'the Lord, from the divine in himself, wholly expelled the evil which he derived from his mother . . .'[14] 'Ignoramus' returned to the attack in the *Magazine*'s final number, making a clear distinction between the Lord's masculine and feminine souls: 'there was not an evil or a false that ever existed in the world, but what the Lord inherited from the mother as to the recipient form in the feminine soul'.[15]

All this helps one to understand the late addition to the *Songs of Experience*, 'To Tirzah', which some critics have found 'obscure':[16]

> Whate'er is Born of Mortal Birth,
> Must be consumed with the Earth
> To rise from Generation free;
> Then what have I to do with thee?

> The Sexes sprung from Shame & Pride
> Blow'd in the morn: in evening died
> But Mercy changd Death into Sleep;
> The Sexes rose to work & weep.

> Thou Mother of my Mortal part
> With cruelty didst mould my Heart,
> And with false self-decieving tears,
> Didst bind my Nostrils Eyes & Ears.

> Didst close my Tongue in senseless clay
> And me to Mortal Life betray:
> The Death of Jesus set me free,
> Then what have I to do with thee?

This, if we set aside the enigmatic second verse, might be an expression of orthodox Swedenborgian doctrine, even according to 'Ignoramus'. The *maternum humanum* supplies only a covering to clothe the divine spirit, and Blake recalls the words of Jesus to Mary (John 2:4): 'Woman, what have I to do with thee?' To this he adds a wider mythic dimension, in the name 'Tirzah', perhaps taken from Revelation 1.11, the name of a city which is rival and opponent to Jerusalem and which becomes for Blake an emblem of 'worldly authority and . . . materialistic thought'.[17] The poem was not added until 1805, and perhaps later, and hence belongs to a period in which Blake may have been becoming reconciled to Swedenborgianism.[18] And in *Jerusalem* he wrote:

> A Vegetated Christ & a Virgin Eve, are the Hermaphroditic
> Blasphemy, by his Maternal Birth he is that Evil One
> And his Maternal Humanity must be put off Eternally
>
> (E247)

However, let us return to 1789. All this debate about the 'divine human' does rather little to prepare us for Blake's beautiful poem, 'The Divine Image':

> To Mercy Pity Peace and Love
> All pray in their distress:
> And to these virtues of delight
> Return their thankfulness.

> For Mercy Pity Peace and Love,
> Is God, our father dear:
> And Mercy Pity Peace and Love,
> Is Man his child and care.

For Mercy has a human heart
Pity, a human face:
And Love, the human form divine,
And Peace, the human dress.

Then every man, of every clime,
That prays in his distress,
Prays to the human form divine
Love Mercy Pity Peace.

And all must love the human form,
In heathen, turk, or jew.
Where Mercy, Love & Pity dwell
There God is dwelling too.

It is a pity to argue about so transparent a poem, but this must be done. Mr F. W. Bateson, in common with other critics, found it to be 'a thoroughly Swedenborgian poem', [19] and Kathleen Raine has concurred: 'There could be no more simple and orthodox statement of the central doctrine of the New Church'.[20] It may therefore seem surprising that the poem, immediately, in its first verse, commences with a refutation of Swedenborg. For Swedenborg had argued in *Divine Love and Divine Wisdom*:

> With Respect to God, it is not possible that he can love and be reciprocally beloved by others, in whom there is . . . any Thing Divine; for if there was . . . any Thing Divine in them, then it would not be beloved by others, but it would love itself . . .

Blake, who was then in his most sympathetic state towards the seer, challenged this with 'False': 'Take it so or the contrary it comes to the same for if a thing loves it is infinite' (E593). The first verse of 'The Divine Image' could not be more explicit in its rejection of Swedenborg's doctrine, and the verses which follow consolidate this. The poem resumes 'the central doctrine of the New Church' in no way.

One can illustrate this by the means of contrast. An early convert to the New Church, whom we have met already, was the Revd Joseph Proud, aged forty-five, who had already served for some twenty-five years as minister of the General Baptists. Converted dramatically to the new faith, he had a little reputation as a poet,[21] and – shortly after visiting London from Norwich in 1789 – he was urged to prepare a volume of original hymns for the use of the public worship of the New Church.[22] He did this with expedition, writing a modest contribution of three hundred hymns in the intervals between breaking the news to his Norwich flock that he was about to leave them to become one of the first ministers of the New Church (in Birmingham). One of his first efforts was, exactly, 'On Divine Humanity',[23] from which these verses are taken:

> . . . Lord, we come to thee,
>   And bow before thy throne;
> In thy Divine Humanity,
>   Thou art our God alone.
>
> Thy esse none can see,
>   That is beyond our sight;
> But thy Divine Humanity
>   Is seen in heavenly light.
>
> Thou art the only God,
>   The *only Man* art thou;
> And only thee our souls adore,
>   At thy bles'd feet we bow.
>
> In essence thou art one,
>   And one in person too;
> Tho' in thy essence seen by none,
>   Thy person we may view . . .

In another hymn, on the same theme, we have these verses:

> But thou art God & God alone,
>   In thy Humanity;
> Before thee, Lord, no God was known,
>   Nor shall be after thee.
>
> Thy human nature is divine,
>   Divine is human too;
> Here God and Man in one combine,
>   And not three Gods, nor two.

One begins to suspect, from a certain barren shuttling of paradoxes, that the doctrine at this point created headaches for the pastor and perhaps dissension among the flock. And this can be confirmed by two lines from a further hymn:

> Why should we fear to say or sing,
>   Our God in Man alone . . .

But the Dutch courage of Mr Proud is immediately covered by an evasive footnote: 'By man alone, understand that God is the only man, strictly speaking, as all mankind are men from him and not in themselves . . .'[24]

Let us now return to Blake's poem, and attempt the painful exercise of reading it with Mr Proud's alternative still in our mind. The instant contrast is between the deference of Proud and the egalitarian humanism of Blake.[25] Without any outrage or rupture of logical or poetic structure, with the greatest quietness, we move from the acceptable (although not to Swedenborg) statement of the first verse to the heresy of the last three. There is indeed some difference in matter between Blake and Proud. Blake passes by altogether the doctrinal issue of the Trinity. And there is an absence in him of that obeisance before 'thy throne' ('Thee we adore, eternal Lord/In thy Humanity') which distances God once more ('beyond our sight'), so that the notion of God's humanity comes through not as authentic but as a metaphysical conjuring trick. 'Thy esse none can see/That is beyond our sight' – but Blake's divine esse can be seen, in human virtues, and only seen there.[26] This is what Blake's song is about, and what it is saying is not so much around the theme of 'divine humanity' as of human divinity: the poem is called 'The Divine Image'. And hence if man worships – but Blake does not use this word, he uses prayers of distress, thankfulness and love – he must worship these qualities as he finds them in himself. Blake is breaking both with the paternalist image of God which (whether a vengeful Father or an all-knowing First Cause or, as with Mr Proud, a somewhat muddled but benevolent gentleman) occupied a position of critical importance within all eighteenth-century ideology, and he was breaking also – and as I think explicitly – with the abasement before 'Jehovah God in his GLORIFIED HUMANITY' as it was demanded by the Confessional of the New Church as expressed in its *Liturgy* (another Hindmarsh product):

> Most merciful Lord Jesus, who in thy DIVINE HUMANITY art the Only God of Heaven and Earth, the supreme Governor of the Universe, and before whom the whole Angelic Host fall prostrate in profound Humiliation, permit us thy sinful Creatures, Worms of the Earth, to approach thy heavenly Majesty . . .[27]

Blake at all times kept his distance from the Swedenborgian doctrine of the 'divine humanity'. The problem of immanence and transcendence, identity and essence, was being worked at in different ways in the early New Church milieu. A contributor to the *New Magazine of Knowledge Concerning Heaven and Hell* tried to explain it by offering a Swedenborgian version of the Lord's Prayer:

Our Father,	O infinite eternal esse,
Who art in the heavens	Manifested in the heavens
Hallowed be thy name	Whom we adore in the existence of thy Divine Humanity
Thy Kingdom come,	Let the divine influx of wisdom
Thy will be done	And love,
As in heaven	Flowing from thee through thy new heavens
So also upon earth.	Be received with a pure affection by each member of thy New Church.
Give us this day	Give us according to our various states of want
Our daily bread . . .	That true nourishment of our souls, that will be our increasing spiritual support to eternity . . .[28]

Nor was this contributor ('Ignoramus' once more) unusual in finding exceptional difficulty in selecting proper spiritual correspondences for such corporeal terms as 'earth' and 'bread'. The characteristic movement is away from the concrete image, whereas Blake leads us back to 'heart', 'face', 'form' and 'dress'. And it is Swedenborg's own writings which are responsible for this evasive movement. 'What Person of Sound Reason', he had asked in the *Divine Love and Wisdom*, 'doth not perceive that the Divine is not divisible?' If he should say

> that it is possible there may be several infinities, Uncreates, Omnipotents and Gods, provided they have the same Essence, and that thereby there is one and the same Essence but one and the same Identity?

This passage had bothered Blake (then in his most sympathetic state towards Swedenborg) a great deal. His annotation runs:

> Answer   Essence is not Identity but from Essence proceeds Identity & from one Essence may proceed many Identities as from one Affection may proceed. many thoughts
> Surely this is an oversight.

> That there is but one Omnipotent Uncreate & God I agree but that there is but one Infinite I do not. for if all but God is not Infinite they shall come to an End which God forbid.

If the Essence was the same *as the* Identity there could be but one
Identity. which is false
Heaven would upon this plan be but a Clock but one & the same
Essence is therefore Essence & not Identity.

(E593)

A consideration of this important note would take us back to
Behmenist and Muggletonian notions of eternity and creation.
But in its immediate relevance it bears upon the problem of the
'divine humanity'. Blake prefers an image which allows 'many
identities' to proceed from one 'essence', just as many thoughts
may proceed from one 'affection': this allows him to think of the
divine essence both as 'one & the same Essence' and also as that
essence expressed in the many identities of men, while still remaining essentially divine.

Swedenborg offered texts which were both diaphonous and
contradictory, and which allowed several positions to be held.
Thus (1) – as endorsed in the principles of the New Church –
it was limited to the doctrine of God taking on mortal form in Jesus
and thus *assuming* divine humanity. As Proud warbled, 'thy esse
none can see' but 'thy Divine Humanity/Is seen in heavenly light'.
But (2) an extension of this could be proposed, in that God makes
himself known to man through heavenly inspiration, working upon
his affections (rather than upon his understanding) and hence his
'esse' enters into man as 'love'. A constant Swedenborgian image is
of the sun as the source of the influx of love, and of man's spirit as
the reflector or recipient of this influx. That part of man enlightened
by love shares in the divine esse and is in that sense itself divine.
Thus Miss Raine cites Swedenborg's *True Christian Religion*:

> A man is an organ of life, and God alone is life: God infuses his
> life into the organ and all its parts: and God grants man a sense
> that the life in himself is as it were his own.[29]

And she concludes that Blake is 'preaching the doctrine of the New
Church'. But Blake's song doesn't sound like this. He sounds as if
he is saying something much blunter: there is nothing in 'The Divine
Image' about God 'infusing' or 'granting' to man 'a sense' of life
being 'as it were' his own. I can't find the words 'as it were' anywhere in the Blake *Concordance*. It sounds as if Blake is saying
exactly what he says in *The Marriage of Heaven and Hell*: 'God only
Acts & Is, in existing Beings or Men' (E39). And that, too, can be
read in two different ways: that God, as some disembodied esse,
only finds embodiment in existing beings or men: or that there is

no God anywhere else. I suspect that Blake fluctuated between contrary states, perhaps emphasising in 1789 the first, the second in 1791–3 and at some time thereafter returning to the first.[30]

In any case, we have a clear idea of how Blake came to his poem. In 1789 when annotating the humanist, Lavater, he was delighted with certain passages. When he fell upon 'He who *hates the wisest and best of men, hates the Father of men; for, where is the Father of men to be seen but in the most perfect of his children?*' he struck out both of the 'hates' and inserted above them 'loves' and underlined the italicised phrase, adding: 'this is true worship'.[31] When Lavater wrote that 'art is nothing but the highest sagacity and exertion of human nature; *and what nature will he honour who honours not the human?*' he underlined again, and noted 'human nature is the image of God'. And, immediately above, Lavater had written: '*He, who adored an impersonal God, has none; and, without guide or rudder, launches on an immense abyss that first absorbs his powers, and next himself*'. Blake underscored the whole passage, and exclaimed: 'Most superlatively beautiful & most affectionatly Holy & pure would to God that all men would consider it' (E586). This prepares us for the annotation to Swedenborg's *Divine Love and Wisdom*, probably in the next year, especially section 11 where the seer comments that the Africans 'entertain an Idea of God as of a Man, and say that no one can have any other Idea of God'. Blake notes approvingly: 'Think of a white cloud. as being holy you cannot love it but think of a holy man within the cloud love springs up in your thoughts. for to think of holiness distinct from man is impossible to the affections. Thought alone can make monsters, but the affections cannot' (E592–3).

There is, of course, a pre-history to all this. The eighteenth century, as is notorious, saw a general movement among the enlightened dissenters through Arianism to Socinianism towards the resting-place of Unitarianism, which entailed the denial of the Trinity and of Christ's divinity. This was one way to a humanist Christ. But the Muggletonians, the Philadelphians and what there was of an articulate antinomian tradition, took, with variants, a different path. Positing only one God, they might see him in the pantheist tradition, as dispersed through all life, or, as did the Muggletonians, as assuming Himself, in the infant Christ, full mortality. Thus Reeve:

There is no other God but the Man Jesus . . . the eternal God, the Man of Glory, who is a distinct God in the Person of a Man . . . Therefore . . . they cannot take the Sword of Steel to slay their Brother, because they know that Man is the Image of God.[32]

Thus also Thomas Tomkinson, some of whose gentle and slightly rationalised versions of the Muggletonian faith were published posthumously. He speaks of God 'begetting himself into a Son . . . God sent forth HIMSELF to be made of a Woman, to redeem us from the Curse of the Law . . .'[33] Both the pantheist and the embodiment-of-God-as-Christ versions were found among eighteenth-century Muggletonians, and they sometimes co-existed in the same mind. I find in a letter of a believer, William Sedgwick, in 1794 the old tension between the two being held:

> Christ is the Light that Lighteth Every man that Commeth into the world yet none but God is Infinite. Notwithstanding tho God the Creater virtuale Dwells in all his Creatures. Nothing is Capable of the Indwelling Infinite power But God alone . . . Even man in his Created Purety tho of the very nature of the Divine Creator yet not Infinite . . .

The argument is close to the discourse preoccupying the New Church, but the emphasis – and where the Muggletonians differed sharply from the Swedenborgians – lay upon Christ's concentrated divinity:

> The Eternal God Left his glorious kingdom Came Down & Enterd The Blessed virgin Mary's whomb. There Desolved his Spritual Body in to seed and Natuer & Quickend into a body of flesh Blood & Bone Like unto man in all Respects (Sins Only Excepted) . . .[34]

Man is the 'Image of God' and he is also the 'ark' or 'tabernacle' of God: and God is Christ. The image of Christ is always that of the sun or of blinding light: as Richard Pickersgill, the Muggletonian painter, wrote in 1803, in heaven 'we shall behold the bright burning Glorious person'.[35] It is such a bright burning glorious infant that Blake shows us in his remarkable (and unprecedented) Nativity, with Christ springing from Mary's womb into the hands of St Elizabeth, with St John the Baptist (also an infant) looking on (Illus. 9). David Bindman finds this treatment to be 'unique in European art': the 'moment of birth is represented as a heavenly burst of radiance'.[36]

> And thine the Human Face & thine
> The Human Hands & Feet & Breath
> Entering thro' the Gates of Birth
> And passing thro' the Gates of Death.

(E171)

37

The pantheist view, which proposed God as some quantum of divine energy dispersed through all life, but more especially in the spiritual nature of men and women, and the notion of God as Christ, are difficult to combine, and perhaps intellectually impossible. Or the difficulty may only be in reconciling these two alternative versions of the same vision. I suggest that, in his later years when he had rejected deism, Blake was often preoccupied with the problem of reconciling, through imagery or myth, these seemingly contradictory visions. Perhaps we have it in *Vala*:

> Then those in Great Eternity met in the Council of God As one Man, for contracting their Exalted Senses They behold Multitude or Expanding they behold as one As One Man all the Universal family & that One man They call Jesus the Christ, & they in him & he in them Live in Perfect harmony . . .
>
> (E306)

Or in his *Descriptions of the Last Judgement*:

> . . . I have seen [those States] in my Imagination when distant they appear as One Man but as you approach they appear Multitudes of Nations . . . I have seen when at a distance Multitudes of Men in Harmony appear like a single Infant sometimes in the Arms of a Female (this represented the Church).
>
> (E546)

And we have it also in the splendid exchange with Crabb Robinson in December 1825:

> On my asking in what light he viewed the great question concerning the Divinity of Jesus Christ, he said; '*He is the only God.*' But then he added – 'And so am I and so are you.'[37]

Crabb Robinson was floored by that, and so in a way are we, although we rejoice at Blake's triumph and have a swift sense of some revealed truth. But what we may actually be sensing is a creative contradiction. Blake is refusing to renounce 'Mercy's lord' or to reduce the gospel to the level of rational historical explanation;[38] but equally he is refusing to sublimate Jesus or his gospel into an abstraction, to tease out from this some bodiless fiction and call this 'God', or to humiliate himself before a divine essence in which all men share. The reply breaks at a bound from the net of the theological disputes of his time, between Arian, Socinian, Unitarian or Deist positions. It conveys a truth of a poetic kind, expressive of a certain equipoise and tension of values, appropriate to lyrical expression. And expressed thus, neither Urizen nor Crabb Robinson could answer it.

Obscurities can arise in the later prophetic books, not just because Blake was managing his art badly, but because he was attempting to reconcile doctrines that could not be logically reconciled. The books plunge into obscurity at exactly those points (of which the problem of the unity and the dispersal of the godhead is one) where Blake was involved in actual doctrinal or philosophical contradictions.

But a contradiction in thought, which derives from an acute tension of contrasting values, neither of which can be abandoned, can be wholly creative. If we will neither deny Christ's divinity nor elevate it above that of mortal creation which shares in the same divine essence, then we have an intense and mystic humanism. If God exists in Men and nowhere else, then the whole cosmic conflict between darkness and light, things corporeal and spiritual, must be enacted within oneself and one's fellow men and nowhere else. This meant above all – and this was perhaps the greatest offence of such a heresy in the eyes of a more vengeful Christian tradition – breaking with any sense of personal conviction in original sin. There had been a fall and a dispersal of the godhead; the godly nature of man now struggled to repair the breach and return to universal harmony, the family of love, Jerusalem. Were man to be called an abject and sinful worm would be (from this standpoint) to blaspheme against the godhead within him. 'Every thing has as much right to Eternal Life as God who is the Servant of Man.'[39]

I cannot see that either Lavater or Swedenborg offers to us the vocabulary or the imagery of 'The Divine Image'. Blake's annotations to them indicate not discovery but recognition and assent, or correction and exposition, of tenets already held. It is a poem which with purity and lucidity holds in tension and reconciles the two positions we have been exploring. From the first verse – and how much is won in the first verse – we are drawn into an ascending circle of mutuality. It was therefore with a delighted shock of recognition that I came across in the *New Magazine of Knowledge Concerning Heaven and Hell*, inserted without preliminaries or explanation, a long extract from Thomas Tomkinson's *A System of Religion*: 'That God ever was, is, and will be, in the Form of a Man':

Can righteousness and holiness act forth themselves without a body? Or do you ever read, that righteousness and holiness were ever acted forth, in, or by any other form but the form of a man? When God said, *Be ye holy as I am holy*: what! must the souls run out of the bodies to be like him? If they did, they would be nothing. Where would mercy and justice, meekness and humility, be found? There could be no such virtues known, or have being, were they not found to center in a body.[40]

Here are our virtues of delight, and here is our human embodiment of the divine. It provides a clearer (and more Blakean) introduction to 'The Divine Image' than does Swedenborg. It is a tantalising piece of evidence. No other theological authority, apart from Swedenborg and contemporary readers of the review, appeared in the two volumes of the magazine. Whose hand brought it to the editor's attention? At least we have evidence that there was one person in that early New Church milieu conversant with Muggletonian writings. 'The Divine Image' might even be called a Tomkinsonian song.

Notes

1. SOUTHEY, *Letters from England*, vol. III, p. 113.

2. HINDMARSH, *Rise and Progress*, p. 13.

3. *New Magazine of Knowledge concerning Heaven and Hell*, vol. I, pp. 16–18.

4. *Liturgy of the New Church* (printed and sold by R. HINDMARSH, 1791).

5. 'Memoirs of Joseph Proud', MSS in Swedenborg Society Conference Library, 1822, pp. 7–8.

6. *New Magazine of Knowledge*, vol. II, p. 237.

7. J. PROUD, *The Fundamental Doctrines of the New Jerusalem* (Birmingham, 1792), p. 15.

8. JOSEPH PRIESTLEY, *Letters to the Members of the New Jerusalem Church* (Birmingham, 1791), p. 31; J. PROUD, *A Candid and Impartial Reply to the Reverend Dr Priestley's Letters* (Birmingham, 1791); R. HINDMARSH, 'Letters to Dr Priestley', *Analytical Review*, 11, Appendix, p. 517, 14, pp. 190–3; J. BELLAMY, *Jesus Christ the Only God* (1792), a reply to Priestley.

9. BELLAMY, p. 51, citing Swedenborg, *Arcana Coelestia*, 2655–2659.

10. BELLAMY, Letter II.

11. BENEDICT CHASTANIER, 'On the Lord's Humanity', *New Magazine*, 2, pp. 305–9. See also 2, pp. 266–8.

12. Ibid., 2, p. 313.

13. Ibid., 2, p. 314: 'M.B.G.'

14. Ibid., 2, pp. 374–6.

15. Ibid., 2, pp. 442–4.

16. As did Sir GEOFFREY KEYNES in his notes to the reproduction of the *Songs* (Oxford, 1967), p. 154.

17. DAVID W. LINDSAY, *Blake: Songs of Innocence and Experience* (Atlantic Highlands, N.J., 1989), pp. 82–3.

18. ALICIA OSTRIKER, *William Blake, The Complete Poems* (Harmondsworth: Penguin, 1977), p. 889, says that poem cannot be earlier than 1803; Erdman (E722) suggests mid-1805 or later. Blake told Crabb Robinson in 1826 that Christ 'took much after his Mother And in so far he was one of the worst of Men'.

19. F. W. BATESON, *Selected Poems of William Blake* (1957).

20. RAINE, *Blake and Tradition*, 1, p. 20. Also RAINE, 'The Human Face of God', in *Blake and Swedenborg*, ed. HARVEY F. BELLIN and DARRELL RUHL (New York: Swedenborg Foundation, 1985), pp. 88–90. Miss Raine is strongly committed to the view that there could not possibly have been any humanist influence on Blake and therefore reads 'The Divine Image' as 'deep eschatological mystery'.

21. His dreadful poem announcing his conversion, *Jehovah's Mercy made Known to all Mankind in these Last Days* was published in 1789 by HINDMARSH. I do not think that all mankind read it. The Old Church could not have received worse references: it was *'sunk, vastated, fallen'*, 'polluted' and 'to Whoredome, gross Adultery is given'.

22. (Ed. E. MADELEY), REVD JOSEPH PROUD, *The Aged Minister's Last Legacy* (1854), p. xi; MS 'Memoir of Joseph Proud', pp. 15–16; at the General Conference, 5 April 1790, Proud announced that he had already written many hymns: *Minutes*, pp. 8–9.

23. This hymn was singled out for special publication in the *New Magazine*, vol. I, p. 288 (August 1790).

24. JOSEPH PROUD, *Hymns and Spiritual Songs for the Use of the Lord's New Church* (2nd edn, 1791), pp. 142, 219–21. The first edition, in 500 copies, was published in 1790.

25. See HEATHER GLEN, *Vision and Disenchantment: Blake's 'Songs' and Wordsworth's Lyrical Ballads* (Cambridge, 1983), pp. 151–6.

26. In the HINDMARSH version of the *Liturgy* it is stated in a footnote that 'the Faces of Jehovah' in Holy Scripture signify 'the Love, Mercy, Peace and Goodness of the Lord'.

27. An *Order of Worship* was drawn up as early as January 1788; HINDMARSH, p. 60. The Liturgy was named for revision at the second Annual Conference, April 1790: *Minutes*.

28. Vol. II, p. 352. Another dreadful version of the Lord's Prayer appeared in the *Order of Worship* in which 'give us this day our daily bread' is given as 'a suitable supply from thy divine human give us momentarily, according to our state of reception'.

29. RAINE, *Blake and Tradition*, vol. I, p. 18.

30. As late as 1820 Blake annotated BERKELEY: *Siris*: 'God is Man & exists in us & we in him'.

31. Blake returns to this in *The Marriage of Heaven and Hell*, Plates 22–3 (E42): 'The worship of God is. Honouring his gifts in other men each according to his genius. and loving the greatest men best, those who envy or calumniate great men hate God. for there is no other God.'

32. JOHN REEVE, *Sacred Remains* (n.d.), p. 83.

33. *A System of Religion*, first published in 1729 from manuscripts found among Tomkinson's papers after his death, pp. 22–3.

34. British Library, Muggletonian archive.

35. Ibid.

36. BINDMAN, *Blake as an Artist*, pp. 121–2,

37. BENTLEY, *Blake Records*, p. 310.

38. In later years he said that Swedenborg 'was wrong in endeavouring to explain to the *rational* faculty what the reason cannot comprehend', ibid., p. 312.

39. Blake's 'Annotations to Thornton', c.1827 (E658).

40. The extract leads vol. I, no. 6 of the *New Magazine* (August 1790), pp. 243–7. It is taken, with some cutting but no alterations, from TOMKINSON's *A System of Religion*, Chapter 2. The Swedenborgians continued to show an interest in Tomkinson: see JAMES HYDE, 'The Muggletonians and the Document of 1729', *The New-Church Review* (Boston, Mass.), 7, 1900, pp. 215–27.

3 Dangerous Enthusiasm

JOHN MEE

In some respects my approach amounts to an archaeology of reading; it includes an effort to seek out the encoded politics of Blake's rhetoric. But it is important to emphasise that my attempt to relate Blake's rhetorical practices to the larger patterns of the Revolution controversy is not an attempt to explain anything away. The chapters below aspire to an historical approach which does not close down but opens up the texts it addresses. Central to this endeavour will be my use of the notion of 'bricolage'; a term which implies diversity in the object of study and looks beyond the attempt merely to fix and limit texts within already unified intellectual traditions. I have developed my understanding of 'bricolage' from Claude Lévi-Strauss's discussion of the distinction between modern and primitive modes of thought in *The Savage Mind*. Lévi-Strauss identified the magical perspective of the latter with the 'bricoleur': 'someone who works with his hands and uses devious means comparable to those of a craftsman'. The response of the bricoleur to a problem is conditioned by 'a heterogeneous repertoire which, even if extensive, is nevertheless limited'. Lévi-Strauss contrasted the bricoleur's use of whatever diverse materials lay at hand with the situation of the engineer, the term he uses to denote a modern, scientific perspective. The engineer seeks to forge new tools to fit each specific task and envisages a language 'wholly transparent with respect to reality'. Crucial to my understanding of 'bricolage' is the fact that, although 'pre-constrained' by 'a heterogeneous repertoire', each time the bricoleur resorts to that language it involves 'a complete reorganization of the structures' that have been inherited. Acknowledging Derrida's point that all textual constructions (including those of the engineer) are always already formed by received languages, I shall be using 'bricolage' to denote an approach which unapologetically recombines elements from across discourse boundaries such that the antecedent discourses are fundamentally altered in the resultant structures.[1]

The historian Iain McCalman has already made an important application of the notion of 'bricolage' in the historical and political milieux with which I am concerned.[2] He has shown how ultra-radicals in the period 1795–1840 produced a variegated political discourse that was an eclectic combination of a variety of received repertoires. These radical bricoleurs produced texts which do not easily fit into any single intellectual tradition, indeed they frequently drew on resources which might seem to the modern scholar to be mutually exclusive. McCalman's paradigmatic example is Thomas Spence, who had a long career as a radical activist. Spence began in Newcastle upon Tyne, where he formulated a theory of land reform and promoted it through cheap tracts and his own debating society. He moved to London, probably in the late 1780s, and became an early member of the London Corresponding Society, producing his own pamphlets, prints, tokens, and the serial *Pig's Meat* (1793–5) to promote the case for revolution. The variety of vehicles that Spence was prepared to use is paralleled in the disparateness of his rhetorical resources. He combined, among other things, the millenarian tendencies of popular enthusiastic culture with the scepticism we associate with the rationalist Enlightenment. Of particular importance to Spence from the latter current was C. F. Volney's *The Ruins* (English translation, 1792). Spence's *A Letter from Ralph Hodge, to his Cousin Thomas Bull* (1795), for instance, contains a dialogue between those whose 'labours support and nourish society' and 'the civil, military, and religious agents of government' which is taken almost word for word from Volney's book. In contrast, *A Fragment of an Ancient Prophecy* (1796) rejoiced in the utopian expectations of the millenarian popular culture, happily quoting the Bible to support its vision of post-revolutionary bliss: 'Then shall the whole earth, as Isaiah saith, be at rest and in quiet; and shall break forth into singing; and they shall say, Now we are free indeed!' We are familiar with similar biblical aspects of Blake's work, but perhaps less ready to admit that strains of Volney's scepticism are also evident.[3]

McCalman's recognition of both of these elements in Spence's work has led him to place Spence within 'a long history of convergence between millenarian religious ideas and popular forms of scepticism and materialism'. Whatever the prehistory of that convergence it surfaces repeatedly in the 1790s. It is a recurrent feature of Daniel Isaac Eaton's *Politics for the People* (1793–5) and can also be traced in Paine's *Rights of Man* (1791–2), where a submerged millenarianism, built up through biblical allusions, is coexistent with a sturdy rationalism. The latter point is exemplified in one of Paine's many direct appeals to the reader: 'Lay then the axe to the root, and teach governments humanity.' What might seem to be a

direct appeal to natural rights theory, calling for the clearing away
of the impediments that have grown up to obscure the original state
of liberty, is, in fact, couched in the language of the Bible (Matthew
3: 10): 'The axe is laid unto the root of the trees therefore every tree
which burgeons not forth good fruit, is hewen down, and cast into
the fire.' The flexibility of Paine's political rhetoric is demonstrated
by his preparedness to turn to the language of popular religion at
a point where he sought to appeal directly to the disenfranchised
reader.[4]

Part of the complexity of Blake's work from the 1790s onwards
stems from the fact that he drew on disparate discourses to create
a bricolage which has features in common with the work of Spence,
Paine, and other radicals. Initially, at least, two separate aspects of
Blake's eclecticism can be identified. The first, which most closely
equates to the notion of bricolage invoked above, is a matter of
seemingly disparate discourses operating in a single text.

From such interactions between discourses Blake constructed a
rhetoric that was alive with political resonances. At the same time
he was also responding to developments which, especially in the
intensely ideological decade of the 1790s, were already emergent
in the discourses themselves. Biblical criticism, for instance, which
might seem the very stuff of dry scholarship, was taken to be
intimately involved with the ideological struggles of the Revolution
controversy. The Bishop of Lincoln at least was convinced that
the defence of the constitution necessitated the protection of the
integrity of the Bible.

> The same captious and restless spirit which leads men to cavil
> at the articles of our religious faith, and to reject the mysteries
> of the Gospel, because they surpass their comprehension, causes
> them to be dissatisfied with our civil constitution, and to represent
> its essential parts as useless and dangerous, because they do not
> agree with their own imaginary ideas of unattainable perfection.

Such suspicions were not just held of the directly political attacks
on the scriptures made by Paine and Volney but also of innovative
biblical scholarship which threatened to subject the text to rational
investigation.[5]

Particular aspects of Blake's rhetoric can be linked with specific
discourses in clear-cut ways. The second aspect of Blakian bricolage
to which I want to draw attention is the facility with which it
produced forms, plots, and figures which stand at significant
confluences between discourses. Sometimes these confluences
preceded Blake's own formulations. The association of the Celtic

bard with the Hebrew prophet, for instance, was a well-established product of syncretic tendencies in literary primitivism, biblical studies, and historiography. But even given these larger trends, Blake seems to have taken a particular interest in such confluences, extending those which were already established, and evolving others which seem uniquely Blakian. A typical example is the complex referentiality of Blake's Tree of Mystery, which makes its first appearance in *The Book of Ahania* (1795). By placing the Tree in a context which links druidism with Christian priestcraft this configuration suggests, like Paine's *The Age of Reason* (1794–5), that Christianity perpetuated barbaric pagan practices. Perhaps less obviously, the image also takes up one of the most emotive and contentious configurations of the Revolution controversy. Burke had presented the British state as the product of an organic and legitimate evolutionary process; in doing so he gave new life to the traditional symbol of the English oak. For radicals this image of natural maturation was a mystification of 'the tree of feudal tyranny' which Paine sought to cut down and replace with the Tree of Liberty. The secret noxious growth of Blake's Tree of Mystery reveals his sense of the corrupt reality hidden by Burke's rhetoric. The point is made even more explicitly in the later works where the image transmutes into 'Tyburn's fatal tree', the gallows on which the power of Burke's established order was most nakedly displayed.[6]

The organisation of an account of Blake's rhetoric around the notion of bricolage provides for a dialectical approach. Aspects traceable to the issues and language of one discourse can also be made sense of in other discursive contexts so that simplistic notions of sources and influence have to be abandoned. Devoting chapters to separate contexts allows for the treatment of particular features of Blake's work from different perspectives. It can accommodate the fact that Blake's anticlerical scepticism admits both of rationalist antecedents and analogues and parallel responses from the populist culture of religious enthusiasm. Yet the notion of bricolage can be pushed beyond an heuristic efficacy in relation to Blake. Many writers involved in the Revolution controversy seem to have shared Blake's rhetorical eclecticism. Ronald Paulson's work on the representation of the Revolution has suggested that the response was necessarily 'a kind of bricolage'. The various new styles of verbal and visual representation which emerged in conjunction with the Revolution were made up from adaptations of received modes in what Paulson sees as an attempt to come to terms with the unprecedented nature of events in France. While Paulson does offer a valid model for much of the discourse of the Revolution, bricolage seems to me to be especially typical of popular radicalism. My point is not that it is a rigidly class-determined strategy, but that those barred from orthodox channels of knowledge and its transmission were particularly disposed to such a procedure.[7]

Ever since E. P. Thompson's *The Making of the English Working Class*, the unprecedented contributions of the disenfranchised lower classes, especially artisans and the petite bourgeoisie, have been seen as one of the most distinctive features of the Revolution controversy. Although there was a popular political culture before the 1790s, it is clear that the London Corresponding Society had among its members many who were freshly involved in the political process with no tested tradition of political discourse standing behind them. The memoirs of activists like John Binns and Francis Place offer evidence of the intellectual awakening experienced by many of these newly involved radicals. It is scarcely surprising that autodidacts and those without formal education were often eclectic in their use of language and prepared to use received protocols in unusual ways. Blake can be numbered among these artisan radicals, though like Thomas Spence he had produced politically aware writings prior to 1789. Not having encountered ideas in the aspic of sanctioned tradition, there was little reason for such figures to write in terms of any homogeneous academic discourse.

T. S. Eliot recognised something of the relevance of this for Blake when he wrote: 'We have the same respect for Blake's philosophy . . . that we have for an ingenious piece of homemade furniture; we admire the man who has put it together out of the odds and ends of the house'. For Eliot, in search of a culturally ratified, unitary tradition of poetry, it was a source of lament that Blake had no available 'framework of accepted and traditional ideas' in which to work. But Blake and many other lower-class radicals of the 1790s rejoiced in their freedom from such a framework. They found in the dominant culture a variety of rhetorical resources which they sought to refashion and recombine in challenging frameworks of their own. Blake was not Eliot's 'naked man'. Along with figures like Spence and Eaton, Blake took full advantage of the potential the complex nexus of languages he inherited opened up for subversion and parody. Many radicals in the 1790s took up the role of the bricoleur; they relished breaking down those discourses which had cultural authority and creating from them new languages of liberation. Blake's attachment to this poetic of transgression receives one of its clearest statements in Plate 14 of his *The Marriage of Heaven and Hell*. There he wrote of his 'printing in the infernal method, by corrosives, which in Hell are salutary and medicinal, melting apparent surfaces away, and displaying the infinite which was hid' (E 39; Pl. 14). So

taken have many critics been with the figural allusion to the
engraving process which produced the Plate that they have often
failed to give due weight to the fundamentally subversive nature
of the method declared here.[8]

Blake's poetic is deeply concerned with the disruption and transformation of hegemonic discourses. Examples are legion. *Europe*, for
instance, invokes and works through Milton's 'Ode on the Morning
of Christ's Nativity', revealing Milton's deferral of 'truth and justice'
to be a compromise with the 'allegorical' rewards and punishments
of the religious establishment. More broadly, there are Blake's trans-
valuations and disruptions of biblical paradigms. What I want to
emphasise here is that while these processes might seem to be
spectacular examples of Blake's peculiar 'Poetic Genius', they are
also typical of the strategies and priorities of a range of radical texts
in the 1790s.

So far I have argued that bricolage is a striking feature of the
organisation of Blake's poetry, a feature shared by many whose
writing responded to and was shaped by the Revolution controversy.
Another quality common to many of the radical texts produced in
the controversy (which might even be seen as an aspect of bricolage)
was a preparedness to reuse the same material in different contexts.
Thomas Spence, for instance, would print songs and ballads both
in his serial *Pig's Meat* and circulate them on separate broadsides.
Similarly, he would reproduce designs on token coins and individual
prints. Much the same is true of Blake. His designs often appear
both within the illuminated books and as separate prints or paintings.
He was also never afraid to rework plots and images in different
texts (and even within a single text). Again this process is clearest in
Blake's use of biblical material. A typical example is the reworking
of the trope of the Deluge or Flood in *The Book of Urizen* (and indeed
across a range of other texts). What is a single event in the Bible
becomes a recurrent metaphor. To some extent this is an extension
of the Bible's own rhetorical procedures. Robert Lowth's influential
Lectures on the Sacred Poetry of the Hebrews (1787), for instance, had
noted the Bible's frequent metaphorical reapplication of events that
had a 'conspicuous place' in Hebrew history. But whereas the Bible
clearly distinguished between its actual account of the Flood and
subsequent uses of the Flood as a trope, Blake presents a series of
deluges none of which is privileged as *the* Flood. I shall argue that
Blake's conception of the Bible involved him in a struggle to liberate
its poetic aspects from the legalistic Word. His development of
the Bible's own procedures can be seen as part of this process,
but Blake's use of the trope of the Flood has a radically different
signification from that of the Bible. In conventional biblical exegesis

the Flood was seen as a type of righteous punishment for the transgression of holy laws. Blake turns this on its head so that the introduction of such punishment becomes part of the primal catastrophe, an example of the 'unrelenting vindictiveness' Paine found in the Old Testament God.[9]

At the root of Blake's attitude to the Bible lies a hostility to the very notion of the pure text, the text which gains authority from its claim to be sacred, invariable, and original. In his annotations to Bishop Watson's *Apology for the Bible* (1798) Blake described 'the Bible or <Peculiar> Word of God' as an 'Abomination' (E 615). Perhaps the paradigmatic expression of Blake's attitude to the whole notion of the sacred text lies in Plate 11 of *The Marriage of Heaven and Hell*, which offers a telescoped account of the origins of 'forms of worship' in the corruptions of 'poetic tales':

> The ancient Poets animated all sensible objects with Gods or Geniuses, calling them by the names and adorning them with the properties of woods, rivers, mountains, lakes, cities, nations, and whatever their enlarged & numerous senses could perceive.
>
> And particularly they studied the genius of each city & country, placing it under its mental deity.
>
> Till a system was formed, which some took advantage of & enslav'd the vulgar by attempting to realize or abstract the mental deities from their objects: thus begun Priesthood.

Notes

1. See LÉVI-STRAUSS's *The Savage Mind* (2nd edn, London, 1972), pp. 16–20. DERRIDA discusses Lévi-Strauss's distinctions in *Writing and Difference* (London, 1978), pp. 279–95.

2. His paper at the 1990 Historicising Blake Conference was an intriguing placement of Blake's work in the milieu of his *Radical Underworld* (Cambridge, 1988). The work done by the notion of bricolage in the following chapters could perhaps have been sustained by the Bakhtinian notion of heteroglossia, which similarly gives weight to a discursive eclecticism across social and discourse boundaries, but since this term tends to be used mainly in relation to the novel and given the precedents of McCALMAN's and RONALD PAULSON's (see pp. 44, 46) use of bricolage, I have decided to retain the latter term.

3. See SPENCE, *A Letter*, 8–12, and *A Fragment of an Ancient Prophecy*, in *Political Works of Thomas Spence*, ed. DICKENSON, p. 46. McCALMAN, *Radical Underworld*, discusses Spence's debts to Volney, pp. 24 and 66, and his popular millenarianism, pp. 63–7.

4. See McCALMAN, *Radical Underworld*, p. 65, and PAINE, *Collected Works of Thomas Paine*, ed. P. S. FONES, 2 vols, i, 266.

5. G. PRETYMAN-TOMLINE, *A Charge delivered to the Clergy of the Diocese of Lincoln* (London, 1794), 15–16.

6. The phrase 'the tree of feudal tyranny' is taken from J. GERRALD's *A Convention the Only Means of Saving us from Ruin* (London, 1793), p. 89.

7. See R. PAULSON, *Representations of Revolution* (1789–1820) (New Haven, Conn., and London, 1983), p. 18.

8. See T. S. ELIOT, *The Sacred Wood*, 7th edn (London, 1980), 156 and 158.

9. See LOWTH, *Lectures*, vol. i, Lecture 9, and PAINE, *CWP*, ii. 474.

4 Infinite London

David Erdman

> O Earth O Earth return!
> Arise from out the dewy grass;
> Night is worn,
> And the morn
> Rises from the slumberous mass.
>
> – Introduction, *Songs of Experience*

The Bard who recites the *Songs of Experience*, written in 1792–93,[1] is capable of seeing 'Present, Past, & Future'; yet he must chide earth's 'lapsed Soul' for the tardiness of spring thaw; and *Earth's Answer* is really, like the questions of Oothoon, an unanswered appeal for help to 'Break this heavy chain, That does freeze my bones around'. 'Cruel jealous selfish fear' (like Fayette's) has chained earth with winter frost; no one can plough or sow; the buds and blossoms are retarded – for Love is held in bondage.

The complaint is essentially that the revolutionary spring torrent, which in 1792 seemed to be 'spreading and swelling . . . to fertilise a world, and renovate old earth' (as Holcroft exclaimed in a prologue in March)[2] is still in England dammed and frozen by cold abstractions and proclamations of 'Thou shalt not'. The Bard is determined that the spring *shall* come; that earth from sleep

> Shall arise and seek
> For her maker meek:
> And the desart wild
> Become a garden mild.

And he trusts that his own art has ritual force: 'Grave the sentence deep.' Yet the poem bearing these declarations was at first a Song of Innocence, moved now into the contrary group to say what it was perhaps no longer easy to write.[3]

Now, in his notebook, he wrote a song lamenting that a 'heavy rain' of cruelty, disguised in the specious abstractions of 'Mercy &

Pity & Peace,' has descended on 'the new reapd grain'; the farmers
are 'ruind & harvest . . . ended'.[4] In an earlier and crueler mood
Blake had written and even etched on copper a bitter characterisation of the kind of *Divine Image* which Cruelty, Jealousy, Terror, and
Secrecy were giving to the nation:

> The Human Dress, is forged Iron
> The Human Form, a fiery Forge.
> The Human Face, a Furnace seal'd
> The Human Heart, its hungry Gorge.[5]

But he kept the copper without printing from it, choosing instead to
stay closer to the ruined grain and farmers. With a more intellectual
irony he constructed from the psychological and moral gains of
'mutual fear' and 'selfish loves' a song of *The Human Abstract* to
sing against the *Divine Image* of Innocence.

Blake retained his sense of balance by engraving together his
Songs of Innocence and of Experience as 'contrary states of the human
soul,' and his sense of perspective by treating winter as a season
and life as an arc of Eternity. 'Without contraries is no progression,'
he still asserts. Yet the peculiar anguish of these songs (and several
notebook pieces of the same vintage) derives from the fact that the
historical contraries of peace and war, freedom and chains, have
come to England in the wrong order. For it is only contrary states
of the soul, not of society, that exist in Eternity, and Blake is still
firm in the belief that the blighting Code of War & Lust is historically negatable. The earth will 'in futurity' be a garden; readers 'of
the future age' will be shocked to learn 'that in a former time, Love!
sweet Love! was thought a crime.'

Relatively little of the considerable and increasing store of commentary on the *Songs of Experience* deals with their historical matrix;
yet it would be pedantic here to spell out the application to these
songs of much in the preceding chapters or to go beyond calling
attention to the particular setting of some of their major themes.
Though immeasurably closer than the prophecies to Blake's ideal of
an art that rises above its age 'perfect and eternal,' these great lyrics
soar up from a particular moment of history. The fused brilliance of
London and *The Tyger*, the sharp, poignant symbolism of *The Garden
of Love*, *Infant Sorrow*, and many another 'indignant page' were forged
in the heat of the Year One of Equality (September 1792 to 1793)
and tempered in the 'grey-brow'd snows' of Antijacobin alarms and
proclamations.

The fearful symmetry of the period in its cosmic implications produced Blake's boldest Oothoonian question, *The Tyger*, touched upon

in an earlier chapter. The recurrent negative theme in the Songs is
the mental bondage of Antijacobinism, manifest not in the windy
caves of Parliament or the archetypal howlings of Albion's Guardians
but in the lives of children and youth forced into harlotry and soldiery and apprentice slavery by the bone-bending, mind-chaining
oppressions of priest and king. In *Europe* and *America* Blake sketches
a panoramic view of the youth of England and their parents walking heavy and mustering for slaughter while their minds are choked
by volumes of fog which pour down from 'Infinite London's awful
spires' and from the palace walls and 'cast a dreadful cold Even on
rational things beneath.' In *Songs of Experience* he takes us into the
dismal streets and into schoolroom and chapel to see the effects
of Empire on the human 'flowers of London town.' He describes,
in *The Human Abstract*, the growth of the evil tree which is gallows,
cross,[6] and the abstract Mystery that hides the facts of war. The
roots of this oak or upas tree of perverted Druidism are watered
by the selfish tears of Mercy, Pity, and Peace:

> Pity would be no more,
> If we did not make somebody Poor:
> And Mercy no more could be,
> If all were as happy as we;
>
> And mutual fear brings peace;
> Till the selfish loves increase.

This tree grows 'in the Human brain,' planted there by priest and
king, who use the virtuousness of pity as an excuse for poverty and
who define peace as an armistice of fear – and thus 'promote war.'[7]

It is instructive to note that ideas like these were widely propagated in the latter part of 1792 by an Association for Preserving
Liberty and Property against Republicans and Levellers – expressly
to persuade 'the minds of ignorant men' that all causes of discontent
were either inescapable or wholly imaginary, and to prepare these
minds for the eventuality of England's being 'dragged into a French
war.'[8]

These pamphleteers were in favor of the mutual fear and 'military
policy' that temporarily bring peace and ultimately bring war.[9] And
they bluntly defended the inequality that supports pity and mercy.
Both the Bible and 'experience,' they said, tell us that 'society cannot
exist without a class of poor.' Consequently it is our duty to teach
the poor that their sufferings are necessary and natural and not to
be remedied by laws or constitutional changes – that it is in fact the
object of our maligned and 'most excellent Government to alleviate

poverty' by 'poor laws, work-houses and hospitals'.[10] Blake's suspicion that 'Churches: Hospitals: Castles: Palaces' are the 'nets & gins & traps' of the 'Code of War'[11] is confirmed by these antilevellers: 'Every step . . . which can be taken to bind man to man, order to order, the lower to the higher, the poor to the rich, is now a more peculiar duty; and if there are any means to prevent the spreading of dangerous and delusive principles, they must be sought for in education. [Hence the need for] Foundation Schools, Hospitals, Parish Schools, and Sunday Schools.'[12]

Blake's counterargument is that if there were not 'so many children poor' there would be no need for institutions and moral code – and no ignorant men for sale to the fat fed hireling. Poverty appalls the mind, making youth sufficiently docile to be led 'to slaughter houses' and beauty sufficiently desperate to be 'bought & sold . . . for a bit of bread' (N.107). There can be no vital bond of man to man in such 'a land of Poverty!' Starvation demonstrates the absurdity of the anti-vice campaign, for the church remains spiritually and physically a cold barn, to which *The Little Vagabond* rightly prefers the warm tavern.[13] The harlot's curse will weave Old England's winding sheet, and ultimately the raging desire for bread will undermine the whole misery-built London of spire and palace.

Boston's Angel asked, 'What crawling villain preaches abstinence & wraps himself In fat of lambs?' The chimney sweep, a 'little black thing among the snow,' answers that it is

> God & his Priest & King,
> Who wrap themselves up in our misery [*deleted reading*]
> And because I am happy & dance & sing
> They think they have done me no injury.[14]

King, priest, god, and parents do not reckon the revolutionary potential in the multitude they are stripping naked. Yet even the sheep puts forth 'a threatning horn' against the tithing priest (N.109). As for the chimney sweeper, his father and mother have turned a happy boy into a symbol of death. Once a year he still does dance and sing – on May Day, when London streets are given to the sweeps and milkmaids to perform for alms in grotesque symmetry.[15] *The Chimney Sweeper* is saying to the London citizen: you salve your conscience by handing out a few farthings on May Day, but if you really listened to this bitter cry among the snow you and your icy church would be appalled.

When we turn now to *London*, Blake's 'mightiest brief poem,'[16] our minds ringing with Blakean themes, we come upon infinite curses in a little room, a world at war in a grain of London soot.

On the illuminated page a child is leading a bent old man along
the cobblestones and a little vagabond is warming his hands at a fire
in the open street. But it is Blake who speaks.

London

> I wander thro' each charter'd street,
> Near where the charter'd Thames does flow.
> And mark in every face I meet
> Marks of weakness, marks of woe.
>
> In every cry of every Man,
> In every Infants cry of fear,
> In every voice; in every ban,
> The mind-forg'd manacles I hear
>
> How the Chimney-sweepers cry
> Every blackning Church appalls,
> And the hapless Soldiers sigh,
> Runs in blood down Palace walls[17]
>
> But most thro' midnight streets I hear
> How the youthful Harlots curse
> Blasts the new-born Infants tear
> And blights with plagues the Marriage hearse

In his first draft Blake wrote 'dirty street' and 'dirty Thames' as
plain statement of fact, reversing the sarcastic 'golden London' and
'silver Thames' of his early parody of Thomson's *Rule Britannia*.
And the harlot's curse sounded in every 'dismal' street. The change
to 'charter'd' (with an intermediate 'cheating')[18] mocks Thomson's
boast that 'the charter of the land' keeps Britons free, and it suggests
agreement with (perhaps was even suggested by) Paine's condemnation of 'charters and corporations' in the Second Part of *The Rights*

of Man, where Paine argues that all charters are purely negative in effect and that city charters, by annulling the rights of the majority, cheat the inhabitants and destroy the town's prosperity – even London being 'capable of bearing up against the political evils of a corporation' only from its advantageous situation on the Thames.[19] Paine's work was circulated by shopkeepers chafing under corporation rule and weary, like Blake, of the 'cheating waves of charterd streams' of monopolised commerce (*N*.113).

In the notebook fragment just quoted Blake speaks of shrinking 'at the little blasts of fear That the hireling blows into my ear,' thus indicating that when he writes of the 'mind-forg'd manacles' in every cry of fear and every ban he is not saying simply that people are voluntarily forging manacles in their own minds. Hireling informers or mercenaries promote the fear; Pitt's proclamations are the bans, linked with an order to dragoons 'to assemble on Hounslow Heath' and 'be within one hour's march of the metropolis.'[20] A rejected reading, 'german forged links,' points to several manacles forged ostensibly in the mind of Hanoverian George: the Prussian manoeuvers on the heath, the British alliance with Prussia and Austria against France, and the landing of Hessian and Hanoverian mercenaries in England allegedly en route to battlefronts in France.

Blake may have written *London* before this last development, but before he completed his publication there was a flurry of alarm among freeborn Englishmen at the presence of German hirelings. 'Will you wait till BARRACKS are erected in every village,' exclaimed a London Corresponding Society speaker in January 1794, 'and till subsidized Hessians and Hanoverians are upon us?'[21] In Parliament Lord Stanhope expressed the hope that honest Britons would meet this Prussian invasion 'by OPPOSING FORCE BY FORCE'. And the editor of *Politics for the People*, reporting that one Hessian had stabbed an Englishman in a street quarrel, cried that all were brought 'to cut the throats of Englishmen'. He urged citizens to arm and to fraternise with their fellow countrymen, the British common soldiers.[22]

The latter are Blake's 'hapless Soldiers' whose 'sigh Runs in blood down Palace walls' – and whose frequently exhibited inclination in 1792–1793 to turn from grumbling to mutiny[23] is not taken into account by those who interpret the blood as the soldier's own and who overlook the potentially forceful meaning of 'sigh' in eighteenth-century diction.[24] In the structure of the poem the soldier's utterance that puts blood on palace walls is parallel to the harlot's curse that blasts and blights. And Blake would have known that curses were often chalked or painted on the royal walls. In October 1792 Lady Malmesbury's Louisa saw 'written upon the Privy Garden-wall, "No coach-tax; d——Pitt! d——n the Duke of Richmond! *no King!*"'[25]

A number of cognate passages in which Blake mentions blood on palace walls indicate that the blood is an apocalyptic omen of mutiny and civil war involving regicide. In *The French Revolution* people and soldiers fraternise, and when their 'murmur' (sigh) reaches the palace, blood runs down the ancient pillars. In *The Four Zoas*, Night I, similar 'wailing' affects the people; 'But most the polish'd Palaces, dark, silent, bow with dread.' 'But most' is a phrase straight from *London*. And in Night IX the people's sighs and cries of fear mount to 'furious' rage, apocalyptic blood 'pours down incessant,' and 'Kings in their palaces lie drown'd' in it, torn 'limb from limb'.[26] In the same passage the marks of weakness and woe of *London* are spelled out as 'all the marks . . . of the slave's scourge & tyrant's crown'. In *London* Blake is talking about what he hears in the streets, not about the moral stain of the battlefield sigh of expiring soldiers.

In Blake's notebook the lines called *An Ancient Proverb* recapitulate the *London* theme in the form of a Bastille Day recipe for freeing Old England from further plagues of tyranny:

> Remove away that blackning church
> Remove away that marriage hearse
> Remove away that —— of blood
> Youll quite remove the ancient curse

Where he might have written 'palace' he cautiously writes a dash.[27] Yet despite the occasional shrinking of Blake as citizen, Blake as prophet, from *The French Revolution* to *The Song of Los*, from 1791 to 1795, cleaved to the vision of an imminent spring thaw when the happy earth would 'sing in its course' as the fire of Voltaire and Rousseau melted the Alpine or Atlantic snows. In England, nevertheless, the stubborn frost persisted and the wintry dark; and England's crisis and Earth's crisis were threatening to become permanent.

Notes

1. All eighteen of the *Songs of Experience* in *Notebook*, including the *Motto to Songs of Innocence & of Experience*, precede the draft of *Fayette*. In the Prospectus of 10 October, 1793, *Songs of Innocence* and *Songs of Experience* are advertised separately. But all extant copies of the latter have a publication date of 1794 and appear not to have been issued except in combination with, or to complement earlier copies of, *Songs of Innocence*.
   The Bard's plea, *Introduction*, is not in *Notebook*, but it must have been drafted before *Earth's Answer*, which is.

2. Prologue to *Road to Ruin* as read 1 March, 1792; quoted in *London Chronicle* of March 3.

3. *The Little Girl Lost.* This and *The Voice of the Ancient Bard,* transferred from *Songs of Innocence,* carry over into *Songs of Experience* a bardic optimism that is not explicit in the *Introduction.* But *The School Boy* must have been similarly transferred because it was too gloomy for *Innocence.*

4. *N.*114: 'I heard an Angel singing.'

5. *A Divine Image*: a.

6. *A Little Girl Lost.*

7. *The Human Abstract* and draft called *The Human Image* (*N.*107) in which the 'mystery' is discussed that 'The priest promotes war & the soldier peace.' Cf. Marg. to Watson, iv: E601/K384. For a discussion of the relations of these poems and of the internal evidence for an early date for *A Divine Image* (confirmed now by script) see ROBERT F. GLECKNER, 'William Blake and *The Human Abstract,' PMLA,* LXXVI (1961), 373–9.

8. I quote from *Politics . . . Reflections on the Present State of Affairs,* by a Lover of His Country, Edinburgh, 1792. For the Association, see *London Chronicle,* 27–29 November, 1792.

9. Politics. On the one hand, peace is 'an object of desire' most effectually approached, we are told, by 'a military policy' and increased armaments; on the other hand, if our 'great empire is insulted by the impudent memorials of a set of plunderers' (the rulers of France) war will be 'necessary and unavoidable.'

10. WILLIAM VINCENT, *A Discourse to the People,* London, 1792.

11. *Song of Los.*

12. Vincent.

13. A curious 'mark of weakness' appears in Blake's own publication. In etching the *Vagabond,* Blake bowdlerised the fourth line, changing 'makes all go to hell' to 'will never do well,' thereby introducing a bad rime and an ambiguity rather than defy the moral code of the Vice Society. The first notebook draft (*N.*105) reads:

> Dear Mother Dear Mother the church is cold
> But the alehouse is healthy & pleasant & warm
> Besides I can tell where I am usd well,
> Such usage in heaven makes all go to hell.

Even as published, the 'audacity' and 'mood of this wild poem' disturbed Coleridge in 1818. *Collected Letters,* ed. E. L. GRIGGS, Oxford, 1959, IV, pp. 834–8.

14. *N.*103.

15. I refer to an ancient May Day custom, illustrated by Blake in 1784 in an engraving for the *Wit's Magazine,* after Collings. The picture, *May Day,* is still used in works illustrating social customs. Milkmaids danced with pitcher-laden trays on their heads; the sweeps, with wigs to cover their grimy heads, banged their brushes and scrapers in rhythm; and a fiddler or two supplied a tune. Reproduced in *Johnson's England,* ed. A. S. TURBERVILLE, Oxford, 1933, I, p. 174.

16. Oliver Elton's phrase, I forget where.

17. The poem originally ended here. See *N.*109.

18. The 'cheating' variant is in *N*.113.

19. PAINE, I, 407; NANCY BOGEN (*Notes and Queries*, XV, January, 1968) finds Paine also calling 'every chartered town . . . an aristocratic monopoly' in the First Part (1791) as well. On chartered boroughs see COWPER, *The Task* iv.671; also JOHN BUTLER, *Brief Reflections*, 1791, a pamphlet reply to Burke cited in J. T. BOULTON, *The Language of Politics in the Age of Wilkes and Burke*, Toronto, 1963, p. 193.

20. *Gazette*, 1 December, 1792. In the note just cited, Mrs. Bogen suggests that Blake's choice, in the Thames poem, of the Ohio as the river to wash Thames stains from a Londoner 'born a slave' and aspiring 'to be free' was influenced by GILBERT IMLAY's *Topographical Description*, London, 1792. On the Ohio Imlay found escape from 'musty forms' that 'lead you into labyrinths of doubt and perplexity' and freedom from priestcraft which elsewhere 'seems to have forged fetters for the human mind'.

21. Address at Globe Tavern, 20 January, 1794 (pamphlet).

22. D. I. EATON, *Politics for the People*, II, no. 7, 15 March, 1794.

23. The Royal Proclamation cited efforts to 'delude the judgment of the lower classes' and 'debauch the soldiery'. Wilberforce feared that 'the soldiers are everywhere tampered with.' Gilbert Elliot in November 1792 expressed a common belief that armies and navies would prove 'but brittle weapons' against the spreading French ideas. Elliot, II, 74. Through the winter and spring there were sporadic attacks of the populace on press gangs and recruiting houses. Mutiny and rumors of mutiny were reported in the *General Evening Post*, 20 April, 20 July, 3, 7, 31 August, 28, 30 October, 1793. In Ireland the mutiny of embodied regiments broached into a small civil war. See also Werkmeister, items indexed under 'insurrection, phantom,' and 'Ireland.'

24. DAMON, p. 283, reads it as the battlefield 'death-sigh' which morally 'is a stain upon the State.' JOSEPH H. WICKSTEED, *Blake's Innocence & Experience*, New York, 1928, p. 253, has it that the soldier who promotes peace is quelling the 'tumult and war' of a 'radically unstable' society. But Blake was not one to look upon riot-quelling as a securing of freedom and peace! ALFRED KAZIN, *The Portable Blake*, New York, 1946, p. 15, with a suggestion 'that the Soldier's desperation runs, like his own blood, in accusation down the walls of the ruling Palace,' comes closer to the spirit of indignation which Blake reflects.

25. ELLIOT, II, 71. Verbally Blake's epithet may be traced back, I suppose, to 'hapless Warren!', Barlow's phrase for the patriot general dying at Bunker Hill (changed to 'glorious Warren' in 1793).

26. *F.R.*24–246; *F.Z.*i:14:15–18.

27. *N*.107. Blake's dash, an unusual mark for him, replaces an earlier 'man' which replaced a still earlier 'place'. The 'man of blood' would be the king, but Blake wanted the *place*, i.e. the Palace, and so settled for a dash.

5 Producers and Devourers

STEWART CREHAN*

Blake's brilliant intelletual satire and revolutionary tract, *The Marriage of Heaven and Hell* (*ca.* 1790–3) has attracted much critical commentary, but only a few interpretations have attempted to locate the work in its social context. One is Sabri-Tabrizi's *The 'Heaven' and 'Hell' of William Blake* (1973). Sabri-Tabrizi makes a number of important points, most of which seem to have been ignored by subsequent critics. The first is that 'Heaven' and 'Hell' 'represent social classes and conditions.' 'Heaven' is the world of 'the rich and propertied or higher clerical class,' 'Hell' is that of the poor and working class. This view is based on the discovery, through close reading, that Emmanuel Swedenborg's descriptions of Hell in his *Heaven and Hell* draw heavily, if unconsciously, on his knowledge of the coal mines he owned. Swedenborg's Heaven, on the other hand, is an idealised picture of the spacious world of the leisured upper classes. Since Blake's *Marriage* is in large part a satire on the writings and teachings of the founder of the New Church, Sabri-Tabrizi argues that Blake has seen through its theology as the worldly, predestinarian argument for an unjust social order. Whereas Swedenborg justified the condemnation of his 'infernal spirits' (or workers) to a life in the 'Hell' of his mines, Blake's sympathies are with those same spirits (whom he calls Devils, or producers), whose class-biased presentation he has exposed by his critical reading of the Swedish theologian's work. Swedenborg's New Church remains a defence of the older order; the 'revival' of Blake's 'Eternal Hell' is a positive response to the revolutionary upsurge of the oppressed.

Sabri-Tabrizi's thesis provides the starting-point for a critique of the usual run of idealist interpretations, according to which *The Marriage* is simply a celebration of creative energy and the active imagination in opposition to reason and 'materialistic' philosophy. In his commentary on the facsimile edition of *The Marriage* (Oxford

---

* From *Blake in Context*. © 1984 by Stewart Crehan. Gill and Macmillan Ltd., 1984. Humanities Press International, Inc., Atlantic Highlands, NJ.

University Press and the Trianon Press, 1975), for example, Geoffrey Keynes offers us the fully-rounded philosophy of an individual working in a socio-political vacuum: 'To him [i.e., Blake] passive acceptance was evil, active opposition was good. This is the key to the meaning of the paradoxes and inversions of which the whole work consists.' But *who* and *what* was Blake, and for whom was he writing? Can he be seen as some timeless, classless genius, ladling out universal prescriptions for everyone to follow? If, as Keynes says, Blake held to the principle that 'active opposition is good,' he must surely have welcomed the 'active opposition' of the *ancien regime* to the Third Estate, the 'active opposition' of the Tories to the movement for political reform, and the 'active opposition' of Pitt to the French Republic in 1793 in the form of war preparations. Torn from its social and political context, Blake's *Marriage* is emptied of its living, revolutionary significance. The 'active/passive' dualism makes little sense if we do not see that Blake was on the side of active, Republican-minded citizens, not 'active' oppressors.

Reason and Energy, on the other hand, do have a universal significance. With these terms, Blake anticipated Freud's analysis of the ego and the id and their interrelations. Blake's polarities, like Freud's, draw attention to the *inner dynamics* of the psyche, overturning the mechanistic, undialectical model of the mind as comprising only the conscious and the pre-conscious, or latent memory. 'Energy is the only life, and is from the Body; and Reason is the bound or outward circumference of Energy' conforms closely to Freud's topography, outlined in *The Ego and the Id* (1923), of the id as passion, bodily instinct and unconscious drives, and the ego as reason and common sense, or 'that part of the id which has been modified by the direct influence of the external world'. When Blake writes that those 'who restrain desire, do so because theirs is weak enough to be restrained,' and that 'the restrainer or reason usurps its place & governs the unwilling,' he is putting forward a theory of repression, which for Freud is the essential mechanism whereby the unconscious, including the pleasure principle, or 'desire' (what Freud calls the libido) is governed and tamed by the reality principle. Blake asserts: 'The tygers of wrath are wiser than the horses of instruction,' and 'the chains are the cunning of weak and tame minds which have power to resist energy'. Freud confirms: 'in its relation to the id [the ego] is like a man on horseback, who has to hold in check the superior strength of the horse; with this difference, that the rider tries to do so with his own strength while the ego uses borrowed forces.' (Note that the Freudian id as instructed horse has been tamed; Blake's tygers have not.) Freud's categories are shorn of overt political meanings, though not of political implications;

Blake's, however, are political through and through. Those who govern society and restrain the masses are the ones who, with their fiendish self-righteousness, have most effectively governed and restrained desire in themselves. This does not mean that they are therefore more rational, or that those who do not restrain desire in themselves are correspondingly less rational. If Reason is the outward circumference of Energy, then it may, by enclosing Energy in a narrower, more confined space, succeed in reducing it to 'the shadow of desire', but in doing so it also diminishes itself. Such a law applies to political and social as much as it does to psychological repression. The typical ruling-class personality may be very good indeed at governing, taming and repressing, but in all other respects (such as in the sexual act, practical work that involves the body as well as the brain, artistic creation and all feats of the imagination) it may well be worse than useless.

'The Argument' of *The Marriage* opens cryptically:

> Rintrah roars & shakes his fires in the burdened air;
> Hungry clouds swag on the deep.

Sabri-Tabrizi argues at length that 'Rintrah' is Urizenic, a reactionary force; Keynes, on the other hand, says: '"Rintrah" may be understood as "Wrath," the wrath of the poet-prophet, Blake himself.' In the poem *Tiriel* (1789), Tiriel, the blind tyrant, calls upon 'Thunder & fire & pestilence' to punish his rebellious sons:

> He ceast. The heavy clouds confusd rolld round the lofty towers
> Discharging their enormous voices. At the fathers curse
> The earth trembled fires belched from the yawning clefts
> And when the shaking ceast a fog possesst the accursed clime
> The cry was great in Tiriels palace.

In 1788 there had been an 'aristocratic revolt' against Louis XVI, sparking off popular riots. In 1789 the political rift widened: it was not a dispute between the wealthy privileged orders and the King, but (as Rude puts it) a *war* between the Third Estate and the two other orders. As the economic and political crisis deepened, the voice of the people began to be heard. Encouraged by outside popular pressure, the Third Estate (in effect, the revolutionary bourgeoisie) arrogated to itself the title of the National Assembly. This revolutionary act brought the masses further into play: on 14 July the Bastille itself fell.

Just as Tiriel's thunderous, fiery and pestilential curse on his 'sons' makes the 'earth' tremble and fires belch 'from the yawning clefts' (echoed in the volcanic fires of the title-page to *The Marriage*), so the ideological and political conflicts between the minority ruling orders in France awakened deeper fires from 'the yawning clefts' in society as a whole. Dismissing Sabri-Tabrizi's interpretation of the opening lines of 'The Argument' as an allusion to the sulphurous, smoky air of Swedenborg's infernal coal mines, we can grasp the dialectical movement that the opening of Blake's *Marriage* enacts:

> Rintrah roars & shakes his fires in the burdened air:
> Hungry clouds swag on the deep.

> As a new heaven is begun, and it is now thirty-three years since its advent, the Eternal Hell revives.

(Thirty-three years is the time that has elapsed since the date of the New Jerusalem as announced by Swedenborg – that is, 1757, the year of Blake's birth – and it is also the age of Christ when he died.) Rintrah roars and hungry clouds 'swag on the deep'; 'a new heaven is begun' and 'the Eternal Hell revives'.

The dialectic here is that of the class struggle. The 'above' and 'below' of 'burdened air' and 'deep,' 'new heaven' and 'Eternal Hell' indicate relationships of dominance, but the unity of opposites is not only political, the dominance of rulers overruled: it is based on the *appropriation* by the ruling few of what the governed many create. The line: 'Hungry clouds swag on the deep' refers to an imminent thunderstorm at sea, in which 'hungry' clouds, filled with too much moisture absorbed from 'the deep', burden the air and are about to burst. (The dialect word 'swag,' meaning to hang swaying like a 'bundle' or 'fat belly' and from which is derived the noun 'swag,' meaning booty, and possibly 'swagger,' meaning to strut, has a radical force that the word 'sway' would have lacked.) Later on, in 'The Voice of the Devil' (plates 5–6), Blake gives us the 'history' of the usurpation of power by 'Reason' from two ideological viewpoints, that of the rulers and that of the ruled: 'It indeed appear'd to Reason as if Desire was cast out, but the Devil's account is, that the Messiah fell, & formed a heaven of what he stole from the Abyss.' Here 'the Governor, or Reason' (Milton's 'Messiah') is the 'fallen' usurper; the 'Heaven' of the rationalists (whom Blake the libertarian sees as ideologues for an existing social order) was formed out of the *stolen* products that those deep in the social 'Abyss' created. (It is worth remembering at this point that Blake's 'diabolical' wit and mode of argument defy logical or systematic analysis. There is much in *The Marriage* that is comic, while Blake's satiric 'Devil' persona delights in a disruptive presentation, throwing off brilliantly memorable verbal sparks with that subversive intellectual audacity that is typical of a certain kind of anarchic individualism, or what Blake would have called 'Poetic Genius', possessed only by those who follow their 'Energies'.)

Plates 16–17 are a highly suggestive amalgam of related ideas presented in extremely condensed form. Taken with the passages so far discussed, they further illuminate the Blakean dialectic:

> The Giants who formed this world into its sensual existence and now seem to live in it in chains, are in truth the causes of its life & the sources of all activity; but the chains are the cunning of weak and tame minds which have power to resist energy, according to the proverb, the weak in courage is strong in cunning.
>
> Thus one portion of being is the Prolific, the other the Devouring: to the devourer it seems as if the producer was in his chains; but it is not so, he only takes portions of existence and fancies that the whole.
>
> But the Prolific would cease to be Prolific unless the Devourer, as a sea, received the excess of his delights . . .
>
> These two classes of men are always upon earth, & they should be enemies: whoever tries to reconcile them seeks to destroy existence.
>
> Religion is an endeavour to reconcile the two.

The deeper implications of this passage will be examined later. The argument is as follows: the 'Giants who formed this world into its sensual existence' and are 'the sources of all activity' seem to live in it in chains. These chains 'are the cunning of weak and tame minds' who have power to resist the energy of prolific creators. But the chains, we are told, are in fact illusory. It is only through the myopic, false consciousness of the devourer that the producer seems to be in his chains. Far from chaining him, this dependence on the devourer releases the producer's prolific energies. The unequal relationship turns out to be absolutely necessary, since for the producer to produce to excess, he must have devourers who can receive 'the excess of his delights'. (We shall return to this paradox later.) Finally, we are told that producers and devourers are 'two classes of men' irreconcilably opposed, and that it is the utopian mission of 'religion' to achieve a reconciliation between them (that is, by blurring or smoothing the class contradictions).

The question arises: Who are Blake's 'Giants' and prolific producers? Are they, as Sabri-Tabrizi argues, the poor and the working class? Before attempting an immediate answer, let us set against Blake's radical historiography a more consistent exposition by a writer with whom he is now often (and often too loosely) compared – Gerrard Winstanley, the writer who has a prime claim to the title of the first English socialist. Winstanley's *The True Levellers' Standard Advanced* (1649) opens:

> In the beginning of time, the great creator Reason made the earth to be a common treasury, to preserve beasts, birds, fishes and man, the Lord that was to govern this creation. . . .
> But since human flesh (that king of beasts) began to delight himself in the objects of the creation, more than in the spirit of reason and righteousness . . . he fell into blindness of mind and weakness of heart, and runs abroad for a teacher and ruler. And so selfish imagination . . . did set up one man to teach and rule over another. . . . And hereupon the earth . . . was hedged into enclosures by the teachers and rulers, and the others were made servants and slaves: and the earth, that is within this creation made a common storehouse for all, is bought and sold and kept in the hands of a few, whereby the great creator is mightily dishonoured, as if he were a respecter of persons, delighting in the comfortable livelihood of some, and rejoicing in the miserable poverty and straits of others. From the beginning it was not so.

Winstanley presents an unambiguous and lucid account of how mankind came to be divided into classes: 'teachers and rulers' on the one hand, and 'servants and slaves' on the other, arose on the basis of private property in the means of production, which for Winstanley is always the land and the means for tilling it. A spokesman for the dispossessed landless labourers of the seventeenth century, Winstanley anticipates the method of modern historical materialism. His 'contraries' compare interestingly with Blake's: it is not Reason that usurps Desire, but 'selfish imagination' that usurps 'the great creator Reason', while instead of 'the Devouring' and 'the Prolific' we have 'teachers and rulers', 'servants and slaves' – explicit class categories.

The originality of Blake's terms shows that he is trying to describe a new historical phenomenon – in particular, the Radical, plebeian intellectual and self-educated artist or craftsman who is now emerging as a potent force for change. (The revival of 'the Eternal Hell' of Radicalism, dead since 1784, occurred in 1790 when Horne Tooke got 1,779 votes at the Westminster election. Westminster, where Blake lived, 'was one of the few "open" constituencies in the south of England, with a householder franchise which admitted many master-artisans and some journeymen to the vote'.) In other words, the 'producer' whom *The Marriage* chiefly celebrates is not the

dispossessed labourer, peasant or 'chained' servant, but the prolifically creative, Radical artist-craftsman or artisan who, as an 'active
citizen' (at least in Westminster), struggles to free himself, his
fellow-producers, and hence society as a whole, from the economic,
political, moral and aesthetic constraints of the old aristocratic,
monarchical system.

The poetic resonance of Blake's categories ('Giants', 'Prolific',
'Devouring') – that is, their lack of historical concreteness and
social specificity (which are the hallmark of other radical writers
from Winstanley through Rousseau to Paine) – is indicative of an
individualistic and subjective desire for liberation. In the passage we
have quoted, the deep structure of Blake's argument, with its idea
of a usurpation giving rise to dialectical oppositions, is the same as
Winstanley's. Like many 'liberation' texts, it offers an explanation of
the present order in terms of an historical usurpation leading to a
system that is the 'contrary' or polar inversion of an original human
condition. Man's original creative energies have been usurped by
rational scepticism, the dominance of 'Hell' by that of 'Heaven',
the paramountcy of 'Giants' by the rule of 'weak and tame minds'.
The rhetorical method, vocabulary and style of Blake's illuminated
text, however, with its sudden breaks and transitions, its mixing of
modes (such as poetry, philosophy and satire), and its proliferation
of linearly related, 'contrary' categories (Reason/Energy → Soul/
Body → Restraint/Desire → Angel/Devil → Devourer/Producer,
etc.) enact an urgent, *subjective* need to break with the old forms, not
only through a radical philosophy or radical politics, but through
a radical aesthetic. The visual impact and originality of *The Marriage*,
with its plenitude of pictorial and typographical meanings, the
power of its language (where new associations, based on semantic
transformations, are deliberately exploited), are as important to
Blake as any 'objective', prosaic meaning. This is not simply a
question of aesthetics, for politics and aesthetics are always intertwined. The aesthetics and style of *The Marriage* cannot, then, be
excluded in the attempt to define its class viewpoint and the social
conditions of its appearance: its readers must produce its meanings.

Our task has been made easier in one way by the self-
consciousness of the text. The first 'Memorable Fancy', relating
in travelogue style how the narrator has collected some 'Proverbs
of Hell', is an ironic parody of Swedenborg's 'Memorable Relations'.
This has led readers and critics into not taking the narrator seriously, that is, literally – the 'Blakean' Hell being thought of only
metaphorically and not as a real place. In fact, Blake's Hell does
have, and indeed *must* have, a real social location. (This is to read
The Marriage, as Blake's Devil reads the Bible, in its 'infernal or

diabolical sense'. There are too many 'Angelic' readers of Blake.)
The text reads as follows:

> As I was walking among the fires of hell, delighted with the
> enjoyments of Genius, which to Angels look like Torment and
> insanity, I collected some of their Proverbs; thinking that as the
> sayings used in a nation mark its character, so the Proverbs
> of Hell show the nature of Infernal wisdom better than any
> description of buildings or garments.

The narrator (a mock-genteel persona) has discovered in this 'Infernal
wisdom' a rich subculture (or what might be termed a 'counter-
culture' or 'radical culture'). He is conveying to us some of the oral
literature ('sayings') of a nation within a nation. In this sense, we
are being asked to attribute the 'Proverbs of Hell' not to the genius
of a single individual, but to the 'Infernal wisdow' of the creative
majority. (It is interesting to note, incidentally, that Blake did not
sign *The Marriage* with his usual 'The Author & Printer W Blake.')
The proverbs are meant to be taken as the varied living utterances
of 'Devils' whose physical (and in this must be included sexual)
energies (Energy being 'the only life' and 'from the Body') are the
inexhaustible wellsprings of infernal culture, a culture that is both
Jacobin and antinomian. As Lindsay points out, 'English Jacobins
called the Devil the first Jacobin'.

Infernal culture, expressing the energy of active producers, is,
however, essentially individualistic, despite the solidarity the real,
historical 'Devils' might have displayed as a class, their sense of
community, or the interdependent nature of the productive process.
Blake lived, in fact, in an extremely competitive environment. On
28 May, 1804 he told Hayley: 'In London every calumny and false-
hood utter'd against another of the same trade is thought fair play.
Engravers, Painters, Statuaries, Printers, Poets, we are not in a field
of battle, but a City of Assassinations.' The proverb: 'The most
sublime act is to set another before you' suggests that for a Devil,
taking a back seat requires some effort (though a Devil in the fifth
'Memorable Fancy' says that the worship of God is 'Honouring his
gifts in other men, each according to his genius, and loving the
greatest men best'). 'No bird soars too high, if he soars with his
own wings' assumes that each man's gifts are *his own*, not God's or
society's; 'The apple tree never asks the beech how he shall grow;
nor the lion, the horse, how he shall take his prey' combines both
the idea of sovereign intellect's independence from 'the horses
of instruction' and the principle that each man must follow his
individual genius. Both A. L. Morton and Christopher Hill have

emphasised Blake's connection with the 'left-wing' radicals of the seventeenth century. However, in *The Marriage* he is arguably closer to the anarchic individualism of the Ranters (whose support derived largely from freed migratory craftsmen, men who were 'unattached and prepared to break with tradition,' according to Morton) than he is to the Diggers' peasant collectivism, whose spirit still lives in the writings of Gerrard Winstanley, a man of profound socialist instincts.

The third 'Memorable Fancy' informs us that the culture of 'Hell' is not only oral, but includes technical means for spreading its 'Infernal wisdom' (something Pitt and the Tories, with their spies and censors, were eager to put an end to). The visit to a 'Printing house in hell' takes us through the process of the transmission of knowledge 'from generation to generation.' The printing house is, on one level, Blake's own workshop. But to argue (with one critic, W. J. T. Mitchell) that it is Blake's own 'cavernous skull that is being cleared of rubbish . . . [and] made infinite by imaginative labor'; that the 'books which result from this labor come from a printing house in a cave, but they also come out of a *head*,' while passing over the reference to the work of the type-founder (in the *melting* of '*metals* into living fluids' which are then *cast* 'into the expanse'), obscures the premise that creative labor, or Energy, 'is from the Body,' and that such work cannot occur merely in the 'cave' of one's own skull, but is practical and social.

Behind Blake's account of how books are made, with its allegorical personifications (reminiscent of alchemical texts), lies an urban, radical culture, a world of political theorists, journalists and pamphleteers, also engaged in 'clearing away the rubbish' of dead ideas; a milieu of 'progressive' illustrators, decorative artists, poets, painters, engravers, type-founders, compositors, copperplate printers, bookbinders, booksellers, antiquarians and librarians. Blake's own 'infernal method' of printing was a stereotype process he himself (soaring with 'his own wings') developed, though others had hit on the idea independently. (In this period, technical innovation and experiment were invariably carried out by practical men: apart from Watt's modifications to the steam engine, which were the result of formal scientific experiment, and industrial processes such as bleaching and dyeing, which were the result of advances in chemistry, none of the major inventions of the industrial revolution were the results of advances in theoretical science.) Blake deserves the appellation of Renaissance Artist, however, since he combined in his work the trades of copperplate printer, bookbinder, bookseller, print-seller, painter, engraver and philosopher, together with the unclassifiable pursuits of prophet and poet, though perhaps 'Poetic Genius,' being the whole man, embraces all these activities.

Blake's 'Prolific' or 'Devils', then, are not producers of the means of subsistence, though most are practical men who use their hands; they are, in the main, producers of *art* and of *ideas*, men of 'Poetic Genius' who have allied themselves with the energy and the cause of the working masses. They are, in sum, the new petty-bourgeois and lower-class democratic intelligentsia. The printer and the bookseller (the latter often combining the functions of proprietor and publisher), were key figures in this radical milieu. Prolific booksellers and publishers in Paternoster Row and St Paul's Churchyard – men such as Joseph Johnson, who published Wordsworth and Mary Wollstonecraft as well as Paine's *Rights of Man* – were of central importance to the whole cause of English Radicalism. 'It is to such men,' wrote the author of *The Young Tradesman* in 1824, '[that] our men of genius take their productions for sale: and the success of works of genius very frequently depends upon their spirit, probity, and patronage . . . it is by the diffusion of knowledge by books that all species of tyranny and oppression can be most effectively resisted' (a view, of course, that ignores the role of newspapers, and also presumes a literate population). Blake's allegorical description of 'the method in which knowledge is transmitted from generation to generation' could be seen as supporting that view; however, after 1790 (when Johnson had printed, but did not publish, Blake's *French Revolution*) Blake was always his own printer and bookseller – not out of some Crusoe-like, do-it-yourself crankiness, but for important artistic and ideological reasons.

The role of the printer (whether copperplate or using type) in artisan London (in which 'the chief trades,' according to Sir John Clapham, were, apart from the building trades, the 'shoemaker, tailor, cabinet-maker, printer, clockmaker, jeweller, [and] baker') was significant in various ways. W. H. Reid, truly one of Blake's Tory 'Angels,' tells us that Swedenborgianism as an 'infidel' movement originated 'in a printer's job' in the parish of Clerkenwell. Its next appearance was 'in an alley in Little Eastcheap, partly in the modern and fashionable form of a debating society: but, instead of preachers collecting the people, these people were so hard run to collect preachers, that for a considerable time the office was generally confined to the printer alluded to, and one of his relatives.' (*The Marriage of Heaven and Hell* was conventionally printed; Blake printed and coloured his copies of *The Marriage of Heaven and Hell* in a singularly unconventional 'printer's job'.)

We know that Blake attended an early London meeting of the Swedenborgian New Church in 1789, and that within a year he was satirising Swedenborg in *The Marriage of Heaven and Hell*. Two other men, one a carpenter called John Wright, the other a copperplate printer called William Bryan, also recorded their disillusionment with the New Church. Wright tells us of his visit to the 'Jerusalem Church' in 1788, in Great Eastcheap:

> The Sunday following, so called, I went to the place, where I saw nothing but old *forms* of worship established by *man's will*, and not according to the will of GOD, although called by that blessed name of *New Jerusalem*, in which these old forms have neither part nor lot. I saw no one there, except the preacher, whom I knew; he had been a preacher among *John Wesley's* people.

This compares closely with Blake's rejection of Swedenborg's 'old forms' in *The Marriage*: 'And lo! Swedenborg is the Angel sitting at the tomb: his writings are the linen clothes folded up.' In October 1788 Wright and Bryan felt the call for a radical change in their lives. As Wright puts it: 'a burning wind is spreading over the earth, and wouldest thou leave to its ravages those whom thou canst save?' In 1789 the Holy Spirit told both men to visit 'a Society at *Avignon* who were favoured with divine communications'. Bryan records the event:

> The 23rd of the month called January, 1789, in the morning, having made all things ready for my work, which was then copper-plate printing, I found a stop in my mind to go on with it. Waiting a little, I took some paper to wet for another plate, but found the same stop: then I perceived that it was of the Lord. Retiring into my little room, I sat down, endeavouring to get my mind into perfect stillness, when a voice spoke in me, commanding me to prepare for my journey, that night.

The humble copperplate printer, who has to make prints from plates others have engraved, hears the voice of the Lord telling him to leave his work and embark on a journey. William Blake, an engraver who felt the same need for radical change, continued the ideological struggle (which, particularly in England, so often took a sectarian form) through his art, 'printing', as he says in *The Marriage*, 'in the infernal method, by corrosives, which in Hell are salutary and medicinal' – that is, exposing reactionary dogma with corrosive, burning acid in his new etching process. Instead of God's voice, it is 'The Voice of the Devil' that *he* hears. Blake's antinomian and immanentist rejection of a Lord who is above or without (he has learned from Swedenborg that the divine and the human are one, and hence that 'All deities reside in the human breast') was the first step in overcoming that mental self-division of those who saw their lives, minds and actions governed by 'the Lord', 'Angels', 'the Holy Spirit' and so forth.

Blake's increasing self-sufficiency as an artist-craftsman is mirrored in his philosophical independence and a conviction that the rule of kings and priests is ending, a conviction that has, of course, to be seen as part of the wider revolutionary movement. As Reid puts it, the 1790s were a new era in England 'because it delineates the first period in which the doctrines of Infidelity have been extensively circulated among the lower orders'. Although Reid includes Swedenborg among the 'Infidels', Blake puts him with the religious conformists: 'He conversed with Angels who are all religious, & conversed not with Devils who all hate religion, for he was incapable thro' his conceited notions.' Blake corroborates Reid in one respect, however, for his Devils, like Reid's 'infidel' lower orders, 'all hate religion'.

William Sharp, a friend of Blake and a follower of the millenarian Richard Brothers and later of Joanna Southcott, was an engraver whose struggle for independence (not wholly achieved in terms of an original art, however) closely parallels that of Blake, and tells us something about the conflict between 'producers' and 'devourers' within the print trade itself. According to W. S. Baker, Sharp 'became dissatisfied with the remuneration he received from the print dealers'. (Normally the engraver merely copied an artist's design, which was then printed on a press belonging to the copperplate printer, after which the prints were sold to the print-dealer or printshop owner.) Just as Blake was able to buy a printing press on the death of his father in 1784, so Sharp,

> becoming possessed of some property, by the decease of a brother, began to publish his own works. Soon afterwards, about the year 1787, that date appearing on his print of 'Zenobia,' he moved to a larger house in Charles St., near the Middlesex hospital.

Sharp, like Blake, had at least broken free of the chains of the print-dealers, who exerted a financial and aesthetic hold over artists and engravers. Catering for the tastes and fashions of middle-class print-buyers (part of the great consuming – that is, 'devouring' – public), the dealers, like the orthodox patrons and connoisseurs, took aesthetic 'portions of existence' and fancied those the whole. Sharp, like Blake, showed – once a degree of independence as a creative 'producer' had been achieved – that the interests of the producers were quite different from those of the devourers. Instead of picturesque scenes, copies of paintings by Reynolds, West and the like, he could engrave portraits of the people's heroes, such as Richard Brothers, Tom Paine and Horne Tooke, and publish prints from his own drawings. Such a career brought with it, of course, the threat of punishment in a very real, earthly 'dungeon'. Like Blake later, Sharp was arrested, being brought before members of the privy council in 1794–95 on suspicion of having 'revolutionary principles'.

Unless the artist-craftsman could free himself from the dictates of Tory patrons and the tastes of the buyers (however lucrative that subservience might prove), there could be no cleansed perception, no overflowing fountain of 'infernal' culture. Yet at this point the Romantic paradox appears: to whom could the revolutionary artist convey his 'infinite' perceptions if not to a 'devouring' public? With astonishing far-sightedness, anticipating Marx, Blake is able to perceive the dilemma in terms of an *irreconcilable* enmity between 'two classes of men'. Historically, this enmity can be explained by the fact that the producer became divorced from an abstract, impersonal and unknown public by the mechanism of the market. The Blakean free artist, the man who had freed himself from the oppressor's law and from spiritual repression, and who exercised his Poetic Genius without restraint, had become locked in a 'marriage' of enmity with those passive 'devourers' on whom, as an artist, he had to depend for a living. The contradiction was insoluble: 'These two classes of men are always upon earth.' Whereas Keats, Shelley and Wordsworth showed a certain elitist disdain as poets for 'the foolish crowd' and the 'unthinking' Public, Blake's class position enabled him to see this relationship dialectically. (Yet the Romantic disdain for his readers is there when his 'Devil' says: 'I have also The Bible of Hell, which the world shall have whether they will or no.')

Blake articulates in *The Marriage* and *A Song of Liberty* the same kind of revolutionary spirit that inspired the actions of the citizens of Paris in 1789. Writing at around the same time as Blake, Paine recalled how the masses armed themselves prior to the assault on the Bastille:

> The night was spent in providing themselves with every sort of weapon they could make or procure: Guns, swords, blacksmiths' hammers, carpenters' axes, iron crows, pikes, halberts, pitchforks, spits, clubs, &c. &c. The incredible numbers in which they assembled the next morning, and the still more incredible resolution they exhibited, embarrassed and astonished their enemies. Little did the new ministry expect such a salute. Accustomed to slavery themselves, they had no idea that Liberty was capable of

such inspiration, or that a body of unarmed citizens would dare
to face the military force of thirty thousand men.

Just as the creatively inspired, revolutionary artisans of Paris
had used blacksmiths' hammers, carpenters' axes and iron crows
as weapons, so Blake turned his own art into a weapon. It came
to possess the same qualities of imaginative daring, skill, energy,
resolution, and capacity for seizing the moment that were shown
by the revolutionaries in France. All it lacked (and this was Blake's
predicament as an artist) was the mass readership that Paine was
able to reach. Yet, imaginatively inspired as the citizens of Paris
were inspired, Blake was even able to see his own alienation
from the art-buying and poetry-reading public as a dialectical
contradiction, part of a wider class struggle.

Blake's *Marriage* reflects a new awareness that social existence
is riven by 'yawning clefts', and hence into two opposed ways of
seeing, two ideological camps. To the revolutionary artist, for whom
sharply distinct outlines are an aesthetic imperative, whoever tries
to reconcile these viewpoints 'seeks to destroy existence'. It is with
this *ideological* split that Blake's *Marriage* is chiefly concerned. Just
as a 'fool sees not the same tree that a wise man sees,' so devouring
Angels and prolific Devils perceive the world in wholly different
ways. Blake's Angel sees the French Revolution as a terrifying
monster rising from the depths of society, a Leviathan whose
'mouth & red gills' hang 'just above the raging foam, tinging the
black deep with beams of blood'. (The 'Hungry clouds' that 'swag
on the deep' in the opening free-verse 'Argument' have now burst:
'the deep', from which those devouring clouds absorbed their
moisture, and from which the upper-class Anglican clergy stole in
order to form their 'Heaven', has now turned into a 'raging foam'.)
The Angel hears and sees in the Revolution 'a terrible noise' and a
huge monster; but Blake finds himself 'sitting on a pleasant bank
beside a river by moonlight, hearing a harper, who sung to the
harp'. What to conservative Angels is a cacophony of noise (the
noise of the 'rabble') is to him pleasant music.

Blake's preoccupation with ideology and modes of perception,
reflecting his class position, also informs his account of the origin
of priesthood:

The ancient Poets animated all sensible objects with Gods or
Geniuses, calling them by the names and adorning them with the
properties of woods, rivers, mountains, lakes, cities, nations, and
whatever their enlarged & numerous senses could perceive. . . .

Till a system was formed, which some took advantage of, &
enslav'd the vulgar by attempting to realise or abstract the mental
deities from their objects: thus began Priesthood:
Choosing forms of worship from poetic tales.
And at length they pronounc'd that the Gods had order'd such
things.
Thus men forgot that All deities reside in the human breast.

The original-state-*versus*-usurpation idea is in line with previous
'radical' explanations of the origin of priesthood. But for writers
such as Winstanley, Diderot and Rousseau, those priests who
'enslav'd the vulgar' by using religion to defend an unjust social
order were – in the words of the English radicals of the seventeenth
century – pre-eminently '*tithing* priests,' whose reliance on rent,
tithes, and feudal dues made them obvious targets for class hatred.
Blake's explanation: 'thus began Priesthood,' is, of course, an idealist
one: ideology (the abstraction of 'mental deities from their objects')
precedes class formation ('Priesthood'). Nevertheless, Blake anticipates Marx by showing how a 'fantastical realm' of institutionalised
ideas is directly linked to the rise of an unproductive class.

The antinomy of producer and devourer in *The Marriage* contains
an important ambiguity, which has so far only been touched upon.
That is, it can be read either as producer/consumer or as producer/
exploiter. Both meanings are present. The ambiguity exists for us,
where it did not exist for Blake, because the historical distinction
between wage worker and capitalist – particularly in London, that
vast hive of small workshops – had not yet sufficiently hardened.
In Blake's later work, the ambiguity is partly resolved.

The ideological moment of *The Marriage* can also be felt in Blake's
doctrine of 'contraries' and in his notion of 'excess'. Blake's dialectic,
which owes more to the spiritual 'contraries' of Jacob Boehme than
it does to the alchemical (and hence, more 'materialist') contraries of
Paracelsus, is both radical and conservative. Underlying the whole
satiric purpose of *The Marriage* is the semantic transformation of
terms such as 'good' and 'evil', 'Heaven' and 'Hell'. But does the
transformation (the 'Evil' of Energy becoming 'Eternal Delight')
leave us with a new set of eternally fixed oppositions, such that
idealist readings of *The Marriage* appear as the most 'natural' ones
to take? If the 'contraries' of Heaven and Hell, Reason and Energy,
are eternally 'married', locked together for all time, then does this
not also apply to those 'social classes and conditions' which, as
Sabri-Tabrizi has argued, they represent? This surely turns Blake
into a Swedenborgian. *A Song of Liberty* clearly calls for the *ending*
of tyranny, Empire, and the rule of 'the lion & the wolf'. Yet the

ambiguity (Is *class* society, though perceived from the 'abyss' up and not from the top down, nevertheless reaffirmed, when the class struggle is seen as eternal?) remains. Given its historical and political context, *The Marriage* could not have gone as far in its critique as Winstanley did almost 150 years before.

Finally, the notion of 'excess', that well-known agent of social disorder, needs to be set in its ideological context. At one level, 'excess' is going 'beyond' or transcending oneself; a kind of Dionysiac ecstacy or surplus energy that cannot be contained or rationalised, a feeling of being at one with prolific creation. This has nothing in common with hedonism or libertinism, the moralist's idea of excess as intemperance or overindulgence. The proverb: 'The road of excess leads to the palace of wisdom' contains at one level the Dionysian belief that another, higher order of 'wisdom,' of spiritual knowledge and perception, can be attained through libidinal 'excess' or ecstatic self-abandon. Excess is, of course, fundamental to the spirit of Romanticism. Yet instead of viewing it as part of the universal human need for transcendental experiences (which can only be realised outside the work process), the principle of excess, looked at from a more 'earthly' angle, might be seen to have an *immanent*, work-oriented side to it.

In *The Marriage*, Blake says: 'the Prolific would cease to be the Prolific unless the Devourer, as a sea, received the excess of his delights' (where 'as a sea' has an ironic twist). A. S. Vasquez points out that under the new, 'freed' conditions of artistic production, the Romantic artist 'had to produce a number of works that exceeded, in quantity and economic value, what he needed in order to survive'. Blake's notion of creative excess, either as a productive surplus ('the excess of his delights'), or as a prolific, bountiful giving, in the sense in which God and nature are prolific and bountiful (hence: 'The lust of the goat is the bounty of God') can be connected with an important shift in eighteenth-century economic thought, as the dominance of mercantile gave way to industrial capital.

Mercantilist theories had derived the source of profit (or excess wealth) from the circulation sphere, that is, exchange of commodities (buying cheap and selling dear). Profit (always a definite, measurable quantity of money) owed its existence to the laws of the market and to the business skills of the merchant. The Physiocrats, on the other hand, saw that mercantile profit could not involve the creation of *new* wealth, since it was simply a redistribution of wealth already created, and therefore, as Blake might have put it, 'unable to do other than repeat the same dull round over again'. The source of society's wealth, and hence of the social surplus, thus lies in the sphere, not of *exchange*, but of *production*. It is through the agricultural producers, those who tap the inexhaustible bounties of nature, that a marketable surplus is created, and *this* surplus is not merely monetary profit; it is the living and essential foundation upon which the whole of civilised life – in other words, the aristocracy, the clergy, commerce, the professions, and the whole of urban life – depends.

In Physiocratic theory (so-called because of the importance it attached to nature, *phusis* in Greek), the farmer is only able to create a surplus (i.e., what is surplus to his needs) through the bounty of nature. It is not labour but nature itself that is prolific. Man only intervenes; he taps the vital source. He becomes prolific by virtue of his closeness to nature. The natural process of germination, growth, flowering and bearing fruit, made possible by the combined action of nutrients in the soil, heat from the sun and moisture from the rain, is the basis of life and hence of all wealth; it is the overflowing fountain in the human economy. The Rousseauesque 'natural man', simple, free and spontaneous; the Romantic cult of nature; the quasi-mystical notion of prolific nature working through man (as opposed to man working on nature); even Wordsworth's characterisation of poetry as 'the spontaneous overflow of powerful feelings' (where the 'feelings' are 'nature's') – all these can be connected with the Physiocrats' discovery that prolific nature and the farmer are the source of the social surplus.

Physiocratic theory emerged at a time when the bourgeoisie, not yet a class acting for itself, was incapable of carrying through a major political change, yet the theory contained a systematic and far-reaching critique of existing society, which could now be seen to be divided into productive and unproductive classes. Those who were productive produced in excess of their requirements. The unproductive classes merely consumed, distributed or changed the form of the surplus produced by the productive classes. For the representatives of the bourgeoisie and petty-bourgeoisie, however, such a theory was in need of drastic modification, since it made all the non-agricultural classes dependent and even parasitic upon the bounties of nature, made serviceable by the investment and labour of the farmer. Adam Smith extended the Physiocrats' categories to every sphere in which *productive capital* was employed, these spheres being agriculture, trade and manufacture. (Here it is *capital*, not simply labour itself, that is productive.) The concept of productive labour was held to mean any labour that was *put to work by capital* (since capital involves an increased return on investment).

The position of the Physiocrats and followers of Rousseau might be summed up in the maxim: 'Where nature is not, man is barren'. Blake's 'proverb of Hell' is a reversal of this: 'Where *man* is not, *nature* is barren'. In a craft and artisan environment, the emphasis shifts from the fertility of nature to human productivity, from prolific nature to prolific work. The craftsman does not rely on the bounties of nature in order to be prolific or productive, but on his own *human* energies. (The Physiocrats would retort: Then how does he eat? To which Adam Smith would reply that any commodity, even a book, has an economic value.)

In Blake's mythological epics, the most 'progressive' figures are Los, a blacksmith-prophet, and his female 'Emanation', Enitharmon, who weaves at her loom. In *Milton* it is Los who must first 'forge the instruments / Of Harvest' (the plough and harrow) for Palamabron the ploughman – a nice reversal of the Physiocratic order. It is not the ploughman – who is also Blake the engraver, ploughing 'furrows' on a copper plate with his graving tool – who is the guiding creative force in Blake's scheme of things, but Los, struggling to create 'Definite Form' with 'Hammer & Tongs' as he labours 'at his resolute Anvil'. Los, not Palamabron, is the archetype of the creative producer. (There is an interesting parallel here with the Nigerian dramatist, novelist and poet Wole Soyinka. Ogun, the Yoruba god of iron and of all those who work with iron, is the poet's guiding inspiration and source of creative energy. See, for example, the long poem *Idanre*, where Ogun is celebrated as divine creator and destroyer.)

In Blake's poetic myth Adam Smith is rebutted along with the Physiocrats, since labour that is unwilling or is carried out in the service of some master can never be creative, just as any artistic work that is the slave of 'fashionable Fools' or a particular, ready-made market will be on the side of that 'Class of Men whose whole delight is in Destroying'. Nor is art quantifiable. It is (to use Marx's terms) a use-value, not an exchange value. Thus what Blake means by being 'prolific' is not producing a merely *quantitative* excess, but striving for a better world through genuine works of art, combinations of words, sounds and images that awaken a new, enlarged perception of reality, and whose creation springs from a deep physical and emotional need, which is also a *social* need.

Blake's class affinities and his own work process – preparing the copper plate, seeing his reflection as a 'mighty Devil' in its mirror-like surface, applying the 'corrosive fires' of acid or ploughing its surface with his burin, making the imprint by turning the wheel of his press, mixing his colours – all this called up a poetic reverie that, while it actively participated in and urged on the work, also evoked other kinds of work, and at the same time inspired certain archetypal images and symbols. As Gaston Bachelard has shown, this kind of reverie or day-dreaming has a phenomenological aspect, in that, while he is freely associating, the 'dreamer' is physically working with actual material substances. By getting to know their inner life, their secret virtues and mysterious habits (such as the extent of metallic resistance to the pressure of the cutting edge, the quantity of water and pigment needed to get the right viscosity, etc.) the 'mystical' artist-craftsman sees them obeying his will, which to him is spiritual and not governed by mechanical laws. His spiritual will enters these substances, and they in turn enter him. Thus a dialectic unfolds. His artistic will is akin to that of a creator-god, yet a god who is *in* his creation: the artist engages, at an imaginative level, in the work of cosmic creation and the cosmic process itself, in which he is both maker and made. In his cosmic mythology, he comes to see that the creation – which includes himself – is only kept going by his own kind of imaginative labour. Without it, the sun would not rise, or give off spear-like rays like those from a blacksmith's hammer when it sets. Thus the Paracelsan, hermetic view that man's reason alone cannot penetrate nature's mysteries. Their unveiling must bring into play deeper levels of the psyche. In the alchemical work of imaginative creation, 'matter' is infused with 'spirit', including that of the divine artist himself. His energetic will fashions, animates and gives inner meaning to his creation, which appears infinite to all those who give themselves, as Los gives himself, through inspired, imaginative labour. This process – especially when fire and considerable energy are required – is one of conflict and struggle, as Bachelard says:

> If passively, as an idle visitor, you find yourself in the stifling atmosphere surrounding a china kiln, then the *anguish of heat* [cf. Blake's 'furnaces of affliction'] takes hold of you. You retreat. You do not want to look any longer. You are afraid of the sparks. You think it is hell.
>
> Nevertheless, move closer. Take on in your imagination the work of the artisan. Imagine yourself putting the wood into the oven: cram the oven with shovels-full of coal, challenge the oven to a duel of energy. In short, be ardent and the ardor of the hearth will shoot its arrows in vain against your chest; you will be invigorated by the struggle. The fire can only return your blows. The psychology of *opposition* invigorates the worker. . . .
>
> Take away dreams and you stultify the worker. Leave out the oneiric force of work and you diminish, you annihilate the artisan. Each labor has its oneirism, each material worked on contributes its inner reveries. . . . The oneirism of work is the very condition of the worker's mental integrity.

Under conditions of capitalist production, with its increasing division of labour, where labour is *abstract* labour, 'creative labour' becomes less and less possible. (One of the characteristically 'Urizenic' features of bourgeois economic science is the way it turns human needs into dehumanising constraints, the whole man's creative excess into calculable 'portions' called profit margins.) On the other hand, the 'craft' viewpoint tends to belittle the working class (not fully born as an organised movement in Blake's time) as an agent of its own liberation; dehumanised by the new work discipline, with its reduction of factory worker into 'hands', the exploited labourers have to rely on the visions of the inspired few. Yet Blake's viewpoint as a direct producer allowed him to see with 'prophetic' insight that labour (one of the most frequently used words in his longer poems), though enslaving under conditions of enforced drudgery, is at the same time the key to man's liberation – *labour*, not merely 'imagination', and certainly not *nature*.

6 *Jerusalem* and Nationalism

SUSAN MATTHEWS

One of Blake's many roles in contemporary popular culture is as the author of a nationalist hymn. Long the anthem of the Women's Institute, the lyric 'Jerusalem' has recently been claimed in competing political contexts. Played before Tory Party press conferences in the run-up to the post-Falklands election, 'Jerusalem' became a national hymn alongside 'Land of hope and glory' and 'Rule Britannia'. In 1990 the Labour Party conference for the first time ended with a rendering of Blake's 'Jerusalem' by a soprano, an innovation which might signal alternatively a change in Labour or in the politics of nationalism. The myth of England as a chosen land which seems to provide some part of the emotive power of the lyric 'Jerusalem' reappears in Blake's last epic, *Jerusalem*. The elaborate edifice of the poem not only tells and retells stories of the Fall but also uses Albion as the figure of the British people. The myth of *Jerusalem* seems on many levels to have the makings of a myth of national supremacy. Yet the cultural meaning of 'Blake' today is not only that of the author of a nationalist hymn but also that of Erdman's 'Prophet against Empire', according to Eagleton, one of the three canonical poets who will 'Smash the ruling class yet' (Eagleton, 1986 p. 185). Moreover, any attempt to re-insert *Jerusalem* into the nationalist language of the early years of the nineteenth century is fraught with difficulty.[1] This essay sets out to suggest both the continuities between Blake's writings and contemporary discourses of nationalism and ways in which nationalist languages, particularly within the poetry, are distorted, changed in meaning and finally rejected.

Whereas nationalism has in recent times seemed the preserve of right-wing politics, some versions of the Left now seek to reclaim it. Academic discourse is simultaneously rediscovering forms of popular nationalism in the crucial period following the French Revolution. E. H. Hobsbawm's *Nations and Nationalism* (1990) traces the association of nationalism with socialism. And whereas Britain's confrontation with Napoleonic France was seen by Tom Nairn as a counter-revolutionary war which used patriotism to strengthen the conservative social structure (Nairn, 1981), Linda Colley argues that the period saw a rise of popular nationalism: 'Between 1750 and 1830 a wide spectrum of aspiring social groups and sectional interests throughout Britain found patriotic and nationalist language invaluable' (Colley, 1986 p. 117). She suggests that 'it was the dominant landed class which most turned its back on the nation and sought and found refuge in the language of class' (ibid. p. 117).

I

The absence of national monuments of the period celebrating British heroes or victories in the Napoleonic wars is taken by Linda Colley as evidence of the wariness of the state towards the potentially subversive force of nationalist discourse. As she points out, nationalist rhetoric is often adopted by radical causes in the period, as in *The Radical Reformers' New Song Book: Being a Choice Collection of Patriotic Songs* dating from the Peterloo era (ibid. p. 116). This account might be seen as being confirmed by Blake's involvement in one of the most notable projects for a public monument. In 1799 he engraved three designs by Flaxman for *A Letter to the Committee for Raising the Naval Pillar or Monument* which proposed the erection of a monumental statue at Greenwich. The *Letter* takes as model the public art of ancient Athens:

> A statue might be raised like the Minerva in the Athenian citadel, whose aspect and size should represent the Genius of the Empire: its magnitude should equal the Colossus of Rhodes; its character should be Britannia Triumphant.
>
> (Flaxman, 1799 pp. 7–8)

It is not just nation but empire that the monument celebrates:

> We may state, then, that Great Britain having increased its dominion by sea and land, taken together, to as great an extent as the Roman Empire at its utmost height; possessing a proportionate commerce, having conquered all enemies at sea in a series of unequalled victories, and controuling the fate of great part of the globe by its power, is desirous to raise a National Monument of such extraordinary success, prosperity, and favour of Divine Providence.
>
> (ibid. p. 9)

Whereas the statue is modelled on the 'Minerva in the Athenian citadel', the power of Great Britain is compared with that of the Roman Empire. The personification of Britannia, established in the 1750s, represents nation and empire rather than any single national hero, and it is interesting that it is both military and commercial power that is celebrated.[2] But the clearest indication that it is not just Britain's nationhood, but Britain's dominant role in the world that is being claimed is the argument offered for the choice of the site at Greenwich. This is suggested on the grounds that it is appropriate to Great Britain's position in the centre of the world:

> It is also to be remembered, that the port of the Metropolis is the great port of the whole kingdome; that the Kent road is the ingress to London from Europe, Asia, and Africa; and that, as Greenwich Hill is the place from whence the longitude is taken, the Monument would, like the first Mile-stone in the city of Rome, be the point from which the world would be measured.
>
> (ibid. p. 13)

To engrave something is not necessarily to endorse its content. But letters written in the 1790s show that Blake shares the enthusiasm of friends such as George Cumberland and John Flaxman for the art and culture of the ancient Greeks. In sharp contrast to the belief of the late pamphlet that 'Rome & Greece swept Art into their maw & destroyd it' (Blake, 1982 p. 270), ancient Greece provides Blake in the 1790s with an image of a society in which art, the artist and the imagination are rightly honoured. On hearing that Cumberland's plans for a National Gallery show signs of succeeding, Blake predicts that 'the immense flood of Grecian light & glory which is coming on Europe will more than realise our warmest wishes' (Blake, 1980 pp. 16–17).

The naval pillar was never built, but in 1801 James Barry added a naval pillar to the background of his painting *Commerce or the Triumph of the Thames* in his series of large paintings in the Royal Society of Arts, London, in response to the competition for a monument to honour England's maritime victories. In Barry's painting, 'the Thames disperses the manufactures of the Midlands carried by the trailing nereids to the four principal trading continents. Europe offers in return grapes and wine, Asia silks and cotton, America furs, and Africa slaves' (Pressly, 1981 p. 101). Blake is outspoken in defence of Barry in his annotations to Reynolds's *Discourses* and in his reference (later deleted) in his *Public Address* of about 1810 to 'the really Industrious, Virtuous & Independent Barry' (Blake, 1982 p. 576).[3] In these images of London as the centre of the world,

Europe, Asia, America and Africa return to London as commercial centre. An unlikely parallel, or parody, is provided in the production of Blake's Lambeth books of the 1790s as *America* is followed by *Europe* and *The Song of Los* containing 'Africa' and 'Asia'. The four continents are produced from a house near the Thames. The epic, as Bakhtin (1981) has told us, is a form which strives for inclusiveness and for mastery. In *Jerusalem*, London and Golgonooza become the places of silent creation from which the nations of the world emanate:

> All these Center in London & in Golgonooza, from whence
> They are Created continually, East & West & North & South,
> And from them are Created all the Nations of the Earth,
> Europe & Asia & Africa & America, in fury Fourfold!
>
> (Blake, 1982 p. 227)

Blake's myth, like the visual imagery of nationalist art of his time, continually moves out from nation to world in a process which disturbingly echoes not only the revolutionary universalism of the 1790s but also the language of empire.

Blake's most explicit language of nation and of empire occurs in two prose works which date from the years in which *Jerusalem* was being written and in which Britain was at war with France: the *Descriptive Catalogue* provided for his unsuccessful exhibition of 1809 and the notebook draft of about 1810 known as the *Public Address*. In the *Public Address* Blake takes on the role of patriot striving for the regeneration of his country:

> Resentment for Personal Injuries has had some share in this
> Public Address But Love to My Art & Zeal for my Country
> a much Greater.
>
> (Blake, 1982 p. 574)

His concern, he claims, is for the state of the public arts in England, represented particularly in the debased public taste in engraving:

> Whoever looks at any of the Great & Expensive Works <of
> Engraving> that have been Publishd by English Traders must
> feel a Loathing & Disgust & accordingly most Englishmen have
> a Contempt for Art which is the Greatest Curse that can fall
> upon a Nation.
>
> (ibid. p. 577)

As in *Jerusalem*, the language hesitates between the national and the universal. Blake writes:

To recover Art has been the business of my life to the Florentine
Original & if possible to go beyond that Original <this> I thought
the only pursuit worthy of [*an Englishman*] <a Man>.

(ibid. p. 580)

'[A]n Englishman' is written, deleted and replaced by 'a Man'.
Art in England is seen as both deriving from that of Italy and as
rivalling Italy: 'England will never rival Italy while we servilely
copy' (ibid. p. 578). For Blake works within at least three different
models: one which belongs with the syncretic mythographers and
leaps national boundaries, seeing Britain as the true heir to Hebrew
religion and Italian art; another which belongs within the contemporary world of competing emergent nations and empires, and a
third which borrows the sophisticated cosmopolitanism of the liberal
elite. Blake is thus concerned with the concept of English character,
typical of the emergent nationalism in its emphasis on the blunt,
honest, sincere man. Here Hogarth figures as an image of English
originality:

Englishmen rouze yourselves from the fatal Slumber into which
Booksellers & Trading Dealers have thrown you Under the artfully
propagated pretence that a Translation or a Copy of any kind can
be as honourable to a Nation as An Original [Belying] Be-lying
the English Character in that well known Saying Englishmen
Improve what others Invent[.] This Even Hogarths Works Prove
a detestable Falshood.

(ibid. p. 576)

But he is also, along with Hayley, Flaxman and Cumberland, aware
of European culture. Indeed a letter from Flaxman to Hayley in
1784 shows that at this date there was a plan to complete Blake's
education by sending him to Rome (Blake, 1980 p. 3). Perhaps most
surprisingly, Blake uses the language of competing nation states in
the challenge he offers to Buonaparte:

let it no more be said that Empires Encourage Arts for it is Arts
that Encourage Empires Arts & Artists are Spiritual & laugh at
Mortal Contingencies. . . .
    Let us teach Buonaparte & whomsoever else it may concern
That it is not Arts that follow & attend upon Empire[s] but
Empire[s] that attends upon & follows [wherever Art leads]
The Arts.

(Blake, 1982 p. 577)

The opening statement does not seem to fit with the second: 'Arts & Artists are Spiritual & laugh at Mortal Contingencies'. It might be that the empire which 'attends upon & follows The Arts' is thereby translated into something which is not empire. But the apparent meaning is that the arts have a public function in time of war, not just as a propagandist means to defeat an enemy, but as a tool for building empires. Napoleon, who is said to have drawn up a short-list of works of art to be transported back to France on the successful conquest of England, of course did use art explicitly as a symbol of military conquest.[4] The process of high-minded looting, however, began earlier in the postrevolutionary period in France; its politics, from the point of view of English sympathisers, may therefore have been more complex. As Francis Haskell and Nicholas Penny describe, it was in 1794 that 'the Revolutionary administration in Paris first proclaimed the principle that the Louvre, newly established as a public museum, was the rightful home for such masterpieces of art as could be seized from conquered territory' (Haskell and Penny, 1981 p. 108). In 1798, at the request of the French minister of the interior, the authors of a popular vaudeville wrote a song to cele-brate the capture of masterpieces of art, whose refrain was:

> Rome n'est plus dans Rome
> Elle est tout à Paris.

> (ibid.)

This almost seems to be what Blake imagines in the *Descriptive Catalogue* where he argues that his invention of portable fresco would have made it possible to transfer the greatest works of art to England:

> If the Frescos of APELLES, of PROTOGENES, of RAPHAEL, or MICHAEL ANGELO could have been removed, we might, perhaps, have them now in England.

> (Blake, 1982 p. 527)

The civic-humanist call for the encouragement of public art becomes part of the nation's sense of cultural superiority.

II

Yet another form of nationalism appears in the *Descriptive Catalogue*. Here Blake offers that traditional function of epic poetry – the mythic account of the nation's origins:

The British Antiquities are now in the Artist's hands; all his
visionary contemplations, relating to his own country and its
ancient glory, when it was as it again shall be, the source of
learning and inspiration. . . . Mr. B. has in his hands poems of the
highest antiquity. . . . The Artist has written it under inspiration,
and will, if God please, publish it; it is voluminous, and contains
the ancient history of Britain, and the world of Satan and of Adam.

(Blake, 1982 pp. 542–8)

Exactly what Blake is proposing to offer to his public is unclear. At
first he seems to be offering the lost epic literature of the primitive
nation – just as Macpherson did in publishing his 'translation' of
the poems of Ossian. But 'the British Antiquities' are also 'all his
visionary contemplations'. Later it seems as if the ancient poems
have acted as source material for a new 'voluminous' work, for
Blake says: 'The artist has written it'. Blake of course is on record in
the annotations to Wordsworth's *Poems* as accepting Macpherson's
claims (Blake, 1982 p. 665). But his defence may not have quite the
meaning it seems to have: inspiration makes nonsense of arguments
about the date of poems, and makes it quite possible for a modern
poet to write poems of the 'highest antiquity'. What is interesting
about the remarks from *A Descriptive Catalogue* is the attempt to
present to the public a poem of inspiration in nationalist terms,
as 'the ancient history of Britain'.

But what are the British antiquities that Blake uses in *Jerusalem*?
There are several ways in which the poem could be seen as using
national mythology. The Preface to chapter 1 of *Jerusalem* offers to
the public a poem about giants and fairies:

After my three years slumber on the banks of the Ocean, I again
display my Giant forms to the Public. My former Giants & Fairies
having reciev'd the highest reward possible, the [*love*] and
[*friendship*] of those with whom to be connected is to be [*blessed*],
I cannot doubt that this more consolidated & extended Work will
be as kindly recieved.

(Blake, 1982 p. 145)

The references to giants and fairies could be seen as an attempt
by Blake to evolve a distinctively British and popular machinery for
his poem. *Jerusalem* is the only one of Blake's long poems in which
giants and fairies are a significant presence; they appear only once
each in *Milton* and *The Four Zoas*. Richard Hurd in *Letters on Chivalry
and Romance* argued for an association between Gothic elements and

English literature. He claims that the 'religious machinery' of Gothic legend has a greater popular appeal than that of Greek legend, having 'in it something more amusing, as well as more awakening to the imagination' (Hurd, 1762 p. 48). He also discusses the 'current popular tales of Elves and Fairies' as 'even fitter to take the credulous mind, and charm it into a willing admiration of the *specious miracles*, which wayward fancy delights in, than those of the old traditionary rabble of pagan divinities' (ibid. p. 48). Perhaps most important is that he finds Gothic elements in both Spenser and Milton, particularly in Milton's Satan:

> when Milton wanted to paint the horrors of that night (one of the noblest parts of his *Paradise Regained*) which the Devil himself is feigned to conjure up in the wilderness, the Gothic language and ideas helped him to work up his tempest with such terror.
>
> (ibid. p. 52)

But whereas Hurd writes of superstitions fit 'to take the credulous mind', Blake in *A Descriptive Catalogue* describes Shakespeare's use of witches and fairies as poetic metaphors, introducing the examples from Shakespeare in order to support his argument for the seriousness of Chaucer's characterisation: 'Shakespeare's Fairies also are the rulers of the vegetable world, and so are Chaucer's; let them be so considered, and then the poet will be understood, and not else' (Blake, 1982 p. 535).

In *Jerusalem*, Blake seems to create supernatural machinery with a limited or subsidiary role, associated with the vegetable world, and by implication with femininity. It is the *daughters* of Albion who are described as:

> Names anciently rememberd, but now contemn'd as fictions!
> Although in every bosom they controll our Vegetative powers.
>
> (Blake, 1982 p. 148)

Genii, gnomes, nymphs and fairies (sixty-four thousand of each) provide the guards for the gates of Golgonooza, acting like Los's spectre in Chapter 1 as servants. But in Chapter 2, the transformation of the zoas into elements and then into these creatures follows the negative step of the separation and division of Albion's emanation:

> Albion groans, he sees the Elements divide before his face.
> And England who is Brittannia divided into Jerusalem & Vala
>
> (ibid. p. 178)

The Gothic supernatural is used to represent a narrow and distorted image of the true spiritual forces:

> And the Four Zoa's who are the Four Eternal Senses of Man
> Become Four Elements separating from the Limbs of Albion
> These are their names in the Vegetative Generation:
> [*West Weighing East & North dividing Generation South bounding*]
> And Accident & Chance were found hidden in Length, Bredth
> & Highth
> And they divided into Four ravening deathlike Forms,
> Fairies & Genii & Nymphs & Gnomes of the Elements.
>
> (ibid. p. 178)

In the following chapter, giants, witches, ghosts and fairies reappear in the company of druids, and of the northern gods Thor and Friga. There is already a suggestion of mischievous energy in the fairy who introduces *Europe*, but the Gothic supernatural in *Jerusalem* is associated with a more sinister kind of cruelty through the image of sacrifice:

> The Giants & the Witches & the Ghosts of Albion dance with
> Thor & Friga, & the Fairies lead the Moon along the Valley
> of Cherubim
> Bleeding in torrents from Mountain to Mountain, a lovely Victim
>
> (ibid. p. 214)

Blake draws on contemporary ideas of the Gothic supernatural in *Jerusalem* but suggests that they are not the true British antiquities. They are debased forms which result from the loss and division of Albion's emanation, England or Britannia, into the two opposed forms of Jerusalem and Vala. Vala therefore becomes associated with a negative form of femininity.

The feminization of the Gothic supernatural may be in part the result of Pope's use of a comparable machinery in *The Rape of the Lock*, based, according to the Preface on 'the Rosicrucian Doctrine of Spirits': 'According to these Gentlemen, the four Elements are inhabited by Spirits, which they call *Sylphs, Gnomes, Nymphs*, and *Salamanders*' (Pope, 1963 p. 217). The passage from canto II in which Ariel gives orders to his 'Sylphs and Sylphids . . . / Fays, Fairies, Genii, Elves and Daemons' provides a parallel to the account of the work of Los's sons in *Milton* while using a machinery which is more like that of parts of *Jerusalem*. Pope's new machinery is specifically associated with femininity, an association which Blake carries over to Hayley in his role as reader of Pope's Homer:

Thus Hayley on his Toilette seeing the Sope
Cries Homer is very much improvd by Pope.

(Blake, 1982 p. 505)

The British antiquities have become part of feminised, middle-class
polite culture. To these, Blake opposes biblical myth, seen more as
a part of an oppositional British culture, a culture which included
the figures of Richard Brothers, the self-styled 'Prince of the
Hebrews' who planned to establish a kingdom with its seat in
Jerusalem, and Joseph Bichero who predicted the restoration of the
Jews to Jerusalem.[5]

Blake's nationalism could be seen as part of the change which
results in his turning away from the classics, for which he displays
considerable enthusiasm in the 1790s, and yet the national myth
he finds available is coloured by its association with middle-class
polite culture. The address 'To the Public' is filled with irony.[6] Not
only have Blake's earlier works failed to receive 'the highest reward
possible' but, if this is envisaged as the love and friendship of the
select group of Blake's patrons and friends, then the public must be
redefined as the few rather than the many. The 1809 Advertisement
for Blake's exhibition quotes ' "Fit Audience find tho' few" ' MILTON'
(Blake, 1982 p. 527). *Jerusalem* addresses 'The Public', a unifying
term, and yet splits the public into 'Sheep' and 'Goats', implicitly
admitting Blake's loss of the public as audience for his national epic.
The defacement of the plate addressed 'To the Public' often seems
to display Blake's estrangement from his audience. He removes, for
instance, the words which ask for acceptance of author by audience:
'Therefore [*Dear*] Reader, [*forgive*] what you do not approve, & [*love*]
me for this energetic exertion of my talent' (Blake, 1982 p. 145). As
a writer and artist, Blake oddly spans different classes, associated
not only with London's radical underground but also with liberal
middle-class society centred on figures such as his patrons William
Hayley and B. H. Malkin. The public are in danger of becoming the
few of Hayley's circle. The search for the British antiquities is therefore more complex than the adoption of the Gothic supernatural,
and depends on the restoration of Hebrew myth as a challenge
both to the middle-class use of classical and of British myth.

The choice of Albion as the central figure of the national epic
immediately sets up a contrast with the mythology of the national
epic of the type espoused by William Hayley. The project of the
national epic had already been taken up by the liberal establishment. William Hayley, in the 1782 *Essay on Epic Poetry*, called on
poets to create national epics using British legend, attacking those
who deny the suitability of 'the annals of our martial isle' (Hayley,

1968 p. 110). National epic poets, in his account, respond to the appeal of Liberty:

> 'Here,' cries the Goddess, 'raise thy fabric here,
> Build on these rocks, that to my reign belong,
> The noblest basis of Heroic Song!'
>
> (ibid. p. 111)

National sentiment is here seen as in France as a liberal force, belonging within the discourse of civic humanism. Many of the long poems of the period could be seen as belonging within this project for a national epic. *The Prelude* of course discusses plans for a national epic. John Ogilvie's *Britannia: A National Epic Poem in Twenty Books* appeared in 1801 with a preface which refers to Hayley's views on epic, and Joseph Cottle published *Alfred* (1800) and *The Fall of Cambria* (1808). Perhaps the most suggestive parallel to Blake's attempts is provided by the epic ambitions of John Thelwall who in 1801 announced plans for a 'National and . . . Constitutional Epic' *The Hope of Albion, or Edwin of Northumbria*. The poem was never completed, but the fragments published in 1801 show Thelwall using patriotic and nationalist themes. The Argument to Book 1 of *The Hope of Albion* contains an 'Invocation to the tutelary Angel of Patriotism'. But it also contains an account of a negative form of nationalism, 'sullen passions' raised 'in the popular mind':

> scorn, and deadly hate
> Of alien tribes, and national pride that steels
> The obdurate heart, presumptuous, and confounds
> Reason and right; moulding the infatuate herd
> (Their own worst foes!) to the pernicious views
> Of crafty politicians: whence the woes
> That thin the human race – oppressions, wars,
> Famine, and fire, and pestilence; whate'er
> The Good with horror view, the Great with pride.
>
> (Thelwall, 1801 p. 195)

In the preface to the collection which contains the fragment of Thelwall's patriotic epic, he explains that by the time he came to work on the poem he found 'the press teeming, and, perhaps, the public already satiated with NATIONAL HEROICS, which, when his principal work was first projected, was *a desideratum* in English poesy' (Thelwall, 1801 p. xlvi). The project seems to show that the national epic was not necessarily a conservative form, though it may have been one of a writer retired from active politics. The late 1790s see Blake, like Thelwall and Wordsworth, contemplating long poems from a place of retirement.

In most attempts to provide a British mythology, the name of Britain is traced back to a Roman conqueror, Brutus, who seizes the island from giants descended from Albion. Not only did Pope write a fragment of a British national epic on Brutus in 1743, but Ogilvie's 1801 'national epic' *Britannia* also uses the story of Brutus which derives from Geoffrey of Monmouth and appears in Milton's history. Although Blake describes himself as 'believing with Milton the ancient British History' (Blake, 1982 p. 543), he in fact makes a very different use of British myth, rejecting the figure of Brutus as liberator. In Ogilvie's poem, as in Milton's history, liberation can only come to the oppressed natives through the intervention and rule of a Roman soldier. Ogilvie's muse predicts the arrival of a foreign liberator:

> She saw the day
> Approaching near, by Heaven ordain'd, to free
> From thrall the natives, by a foreign host,
> From orient climes, beneath a Chief renown'd
> That spread the sail for Albion: doom'd to crush
> The tyrants of the land.
>
> (Ogilvie, 1801 p. 57)

Blake's Advertisement for his 1809 exhibition describes his painting *The Ancient Britons*: 'Three Ancient Britons overthrowing the Army of armed Romans; the Figures full as large as Life – From the Welch Triades' (Blake, 1982 p. 526). Here Blake presents the Romans as opponents rather than liberators of the Ancient Britons:

> The most Beautiful, the Roman Warriors trembled before and
>   worshipped:
> The most Strong, they melted before him and dissolved in his
>   presence:
> The most Ugly, they fled with outcries and contortion of their
>   Limbs,
>
> (ibid. p. 526)

By choosing Albion, Blake places his myth in an age of giants before the arrival of Brutus, the Roman, or Hercules, the Greek. He thus strengthens the nationalist force of his myth.

But Blake also places the mythic figure of Albion before the events of Hebrew myth. In doing so, he constructs a very different form of Hebraism from that of Richard Brothers or Joseph Bichero. Blake's

notebook commentary on *A Vision of the Last Judgment* describes
what seems to be an earlier version of the mythology of *Jerusalem*
in which 'our Ancestor' is clearly placed before Hebrew history:

> an Aged patriarch is awakd by his aged wife <He is Albion our
> Ancestor <patriarch of the Atlantic Continent> whose History
> Preceded that of the Hebrews <& in whose Sleep <or Chaos>
> Creation began, [*his Emanation or Wife is Jerusalem <who is about to
> be recievd like the Bride of the*>], at their head> <the Aged Woman
> is Brittannia, the Wife of Albion Jerusalem is their daughter>>.
>
> (Blake, 1982 p. 558)

In *The Marriage of Heaven and Hell* in the early 1790s Blake used
the figure of Ezekiel to suggest that the authority accorded to the
Hebrew scriptures creates a form of oppression, one which denies
to the religions and myths of other nations an equal validity and
produces an ideology which supports empire:

> and we so loved our God, that we cursed in his name all the
> deities of surrounding nations, and asserted that they had
> rebelled; from these opinions the vulgar came to think that all
> nations would at last be subject to the jews.
>
> This said he, like all firm perswasions, is come to pass, for all
> nations believe the jews god, and what greater subjection can be.
>
> (Blake, 1982 p. 39)

The passage from the *Vision of the Last Judgment* might be seen as
creating exactly the same scope for misunderstanding as is described
in the 'Memorable Fancy'. Instead of the Hebrew scriptures being
granted priority as they were by the mythographer Jacob Bryant
(who saw all other bodies of myth as derived indirectly and incor-
rectly from them, the Egyptian from the Hebrew and the Greek from
the Egyptian), Blake seems here instead to give priority to British
myth. In the *Descriptive Catalogue* Blake asserts the value of British
myth but does not appear to rank the myths of various nations:

> The antiquities of every Nation under Heaven, is no less sacred
> than that of the Jews. They are the same thing as Jacob Bryant,
> and all antiquaries have proved. How other antiquities came to be
> neglected and disbelieved, while those of the Jews are collected
> and arranged, is an enquiry, worthy of both the Antiquarian and
> the divine.
>
> (Blake, 1982 p. 543)

But when in the Preface to Chapter II of *Jerusalem*, addressed 'To the Jews', Blake returns yet again to this issue something rather strange seems to happen:

> Jerusalem the Emanation of the Giant Albion! Can it be? Is it a Truth that the Learned have explored? Was Britain the Primitive Seat of the Patriarchal Religion? If it is true: my title-page is also True, that Jerusalem was & is the Emanation of the Giant Albion. It is True, and cannot be controverted. . . .
> Albion was the Parent of the Druids; & in his Chaotic State of Sleep, Satan & Adam & the whole World Was Created by the Elohim.
>
> (Blake, 1982 p. 171)

This passage alters the mythic relationships of the passage from *A Vision of the Last Judgment* in a way which modifies the nationalist focus of the myth. In *A Vision of the Last Judgment*, Jerusalem is Albion's daughter and Britannia his wife. In the Preface to *Jerusalem*, it is Jerusalem rather than Britannia who is Albion's wife or emanation. The change might be a result of unease about using the figures of British national myth. Britannia appears only four times in the poem, mostly towards the end, at the stage at which figures who have been misappropriated begin to be cleansed of false associations. The form of Blake's argument in the Preface to *Jerusalem* adopts and then parodies the method of a mythographer such as Jacob Bryant. He sets up a proof of his account, marking the steps of his demonstration in a way which dismisses logic: 'Is it a Truth that the Learned have explored? . . . If it is true, my title-page is also True. . . . It is True and cannot be controverted' (ibid.). The theories developed by Bryant have the effect of creating a hierarchy of groups of myth. Blake's use of his kind of argument about priority could be seen as parodically undoing his logic, mocking the attempt to establish an order of myths. The figure of Albion may be intended in part to avoid the kind of ranking necessary to Bryant, for Albion is placed before creation, before the appearance of such figures as Adam, Satan, Noah or Arthur (with whom he is equated in *A Descriptive Catalogue*). Each of these later figures can be associated with him, since each is a point of origin, the father of a nation; all men are descended from Adam, but all are also descended from Noah. In the sense that the fallen world can be seen as an image of hell, all are also descended from Satan. Spenser in *The Faerie Queene* uses Arthur as an origin in a more limited sense, since he derives queen, realm and race from him. But in attempting to pre-empt all other myths by using Albion as the name of the eternal man, the

way is opened to a reading which turns the poem into a myth
of national supremacy. Albion, dying, at the end of Chapter I
remembers a time when 'Albion coverd the whole Earth, England
encompassed the Nations' (Blake, 1982 p. 170).

The narrator, whose voice introduces Chapter I, is given the
power to restore to the nation the national memories that are lost:

> Names anciently rememberd! but now contemn'd as fictions!
> Although in every bosom they controll our Vegetative powers.
>
> (ibid. p. 148)

Yet the degree of power and authority which is to be accorded
to the rediscovered figures of British myth remains unclear.

III

Blake's unfinished *The French Revolution* seems to create an image
of popular nationalism in the replacement of the king of France
with a figure of the French people. In *Jerusalem*, the figure of the
British people, Albion, takes on an odd dual role as both national
and universal figure. Yet the case for *Jerusalem* as a nationalist epic
does not seem hard to make; its concern with themes of national
identity and regeneration is obvious. The question is rather what
kind of nationalism, or whose nationalism, the poem represents.
Is its nationalism always ironic – an attempt perhaps to use and
manipulate the nationalism of the nation at war – or is it an
oppositional nationalism, one which creates an image of the nation
as utopia? The superimposition of the figure of Albion as nation
on Albion as universal man is surely open to two readings, one of
which dissolves the national identity in the universal, but the other
of which becomes an image of empire.

In many places, *Jerusalem* does seem to be a straightforward epic
of national identity. As Los works at his furnaces in the fourth and
final chapter he sees an image which is taken by commentators such
as Stevenson as a sign of the imminent reawakening of Albion,
a clearly positive development.[7] Los cries out:

> What do I see? The Briton Saxon Roman Norman amalgamating
> In my Furnaces into One Nation the English: & taking refuge
> In the Loins of Albion.
>
> (Blake, 1982 p. 252)

Yet this straightforward image of the nation formed from diverse ethnic strands is immediately complicated by the superimposition of biblical myth:

> The Canaanite united with the fugitive
> Hebrew, whom she divided into Twelve, & sold into Egypt
> Then scattered the Egyptian & Hebrew to the four Winds!
> This sinful Nation Created in our Furnaces & Looms is Albion
> (ibid. p. 252)

This parallel implicitly questions the image of national unity: the joining of Canaanite and Hebrew leads to division, betrayal and scattering. The joining of 'Briton Saxon Roman Norman' produces a 'sinful Nation': national strength and unity are not necessarily seen positively here. But if Albion is a 'sinful nation', it is also, according to the Voice Divine, a chosen nation:

> I elected Albion for my glory; I gave to him the Nations,
> Of the whole Earth. He was the Angel of my Presence: and all
> The sons of God were Albions sons: and Jerusalem was my joy.
> (ibid. p. 191)

Albion given 'the Nations / Of the whole Earth' could be read as an image of empire. Albion's despairing words at the end of the first chapter lament the loss of a time in which England as a commercial power was the centre of the world, just as in the proposal for the naval pillar at Greenwich:

> In the Exchanges of London every Nation walkd
> And London walkd in every Nation mutual in love & harmony
> Albion coverd the whole Earth, England encompassd the Nations,
> Mutual each within others bosom in Visions of Regeneration;
> (ibid. p. 170)

The same words are echoed in Jerusalem's lament in the fourth chapter (ibid. p. 234). This apparent celebration of Britain's commercial power is perhaps only surprising in view of the outspoken criticism of the debilitating power of commerce in the *Public Address*:

> <Commerce is so far from being beneficial to Arts or to Empire that it is destructive of both <as all their History shews> for the above Reason of Individual Merit being its Great hatred. Empires flourish till they become Commercial & then they are scattered abroad to the four winds>.
> (Blake, 1982 p. 574)

As so often (and so perplexingly) in Blake's writing similar images reappear in both positive and negative guises. The image of Albion covering 'the whole earth' reappears as a fear of a lost unity, a scattered identity. The fear of a British diaspora runs through *Jerusalem*. Los at work at his furnaces cries, 'O when shall the Saxon return with the English his redeemed brother!' (Blake, 1982 p. 241). Here the German Saxon is imagined as part of the English people, parted from the Anglo-Saxon by history and the North Sea.[8] Los is answered by Albion's daughters speaking from the Euphrates, exiled like the daughters of Jerusalem in Psalms and Lamentations. Los laments that 'The English are scattered over the face of the nations'. The English, unlike the Jews or the Africans, would not seem to be 'scattered over the face of the nations' unless war, empire, trade or the loss of America are imagined as the scattering of the nation.

The nationalist language of *Jerusalem* then seems to be highly complex, and to work in ways which are distinctly different from that of other contemporary nationalist literature. If nationalism rests on organic notions of identity, then Blake's organicism is so radical that it tends to unify not only the disparate parts of the nation but also the world: in the myth underlying *Jerusalem* a time is imagined in which Britain is not an island but is joined to America and in which Canaan and England are the same place. There are also indications that the nationalism of *Jerusalem* parodies and rejects some aspects of the contemporary discourse of nationalism, even that with which Blake in other contexts seems to be associated. The Thames is equally important in the iconography of *Jerusalem* and in Barry's painting for the Royal Society of Arts, yet the figure of the Thames takes on a different identity. Los calls out to Albion:

> Found ye London! enormous City! weeps thy River?
> Upon his parent bosom lay thy little ones O land
> Forsaken. (Blake, 1982 p. 241)

The Thames is envisaged as comforting parent to England's children rather than as receiving slaves from Africa, but also, further upstream, as a youthful river, the place of pleasure:

> Separate Albions Sons gently from their Emanations,
> Weaving bowers of delight on the current of infant Thames
> Where the old Parent still retains his youth.
>
> (ibid. p. 242)

Blake imagines a young figure of the Thames, just as in *Milton* he imagines a youthful figure of Time. There are also indications that

in *Jerusalem* the project for the naval pillar appears in a negative
form. The spectre

> reads the Voids
> Between the Stars; among the arches of Albions Tomb sublime
> Rolling the Sea in rocky paths: forming Leviathan
> And Behemoth: the War by Sea enormous, & the War
> By Land astounding: erecting pillars in the deepest Hell
> To reach the heavenly arches.

(ibid. p. 251)

Leviathan and Behemoth have already been associated in Blake's
Descriptive Catalogue with Pit and Nelson and in the paintings described there become the focus for a parodic account of the heroes
of national myth. The pillars erected 'in the deepest hell' are not
only versions of Pandemonium but more specifically forms of the
naval pillar. Los's work is to destroy such images of national
heroics: Los beheld undaunted, furious

> His heavd Hammer; he swung it round & at one blow,
> In unpitying ruin driving down the pyramids of pride
> Smiting the Spectre on his Anvil.

(ibid. p. 252)

Not only the pillars but the 'pyramids of pride', which might
be seen as versions of the Napoleonic obelisk, are destroyed.

If the myth of Albion is potentially a nationalist myth, however,
Jerusalem also contains an implicit model which focuses again on
the theme of national identity in a way which is far more subtle
than that of the prose works. The model is signalled in the number
of chapters planned for the poem, and in the decision to label them
as chapters rather than books. Although *Jerusalem* is a poem in four
chapters, the title page once announced that it was a poem 'In
XXVIII Chapters'. The division of the final poem into four chapters
has been taken as evidence that the intended model is Milton's brief
epic, the four book *Paradise Regained*. But if 'twenty-eight' is the significant number, and 'Chapter' the important word, then it suggests
instead the model of Acts of the Apostles, one of the two books of
the Bible with this number. The four chapters of *Jerusalem* are each
prefaced by an address to one of the groups which make up the
nation, or the potential audience for Blake's epic. And whereas the
poem as a whole takes Acts as its model, these are versions of the
Pauline epistles. Blake writes 'To the Christians', 'To the Jews', 'To

the Deists' and 'To the Public' instead of 'To the Romans' or 'To the Hebrews'. Like the Pauline epistles, the prefaces rebuke as well as praise. In the Preface 'To the Christians', Blake defines Christianity as 'liberty both of body & mind to exercise the Divine Arts of Imagination' and uses the apostles as his authority: 'The Apostles knew of no other Gospel'. He uses the opposition of flesh or body to spirit which is central to Paul's epistle to the Galatians:

> What is Mortality but the things relating to the Body, which Dies? What is Immortality but the things relating to the Spirit, which lives Eternally! What is the Joy of Heaven but Improvement in the things of the Spirit? What are the Pains of Hell but Ignorance, Bodily Lust, Idleness & devastation of the things of the Spirit[?]
> (Blake, 1982 p. 232)

This plate is headed by a reference to the conversion of St Paul which is a quotation from Acts: 'Devils are / False Religions / "Saul Saul" / "Why persecutest thou me"'. Acts begins with the instructions given to the apostles by Jesus before the Resurrection, and the first is 'that they should not depart from Jerusalem, but wait for the promise of the Father' (Acts 1: 4). *Jerusalem*, Blake's poem, tells of Albion's desertion of his true bride, Jerusalem, for Vala, the figure associated with war and the female will. Moreover, *Jerusalem* tells of the witness of the poet Los (Urthona's spectre) in 'time of trouble':

> Therefore the Sons of Eden praise Urthonas Spectre in Songs Because he kept the Divine Vision in time of trouble.
> (Blake, 1982 p. 193)

Keeping the divine vision in time of trouble is the subject of Acts of the Apostles, of *Jerusalem*, and is also the predicament of the radical artist in the time of a nationalist war. One of the central preoccupations of Acts of the Apostles, as of *Jerusalem*, is the question of identity, of an identity of belief or of custom, nation or race. Acts tells of the opposition of Jewish believers to the mission to the Gentiles, an opposition which is focused on the debate over circumcision. The decision is 'that we trouble not them, which from among the Gentiles are turned to God' (Acts 15: 19). In *Jerusalem*, national identity is discovered in the process of recognising a likeness with another nation, as the map of Britain is superimposed on the map of Israel: identity and otherness become the same. As Golgonooza is built, Los is able to see Palestine in London:

is that
Mild Zions hills most ancient promontory; near mournful
Ever weeping Paddington? is that Calvary and Golgotha
Becoming a building of pity and compassion?

(Blake, 1982 p. 155)

Within the context of *Jerusalem* identities are continually redefined.
Babylon, Jerusalem and Albion become the names of places only
on one level of meaning. As Morton Paley points out, Brothers'
'intention was to establish a kingdom with its seat in Jerusalem'
whereas 'Blake's Jerusalem is to be built in England's green and
pleasant land' (Paley, 1983 p. 132). And once 'Jerusalem' has ceased
to refer to a geographically real place, it is surely just as possible
for England to be generalised by means of the double national and
universal reference of the word Albion in a way which takes it
beyond national myth. Yet to deny Blake's writing any historical
reference seems equally unsatisfactory. The complex politics of
nationalism are present in the nationalist discourses used and transformed within his writings in such a way that it is not possible to
extract a single Blakean view on nationalism from the prose and
poetry. The voice of the patriot from the *Public Address* is not that
of *Jerusalem* or even of any of the voices which go to make up that
many voiced poem. The potentially nationalist discourse of the
Descriptive Catalogue is undercut by the paintings it accompanies.
Yet the language of Blake's poetry cannot entirely redefine its own
terms. The shifts in identity and the shifts in meaning characteristic
of it do not reduce the likelihood that the Eternal Man will seem
to be male and that Albion will be read as a figure of the nation.
While *Jerusalem* works towards a point at which national identities
merge, it nevertheless does so through the form of a national epic
poem.

Notes

1. The most helpful discussion of Blake's nationalism is by MARILYN BUTLER
   (Butler 1988), p. 49.

2. The iconographic establishment of the figure of Britannia is described in
   NEWMAN 1987, pp. 77–9.

3. JOHN BARRELL argues that 'the influence of Barry upon Blake – sometimes as
   mediated, perhaps, by John Opie – is very apparent' (Barrell 1986), p. 227.

4. See HASKELL AND PENNY 1981, p. 67.

5. Richard Brothers and Joseph Bichero are discussed by MORTON D. PALEY
   (Paley 1983), pp. 131–2.

6. See JOHN BARRELL's interesting discussion of Blake's use of the concept 'the public' (Barrell 1986), pp. 253–7.

7. W. H. STEVENSON comments: 'This is one of the first signs of hope; Albion, hitherto shattered and disintegrated, is seen to display in the course of history the power of brotherhood in uniting nations in himself' (Blake 1971), p. 829.

8. W. H. Stevenson's suggestion. See Blake, 1971, p. 808.

7 'Original', 'Character' and 'Individual'

JOHN BARRELL

'Original'

The word 'original' seems to have two distinguishable meanings in Blake's writings on the arts of design, though both of these are related in the definition offered by the *OED* for 'originality': 'the fact or attribute of being primary or first-hand: authenticity, genuineness'. The first of these two meanings is not at all troublesome, and can best be conveyed by saying that an original work or artist is the opposite of a copy, or of a copyist engaged in directly reproducing another man's work or invention. Thus, when Blake says that 'No Man can Improve an Original Invention', his primary meaning in the context of this remark is that no engraver can improve on the work he is engaged to reproduce, as Tom Cooke believed he could improve on Hogarth's designs. It is to this sense of the word that Blake is appealing, when, in a draft prospectus for the engraving of his own 'fresco' of Chaucer's Canterbury Pilgrims, he writes that the engraving 'is minutely labour'd , not by the hands of Journeymen, but by the Original Artist himself'. In this sense also, he writes that an 'original' artist cannot employ 'numerous Journeymen in manufacturing (as Rubens and Titian did) the Pictures that go under his name' (pp. 594–5, 587–8, 583).* Because, for Blake, 'Invention depends Altogether upon Execution', which is 'the Only Vehicle', the 'Chariot' of 'Genius', an original artist cannot remain so when he entrusts the execution, even of what Reynolds would regard as the subordinate parts of a work, to 'the Hands of Ignorant Journeymen' (pp. 446, 453–4, 595).

But even in the examples quoted above, this simple meaning gains an additional force by the use of the word 'original' in a wider sense, in which it is opposed to what we might prefer to call

---

* All page-numbers in this chapter refer to *The Complete Writings of William Blake*, ed. Geoffrey Keynes, London 1966.

'imitation', though Blake usually persists in calling it 'copying'. In this enlarged sense, an artist is original, first of all, when he does not imitate other artists, for 'none but Blockheads Copy one another'; and the work of an artist who forms his style on, or borrows his inventions from, other artists, cannot have that consistency which is a mark of 'authenticity, genuineness': 'The Man, Either Painter or Philosopher, who Learns or Acquires all he knows from Others, Must be full of Contradictions'. But equally, an artist cannot be original if he imitates *nature*. To some extent, Blake's opinion here coincides fully with Reynolds's: it depends on a distinction between those who 'Copy Nature' directly – mere copyists of actual nature – and those who are 'Copiers of Imagination' (pp. 601, 449, 594–5). But the fact that those who copy imagination do not, for Blake, do so in any way that Reynolds could approve, is clear from Blake's inclusion, among the copiers of nature, not only of Rembrandt, but of Reynolds himself. For the central form which for Reynolds was derived empirically by the imagination is for Blake derived by the form of reasoning he describes as 'ratio': the central form is simply 'A Ratio of All we have Known'. The imagination is not involved at all, but simply the powers of calculation and memory; thus 'the Greek Muses', for example, are 'daughters of Mnemosyne, or Memory, and not of Inspiration or Imagination'; and thus the annotations of Reynolds's third discourse, in which he announced the doctrine of the central form, begin with a quotation from Milton's *Reason of Church Government* to the effect that a work of Genius is 'Not to be obtain'd by the Invocation of Memory and her Syren Daughters, but by Devout prayer to [the] Eternal Spirit' (pp. 475, 566, 457).

Blake is not opposed to copying *per se*. It is essential to the education of an artist that he should learn 'the Language of Art by making many Finish'd Copies both of Nature & Art'; and even an original artist must be a copyist, must indeed be a more perfect copyist than an uninspired artist could ever be. 'The difference between a bad Artist & a Good One Is: the Bad Artist Seems to Copy a Great deal. The Good one Really Does Copy a Great Deal', and the more (in an ironic application of Reynolds's sense of the term) his copying is 'Servile', the better a good artist will be. What is more, the works which a good artist produces by copying will be far more 'correct', more 'servile', than those produced by a mere copyist of actual nature or of the images begotten by the ratio upon the daughters of memory, for the images seen by the 'imaginative and immortal organs' of the genius will be far more 'organised and minutely articulated' – will be far more detailed, will require *more* to be copied – than the objects which 'we see reflected in this

Vegetable Glass of Nature', this 'world of Dross', where 'Reality' is 'Forgot', and only 'the Vanities of Time & Space' are 'Remember'd & call'd Reality' (pp. 455–6, 595, 576, 605, 600). For that reason 'Nature' becomes to its 'Victim', its copyist, 'nothing but Blots & Blurs'. What is at issue, then, is not whether but what the artist should copy: and the answer is evidently imagination and inspiration, or 'vision' – the original artist 'Copies That without Fatique' (pp. 595–6, 457). I want now to consider what that vision is, and why to copy it minutely and faithfully should be the mark of an 'original' artist; the question of originality of style, or of manner, I shall defer until after we have examined some other of the terms of the value-language of Blake's writings on art.

Throughout those writings, the influence of Barry upon Blake – sometimes as mediated, perhaps, by John Opie – is very apparent. Blake contemplated, and composed a few lines of, a poem about Barry (pp. 553–4), and on one occasion when – as occasionally he does – Blake finds a thought to admire in the *Discourses*, he suggests that 'Somebody else wrote this page for Reynolds'. Like Barry, Blake believes that the earliest examples of art that have survived bear the marks of being derived 'from some stupendous originals now lost or perhaps buried till some happier age'. These 'wonderful originals' were produced in 'the ancient republics, monarchies, and patriarchates of Asia', and are referred to in the scriptures as the 'Cherubim', which 'were sculptured and painted on walls of Temples, Towers, Cities, Palaces, and erected in the highly cultivated states' (for 'The Bible says That Cultivated Life Existed First, Uncultivated Life comes afterwards') 'of Egypt, Moab, Edom, Aram, among the Rivers of Paradise' (pp. 463, 565, 446).

There are significant differences, however, between Blake's account of the origins of art and Barry's. To begin with, for Blake, the art of the Greeks cannot, as we have seen, be regarded as the product of a rediscovery of the principles of art: though the Hercules Farnese, the Venus de'Medici, and the Apollo Belvedere are 'justly admired', they are 'copies' of the original images of the Cherubim, of the vision, that is, as already mediated by other artists. Secondly, Blake is not obliged, as Barry is, to deduce the original existence of a more perfect art – indeed, for Blake, of a perfect art – from the vestiges of it that survive in the work of those who remembered it, more or less immediately. Blake, 'having been taken in vision' to the ancient states of Asia, 'has seen those wonderful originals', which he can therefore assure us 'were some of them one hundred feet in height; some were painted as pictures, and some carved as basso relievos, and some as groupes of statues', all 'executed in a very superior style' to the works of the Greek artists, or to all except the Torso, which is the only Greek work that Blake believes to have been an 'original' work, a genuine 'invention' (pp. 565–6).

Blake's claim to be an original artist is founded on his vision of, among other things, these originals of art. Whereas if the Greeks copy these originals they produce only imitations, if Blake copies them he will produce works of art equally original; and the difference is that while Blake sees them with his imaginative eye, the Greeks either saw them with their moral, their perishing organs of sight, or did not see them at all, and copied only the memory of them as transmitted perhaps by intermediate copies. But Blake's claim is founded also on a more general capacity for vision, an ability like that of the prophets to receive visions of 'what Eternally Exists, Really and Unchangeably', the 'Eternal Forms' of things 'as they were reveal'd to Mortal Man in the Series of Divine Revelations as they are written in the Bible'. For this reason, Blake can claim to be 'an inhabitant' of Eden, 'that happy country' among 'the Rivers of Paradise' where the originals of art wait to be rediscovered; and for that reason he can state that 'The Nature of my Work is Visionary or Imaginative; it is an Endeavour to Restore what the Ancients call'd the Golden Age'. On the other hand, 'The Man who never in his Mind & Thoughts travel'd to Heaven is No Artist' – the distinction is not between original artists and unoriginal artists, but between artists, all of whom are original insofar as they have access to a vision of the originals of art, or eternal forms, and those who are not artists at all; the 'nature' of all art is 'visionary', 'imaginative', and original (pp. 604–6, 578, 565, 458). Originality does not consist in any quality of novelty that the best artists may display, but in their ability to penetrate through the accidents of time and place to the substances of things, which are discoverable only by imaginative vision. The difference between Reynolds's notion of originality and Blake's does not reside in any greater power in Blake's artist to produce inventions out of nothing, or inventions which originate in his individual self; it depends entirely on the fact that, for Reynolds, substance is discoverable by the imagination working empirically; for Blake, by the imagination working intuitively, seeing into things, through to their original forms.

It seems that this faculty of vision is available to everyone, and that we all have the power to 'see . . . above the shadows of generation and death'. Blake certainly believes that genius is innate, and that it is nonsense to speak of 'Acquiring Invention and learning how to produce Original Conception'; and insofar as 'there cannot be more than two or three great Painters and Poets in any Age or Country', and 'inspiration and vision' are 'the gift of God', it may

seem that originality is a grace vouchsafed only to a happy few
(pp. 578–9, 469, 561). Insofar, however, as the knowledge of ideal
beauty is (as it was for Barry) given by conscience – by 'Con-Science
or Innate Science' (pp. 457, 459) – it seems that, however insuperable
the difficulties interposed to the imagination of most people by the
obstructions of the vegetable world, the vision is accessible to all
who will follow their conscience. Thus, in the account of his 'Vision
of the Last Judgment', he insists that:

> If the Spectator could Enter into these Images in his Imagination,
> approaching them on the Fiery Chariot of his Contemplative
> Thought, if he could Enter into Noah's Rainbow or into his
> bosom, or could make a Friend & Companion of one of these
> Images of wonder, which always intreats him to leave mortal
> things (as he must know), then would he arise from his Grave,
> then would he meet the Lord in the Air & then he would be
> happy (p. 611).

Whether the spectator 'can' do these things seems to depend on the
will rather than on the possession of the faculties necessary to the
apprehension of visions; for it seems that he has an imagination, and
'contemplative thought', and the images of wonder would not (one
presumes) 'intreat' him to do the impossible. Why so many men
should ignore the intreaty, when 'the Whole Business of Man Is the
Arts', is a question we may defer till the end of this note (p. 777).

It is partly because the vision is a gift of God, a grace, that its
minute details must be copied as accurately as they are perceived:
to do anything less would be to reject a part of God's gift. Therefore
the colours must be 'clear' and 'unmudded by oil', and the lines
'firm and determinate' and 'unbroken by shadows'; for the aim is to
display the vision, and not to conceal it, as the original artist will do
if he succumbs to the influence of the painters of Venice or the Low
Countries, who 'cause that the execution shall be all blocked up with
brown shadows', and who 'put the original Artist in fear and doubt
of his own original conception'. For that reason too 'Art can never
exist without Naked Beauty displayed': drapery will conceal the
clarity of the lineaments (pp. 564, 582, 776). The resemblance between
Blake's and Barry's views on the importance of the representation
of detail is clear enough: for Barry, generalised form and drapery
conceal the minute and perfect organisation of the body of the
sublime character, as for Blake they conceal the same quality in the
figures perceived in vision. But the resemblance goes further than
that, as we shall see in the next section.

William Blake

'Character'

Genius and Inspiration, by which the painter has access to 'original conceptions' of the eternal forms of things, are also, according to Blake, 'the Great Origin and Bond of Society': their function is to create, and to confirm, a society which is also, as we shall see, a public. To ask how it is that art performs this function it is necessary first of all to ask what it is that is revealed to the original artist in his visions, and which it is his task therefore to represent. We have already had some intimation of the answer, in Blake's account of the Greek copies of the scriptural Cherubim, which emerged in the form of the Apollo, the Hercules, the Venus de'Medici: the 'Grecian gods were the ancient Cherubim of Phoenicia', which are 'visions' of the 'eternal principles or characters of human life'. The prime task of the original artist is the representation of these characters, and it is for this reason, and not out of any concern with the *unique* character of the artist, that Blake describes the 'Two Grand Merits of the Great Style' as 'Original and Characteristical' (pp. 561, 571, 468). Art is characteristical when it is engaged in the representation of character, and it is 'expressive' when it is engaged in the representation of expression as a function of character, which is the 'stamina' of expression. Both character and expression 'can only be Expressed by those who Feel Them', and neither can exist except in works which employ a 'firm and determinate outline'. But that outline is not characteristic or expressive because it is an indication of the particular character of the artist or the feelings which, as a particular character, he seeks to express; 'expression' is a property not of the artist but of his subject. Outline, therefore, is characteristic, is expressive, because it marks with minute fidelity the characters and expressions of the persons it delineates: that is why Blake can claim that 'there is not one Character or Expression' in his prints 'which could be Produced with the Execution of Titian, Rubens, Correggio, Rembrandt, or any of that Class' (pp. 585, 599).

The most detailed account of character that Blake offers in his writings on art is contained in his description of his painting, *Sir Jeffery Chaucer and the nine and twenty Pilgrims on their journey to Canterbury*. 'Chaucer's characters', writes Blake, 'are a description of the eternal Principles that exist in all ages', and for that reason, in Blake's representation of them, 'every one is an Antique Statue': the Franklin is 'the Bacchus', the Doctor of Physic is 'the Esculapius', the Host is 'the Silenus', the Squire is 'the Apollo', the Miller is 'the Hercules', and so on. I have *quoted* the names of the gods, so as to preserve the definite article that introduces each of them, which serves to suggest that the antique statues have a certain general, or generic character, and that is exactly Blake's point: every one of his pilgrims, like every one of these 'antique statues', is 'the image of a class'. For:

> The characters of Chaucer's Pilgrims are the characters which compose all ages and nations: as one age falls, another rises, different to mortal sight, but to immortals only the same; for we see the same characters repeated again and again, in animals, vegetables, minerals, and in men; nothing new occurs in identical existence; Accident ever varies, Substance can never suffer change or decay.

> Of Chaucer's characters, as described in his Canterbury Tales, some of the names or titles are altered by time, but the characters themselves for ever remain unaltered, and consequently they are the physiognomies or lineaments of universal human life, beyond which Nature never steps.

The notion that Blake's concern with character is a concern with the representation of 'individual' character, uniqueness of appearance, is no doubt partly the result of a belief that minute fidelity to particular detail will inevitably result in the minute discrimination of the particular appearances of individual persons; but that will be true, of course, only if it is nature that Blake is copying, and not eternal forms and principles. It is also partly the result of the assumption that, because Blake believes that the representation of character not only permits but demands a good deal of variety, that variety will (when coupled with minute fidelity) produce a representation of character minutely individualised. But though, for example, Blake claims to have 'varied the heads and forms of his personages into all Nature's varieties', we have already seen that what Nature produces is a taxonomy of generic characters or classes, each varied from the other, but each varied in itself only by 'accidents' which Blake forebears to represent as urgently as if instructed by the early Reynolds – for accidents, of 'time' and 'space', are not realities. In the same way, though the Roman soldiers who appeared in Blake's (now lost) painting *The Ancient Britons* 'each shew a different character, and different expression of fear, or revenge, or envy', and so on, they show these expressions in their identity as characters, and characters are the images 'of a class, and not of an imperfect individual' (pp. 571, 567, 580).

There may appear to be a certain latitude of interpretation offered by this last phrase, at least to the most determined believer in Blake as the celebrator of the uniqueness of individual personality: perhaps it could be argued that though an 'imperfect individual' may be one who is perceived in terms of accident, not substance, and so not as a member of a class, there may be another class of (presumably) perfect individuals, to whom Blake may feel more kindly. I doubt it; but we can consider the point when we consider the term 'individual' in the various meanings which Blake asks it to bear. In the meantime, we can at least dispose of the notion that Blake's 'adherence to an expressive theory of art and a concept of individual identity eliminates the possibility of a standard idea of beauty or hero'. Chaucer's knight, Blake tells us, 'is a true Hero, a good, great, and wise man . . . and is that species of character which in every age stands as the guardian of man against the oppressor'; he is, apparently, not an individual but a 'species of character' which transcends time, place, or whatever is opposed to 'identical existence', where that term is apparently intended to refer to what 'individual examples of one species' have in common, so 'that any one of them may . . . be substituted for any other' (*OED* 'identical'; pp. 567–8).

Blake's characters, his representation of the eternal and substantial forms of human life, are divided between 'good' characters and 'bad'. Thus, if the knight is 'good, great, and wise', and the Parson is an angel, 'an Apostle, a real Messenger of Heaven', others, such as the Pardoner and the Sompnour, are 'Devils of the first magnitude'. The character of Hercules was divided by Chaucer, and so is divided also by Blake, between an angel and a devil: the simplicity, wisdom and strength of the character are attributed to the 'benevolent' plowman; and in this form he represents Hercules 'in his supreme eternal state, divested of his spectrous shadow', which is represented by the Miller, 'a terrible fellow, such as exists at all times and places for the trial of men'. The Pardoner, also, 'is sent in every age . . . for a blight, for a trial of men, to divide the classes of men'. This division of characters into angels and devils is reminiscent of Barry's distinction between character and deformity: between those whose character is represented in a body adapted for the performance of tasks advantageous to men, and those whose bodies are deformed by their adaptation to selfish or destructive ends. In fact, however, both Angels and Devils among the pilgrims have useful and necessary tasks to perform: the Pardoner is not simply a blight, he is 'sent . . . for a trial of men', and so 'he is suffered by Providence for wise ends, and has also his great use'; the Miller exists 'to curb the pride of Man'; the character of the Wife of Bath is 'useful as a scarecrow' (pp. 570–2).

Blake does, however, make two important distinctions in his discussion of character that seem to be related to Barry's distinctions between beauty, character, and deformity. By the first of these, he distinguishes, among the characters of Strength (the Hercules), Ugliness (the Dancing Fawn) and Beauty (the Apollo – for beauty may be a character for Blake, whereas for Barry character is a sublime distortion of beauty), those images of each character which are, and are not, 'the receptacles of intellect'. This distinction relates to his remark that Reynolds 'thought Character Itself Extravagance & Deformity'; for these three characters are fit for representation in high art, only when clearly marked as fit for the different tasks they are 'sent' to perform, and so uncontaminated by any appearance of a propensity to folly, or imbecility, or (in the case of Strength) mere bulk without spiritual energy, of the kind represented for Barry by Roubiliac's statue of Hercules tying a bow-knot. Insofar as these characters are not represented as 'the receptacles of intellect', it seems they cease to be characters: not because mere individuals, but because unfit to fulfil their tasks; and in the same way as, for Barry, the images of deformity, of unfitness to perform 'useful' tasks, are fit subjects only in comic painting, so for Blake these useless variants of generic character are 'a subject for burlesque and not for historical grandeur' (pp. 579–80, 460).

Blake also appears to make a distinction in relation to character which may be derived from Barry's distinction, between the notion of a proper division of labour, among different characters all working to a common end – the perfection of man – or among figures of deformity which treat the tasks they perform as ends in themselves. The error of the Greeks was, according to Blake, that they, and 'since them the Moderns, have neglected to subdue the gods of Priam'. By this he means that the characters represented by original artists – the Cherubim, for example, are properly to be regarded as 'visions of the eternal attributes, or divine names': the separate characters, that is, are attributes of an omnipotent deity, whose powers are distributed among the different classes of men by the same 'natural' division of labour as formed, for Barry, the distinction of characters. As long as the characters are thus regarded as having a common ground of unity, in Christ, they remain as they should do, the 'servants, and not the masters, of man, or of society'; for all the 'Permanent Realities' of things, including the 'eternal principles or characters of human life' are for Blake 'comprehended in their Eternal Forms in the divine body of the Saviour', whose body is the body of the public; and for that reason, insofar as we are characters, we are 'members' of Jesus, in the same way as the different characters represented by the Greek gods are for Barry comprehended in the unity of an omnipotent God. The Greeks, however, by erecting the characters into separate gods, dissolved the ground of their unity and 'separated' them from man or humanity, who is Jesus the Saviour. The sense of common purpose, and of community, was therefore destroyed: the Greek gods became the representatives of tasks pursued as ends in themselves, and so became not the servants of mankind but 'the masters'; and instead of being 'made to sacrifice to Man', they 'compelled' man to sacrifice to them (pp. 571, 605–6, 776).

'Every age', argues Blake, 'is a Canterbury Pilgrimage; we all pass on, each sustaining one or other of these characters; nor can a child be born, who is not one of these characters of Chaucer' (p. 570). For Blake, unlike Barry, generic identity is innate, not the result of education and adaptation; and the function of painting appears to be to represent to us the characters of life, in such a way as enables us to realise our different, innate identities in them. I mean 'different' in two senses: the representation of these 'eternal principles or characters of humanity' is intended to reveal to us how, when we see the images of character stripped of accident, we may all recognise that our different identities are united with those of others in one of the various classes of humanity; and to reveal to us that those classes are indeed various, though finite in number, according to the number of tasks God has sent the various characters to perform. Thus far, and except that the audience are to identify with one or another specific class, rather than with a uniform central form, it seems that Blake's idea of the function of art is close to Reynolds's: art is the 'origin' of society because it reveals to us our common humanity, the ground of social affiliation; it is the 'bond' of society because it continues to do this, continually offering to us images which confirm that common humanity.

But Blake's notion of the function of art goes further than this: its task, as we have already seen, is to 'Restore what the Ancients call'd the Golden Age' (p. 605), and as far as we can deduce from his writings on art, this will be achieved when the 'gods of Priam' are subdued, and we recognise ourselves not only as members of the separate classes of humanity, but as united in a common purpose, and a common sense of identity – when we recognise that the characters we represent are united in Jesus, and, thus understood, are the servants of man and society, and no longer the tyrannous agents of division. In this, Blake's idea of the function of art seems to depart from Reynolds's almost exactly as Barry's did, and in such a way as to acknowledge the need for variety in art and society, but not for the kind of variety which opposes one activity, one character, to another, instead of uniting them. There are, however, important differences between Blake's notion and Barry's. First, though for both men the function of art, and the forms of character, may be grasped by an appeal to conscience, for Blake conscience can go so far as to reveal to the imagination an unmediated vision of the difference and unity of those forms. Second, it was for Barry essential that the forms of character should be represented as engaged in moral actions, so that we can distinguish them from the forms of deformity they may resemble, and perhaps also (if Barry is following, though it is not clear that he is, Alison's associationist theory) so that we will learn to associate them with the performance of acts of virtue. For Blake, as for Reynolds, the point seems to be that by the exhibition of ideal forms, we will learn the grounds of social affiliation; to this end they do not need to be represented in action; but because the idea forms are fitted, are designed for action, Blake believes that they will teach us (as the central forms of Reynolds do not) that the sense of community among the varieties of character is to be achieved by deeds which are of service to a Christian community.

'Individual'

To an art with such a function as this, individuality – or the assertion that one is an individual, a member of no class – can only be an obstruction. Now it is not clear what Blake means when he says that the Pardoner is 'sent' to divide the classes of men: he may be sent to separate the classes from each other, by dividing them from the Saviour who is the ground of their unity; or he may be sent to divide each class into individuals who, seeing only with the perishing mortal organ of vision, see accident and difference instead of substance and identity, and so lose a sense of their common humanity by becoming aware of themselves only as 'individuals', necessarily 'imperfect' because impaired by the process of division. In either case, the 'trial' that the Pardoner makes of men must be accepted and resolved; and it must be resolved in the second case, because, in so far as mortal sight blurs the bounding line which separates one class from another, it returns the world to chaos, and 'the line of the almighty', which marks the lineaments of each class, 'must be drawn out' again before 'man or beast can exist'; for 'where there are no lineaments there can be no character'. It is perhaps worth repeating here that it is because the function of art is to represent character, and not because its function is to represent individuality, that the 'Greatest Artists' are 'the Most Minutely Discriminating and Determinate': individuality, for Blake as for Reynolds, Barry and Fuseli, is accidental, and 'Minute Discrimination is Not Accidental' (pp. 585, 575, 453). For Blake as for Barry, the sublimity of art is the result of the representation of generic character, and if 'All Sublimity is founded on Minute Discrimination', that is because, for both men, the representation of different classes or characters, finely organised and so finely discriminated from each other, is the representation of the 'sublime', the 'stupendous' and 'wonderful' originals of character also represented, according to Blake, in the Cherubim. 'The whole of Art', Blake argues in his annotations to Reynolds, is comprised in an attention to 'Complicated & Minute Discrimination of Character'; this is what the 'Ancients' were 'chiefly attentive' to; and only a reading of the annotations which is based on the assumption that Blake's views were the polar opposite of Reynolds's, and that therefore he was chiefly attentive to the minute discrimination of *unique* characters, could fail to grasp his meaning. The representation of men as mere individuals is for Blake, as for Barry and Reynolds, the humdrum employment of the mere face-painter, whose 'sordid drudgery' is directed to 'facsimile representations of merely mortal and perishing substances' (pp. 453, 466, 576).

There is, however, a large number of uses of the word 'individual' and its derivations in Blake's writings on art where its meaning is clearly not pejorative, and it is to the meaning of the word in these uses that I now want to turn. For when Blake says, for example, of the oak-tree, that its 'Eternal image and Individuality never dies'; when he says that nothing 'can be Changed or Transformed into Another Identity while it retains its own Individuality' (pp. 605, 607); or when he claims that 'Every Class is Individual', or inveighs against those writers who 'militate against Individual Character', or against those who cannot bear 'Individual Merit' in an artist (pp. 460, 453, 593) – is he not surely arguing that there is a value in that individuality which is separable from the generic, which finds expression in images of unique individual characters, and that these may be as much 'eternal images' as the images of generic character?

It will help us to answer these questions if we examine in some detail Blake's account of one of his 'experiment pictures', which he exhibited in 1809 along with *Chaucer's Canterbury Pilgrims* and *The Ancient Britons*. The 'experiment pictures' were works in which Blake was concerned to experiment with colours, but which required him to labour so hard that some of them he could never finish, and in a number of them, at least, he found that his concentration on the effects of colour 'destroyed the lineaments', by which he means that the firm and determinate lines by which the figures were marked came to be concealed by the 'blotting and blurring' which is the only language of art known by those who value colour over line. In his account of these pictures, Blake represents the struggle to preserve the lineaments as a struggle against the 'blotting and blurring demons', among whom he includes Titian, Rubens and Correggio; and it is appropriate therefore that one of the 'experiment pictures' should have been of *Satan calling up his Legions, from Milton's Paradise Lost*. This picture, he explains, was the result 'of temptations and perturbations, labouring to destroy Imaginative power, by means of that infernal machine called Chiaro Oscuro, in the hands of Venetian and Flemish Demons', who 'cause that every thing in art shall become a Machine. They cause that the execution shall be all blocked up with brown shadows. They put the original Artist in fear and doubt of his own original conception' (pp. 581–2).

By Rubens, for example, 'a most outrageous demon', this 'original conception' is 'loaded' with 'hellish brownness'; the special delight of Correggio 'is to cause endless labour to whoever suffers him to enter his mind' – for that reason he established 'manufactories of art', dark satanic mills, where the manual labours of impoverished journeymen are divided in such a way as they are divided by the gods of Priam, so that those employed there are unable to perceive the common end of their separate tasks, the vision which is the unity of those tasks in Christ. The 'spirit of Titian' attempted to persuade Blake of the impossibility of 'executing without a model', to persuade him therefore to copy nature, and in this way he was able to 'snatch away' from Blake 'the vision', his 'original conception'. Instead of the vision, his mind became possessed by the 'memory of nature, and of Pictures of the various schools', and his execution, which should have been 'appropriate' to the 'invention', became the execution not of an 'original' artist but of an imitator, a copyist of nature and of the styles of artists who, if they had ever 'travel'd to Heaven', had been thrown out of it again. And Blake describes the influence of the blotting and blurring demons in such a way as may well seem to invite us to believe that it is his unique personality as an artist that is being threatened and compromised. Rubens, 'by infusing the remembrances of his Pictures and style of execution, hinders all power of *individual* thought'; Titian, by stirring up in Blake the memories of other men's work, persuaded Blake to execute his picture as if he were 'walking in another man's style, or speaking, or looking in another man's style and manner, unappropriate and repugnant to your own *individual* character' (pp. 582–3, my emphases).

To understand the meaning of the word 'individual' here, it will help us if we consult a passage in Book V of *Paradise Lost* in which the angel Raphael begins to recount to Adam and Eve the history of the 'exploits' of the 'warring Spirits' in Heaven: in Blake's universe it was no accident, of course, that the names of the angels Raphael and Michael should have been inherited by the greatest of the

Italian painters, for they, like the angels, are the 'Progenie of Light', opposed to the demons of hellish brownness. In this passage, indeed, Raphael makes a distinction between the loyal and the rebel angels in exactly these terms:

> Hear all ye Angels, Progenie of Light,
> Thrones, Dominations, Princedoms, Vertues, Powers,
> Hear my Decree, which unrevok't shall stand.
> This day I have begot whom I declare
> My onely Son, and on this holy Hill
> Him have anointed, whom ye now behold
> At my right hand; your Head I him appoint;
> And by my Self have sworn to him shall bow
> All knees in Heav'n, and shall confess him Lord:
> Under his great Vice-gerent Reign abide
> United as one individual Soule
> For ever happie: him who disobeyes
> Mee disobeyes, breaks union, and that day
> Cast out from God and blessed vision, falls
> Into utter darkness, deep ingulft, his place
> Ordaind without redemption, without end.
>
> (*Paradise Lost*, Book V, lines 600–15)

The similarity between the plot of this passage, and that of Blake's account of his work on the 'experiment pictures', is clear enough: the blotting and blurring demons, the angels of darkness, tempt Blake, and when he succumbs to their temptation, and loses sight of his original conception, his vision of origins, he is 'Cast out from God and blessed vision', and must fall 'Into utter darkness, deep ingulft'. To disobey God is the same thing as to disobey Christ, in whom the unity of the angels, and (as we have seen) of humanity subsists; and to 'break union' is to dissolve the 'individual Soule' which is the unity of all the 'Progenie of Light' under Christ, and in him.

The word 'individual' is thus used, as it regularly is by Milton, to mean – as the *OED* defines it – 'that cannot be separated, inseparable'; 'forming an indivisible entity; indivisible'. This is the meaning of the word also, for example, in Book IV, where Adam is recorded as saying to Eve:

> to give thee being I lent
> Out of my side to thee, neerest my heart
> Substantial Life, to have thee by my side
> Henceforth an individual solace dear;

Part of my soul I seek thee, and thee claim
My other half.

(*Paradise Lost*, Book IV, lines 483–8)

The meaning of the word in both these passages is perhaps
best conveyed by Johnson's dictionary, which cites them both:
'undivided; not to be parted or disjoined'; for whether he means
to or not, Johnson gives his definition in a form which indicates the
possibility that what '*cannot* be separated' may indeed be separated
– it is not so much that an 'individual soul' cannot be, it should not
be divided, from other souls, or from Christ. It is this meaning that
I am suggesting Blake has in mind when he speaks, in his account
of *Satan calling up his Legions*, of his 'individual character' and his
'individual thought'.

Thus, Blake's 'individual' character is individual, not because
it is uniquely his – as we have seen, no character can be that –
but because, insofar as it is his 'character', it is what constitutes
the ground of his unity with eternity ('characters' are the 'eternal
principles . . . of human life'), with Christ, and so with other men
insofar as they acknowledge their generic character. Indeed, it is
because the visions of artists are visions of (among other things)
these 'eternal principles or characters', that for Blake to lose sight
of the 'blessed vision', of characters and their unity in Christ, is also
to lose sight of his 'individual', his properly indivisible, character,
which in being divided will divide him from others who partake in
the same individual character, and leave him a mere, an 'imperfect'
individual. And to lose sight of his individual character is also to
lose sight of his original conception, his 'individual thought' – the
thought and the conception which, because a vision of the original
and the eternal, is what unites him with eternity.

It is in terms of this definition of the word that 'individual' is
redeemed of its pejorative overtones, but in being so its meaning
becomes the opposite of that notion of uniqueness of personality,
which emphasises difference rather than similarity, and which is the
notion of individuality continually appealed to by those who wish
to oppose Blake's ideas on art to the uniform principles of Reynolds.
When Blake uses the term in that way, in his writings on art, he
uses it as an accusation: it is the 'ignorant Insults of Individuals'
that threaten to hinder Blake from doing his 'duty' to his art
(p. 561). When he uses the term in a positive sense, however, it
seems that we can only understand his use of it as consistent with
his notion of 'character' if we attribute to the word the meaning
which Milton also attributes to it. Thus, if nothing 'can be Changed
or Transformed into Another Identity while it retains its own

individuality', that is because the eternal identity of each thing – its 'substance', as opposed to its accidental qualities – is the characteristic mode of participation in, and indivisibility from, the eternal, ordained for it by God: if it were to change that mode, that identity, it would cease to be what in God's eye it is, and would 'break union'. If the 'Eternal Image and Individuality' of the oak-tree 'never dies', that is because its individuality, in the sense of its inseparability from eternity, is its eternal image, as the singular verb indicates; but as its eternal image is also its generic character, no understanding of 'individual' which is inconsistent with the meaning that Blake clearly attributes to character seems to be invited by the remark.

And that is the nub of my argument: I do not deny that within the local contexts in which the word appears in Blake's writings on art – local contexts, I mean, of a single sentence, or a few phrases – it is sometimes plausible to interpret the word as referring to a notion of unique, personal identity. I can sum up my point by saying that I believe that the first strategy we should adopt towards a writer is to attempt to understand their writings as making coherent sense; and, if we come to believe they do not, our next task is to try to understand how and why they do not. It may be that we cannot read Blake's writings on art as the statement of a coherent set of opinions. I happen to believe that we can; but if we always attribute to the word 'individual' the meaning that is attributed to it in, for example, the *Blake Dictionary* ('The INDIVIDUAL is unique . . . Each Individual is sacred . . . The Individual's duty is to be himself . . .'), we can make no sense of Blake's use of 'character'. If we attribute the meaning I have proposed, it is not only consistent with the meaning of 'character', it positively reinforces the complex reference of that word.

8 A New Mode of Printing

KATHLEEN RAINE

Poetical Sketches, Blake's first collection of poems (including some written in his boyhood), was published in 1783 through the patronage of a Mrs Mathew, a clergyman's wife who had 'taken up' Flaxman, and, on Flaxman's introduction, for a time extended her patronage to Blake. Mrs Mathew and her husband paid half the cost of printing Blake's poems, Flaxman apparently paying the rest. Gilchrist records that Mrs Mathew used to read Homer to Flaxman; but when it became apparent that Blake came not to learn but to teach, his welcome in Mrs Mathew's circle of admirers became less warm. Blake did not suffer patrons gladly, and the comedy of Mrs Mathew was to be repeated fifteen years later (with Flaxman again the well-meaning intermediary) in the episode of his three years' employment by the poet and country squire Hayley. Blake was never an easy man socially. 'A mental Prince', he was proud, argumentative, and violently opposed to current fashion, in his art and his philosophic and religious ideas alike. His only tenable role in his world was that of the venerated teacher he became, in his old age, to the group of young painters known as the 'Shoreham Ancients'.

Artists who work for quick success must rise on a tide of fashion, or possess social graces and tact, or private means. Blake, who was ready to speak his mind to Moser on the subject of 'Venetian and Flemish demons', was 'a priest and king in his own household', but no courtier. A radical in politics, Swedenborgian in religion, with no interest whatever in making money, Blake was clearly destined for worldly failure. He was a man of tireless industry; he carried out his commissions as an engraver laboriously and conscientiously. But his thoughts were elsewhere.

From whatever combination of causes and circumstances, it came about that he was without a publisher for his subsequent books of verse. True, *The French Revolution*, an unreadable verse narrative and commentary whose turgid style recalls Carlyle's later prose work of the same name, was actually set up in type by Blake's friend and employer Johnson the radical bookseller; but it was then considered too dangerous to publish.

The political and moral subversiveness of his early works provides one possible explanation of how Blake came to be his own publisher; but were there deeper reasons? Did he wish to produce books of an entirely new kind? Books as beautiful as some medieval psalter, the words enhanced by decoration of design and colour? Geoffrey Keynes points out that the germinal idea of such books was already in Blake's mind when in about 1784 he wrote his dramatic farce, *An Island in the Moon*. The first part is missing from the manuscript of a passage which begins abruptly:

'. . . thus Illuminating the Manuscript.'
'Ay,' said she, 'that would be excellent.'
'Then,' said he, 'I would have all the writing Engraved instead of Printed, and at every other leaf a high-finish'd print – all in three Volumes folio – & sell them a hundred pounds apiece. They would print off two thousand.'

Far from being a child of necessity, the idea was to make a great deal of money.

Keynes thinks that this idea may have been suggested to Blake by George Cumberland, who early in 1784 wrote to his brother Richard with 'the enclosed specimen of my new mode of Printing – it is the amusement of an evening and is capable of printing 2000 if I wanted them – you see here one page which is executed as easily as writing and the cost is trifling'. Cumberland's letter goes on to point out that you need print no more than are needed at one time, and that the copper plates can be used again – the only difficulty being that work of this kind can only be read with the aid of a looking-glass, as the letters are reversed. 'However we have a remedy for this defect also,' he adds. Can this 'we' conceivably have included Blake, or may Blake have been the real originator of the idea? Cumberland concludes: 'the expense of this page is 1/6 without reckoning time, wh. was never yet worth much to authors, and the Copper is worth I/– again when cut up. In my next I will tell you more and make you also an engraver of this sort, till when keep it to yourself'.

Blake first used the method of 'illuminated printing' in about 1788. Three small tractates entitled *There is no Natural Religion* seem to have been his first experiments in this art. They are crudely executed in comparison with his later work, very small (copper was expensive), and simple in design. The title-page of *Songs of Innocence* bears the date 1789, and it is likely that, satisfied with his new

*Songs of
Innocence*, 1789
Title-page

method, Blake in a hopeful mood began work on the title-page
of his next book of poems.

A contemporary account (by J. T. Smith) tells of visionary aid.
When Blake's brother Robert had died in 1787, Blake had seen his
spirit rising 'through the matter-of-fact ceiling, "clapping his hands
for joy"'. His brother's spirit continued to be present to him. After
Blake 'had deeply perplexed himself as to the mode of accomplish-
ing the publication of his illustrated songs, without their being
subject to the expense of letter-press, his brother Robert stood before
him in one of his visionary imaginations, and so decidedly directed
him in the way in which he ought to proceed, that he immediately
followed his advice, by writing his poetry, and drawing his marginal
subjects of embellishments in outline upon the copperplate with an

119

Songs of
Innocence, 1789
Frontispiece

impervious liquid, and then eating the plain parts or lights away
with aqua fortis considerably below them, so that the outlines were
left as a stereotype'.

Ruthven Todd, with the help of Joan Miró, has experimented in
the production of a reversed image of this kind. This is done by
writing in the varnish on a sheet of paper, then reversing the paper
on to the copperplate, under pressure: a very delicate process.

Blake's watercolour illumination, carried out by hand, also owed
something to supernatural inspiration. According to Gilchrist, 'He
ground and mixed his watercolours himself on a piece of statuary
marble, after a method of his own, with common carpenter's glue
diluted, which he had found out, as the early Italians had before

him, to be a good binder. Joseph, the sacred carpenter, had appeared in vision and revealed *that* secret to him'. Ruthven Todd thinks that 'carpenter's glue' would have been too coarse and that some more refined substance was used. 'The colours he used were few and simple,' Gilchrist continues, 'indigo, cobalt, gamboge, vermilion, Frankfort-black freely, ultramarine rarely, chrome not at all. These he applied with a camel's hair brush, not with a sable which he disliked'.

Blake never printed off his two thousand copies, or made his fortune, but for the rest, Cumberland's letter foretold some of the advantages of the method. He could print copies as he needed them: he continued to print *Songs of Innocence*, and later *Songs of Innocence and Experience*, from time to time to the end of his life, as he did his later books, whenever he found a purchaser. The inks he used were various: blue, green, bluish green, golden brown or black. Occasionally inks of two colours are combined in the same plate. But the unique character of each copy is created by the watercolour 'illumination'. There are great variations: each copy has its own colour-range and is a unique creation. Early copies of *Songs of Innocence* often have the transparency and delicacy of a rainbow, while some later copies are richly sombre, glowing with gold paint, like those medieval psalters which were doubtless Blake's inspiration.

Songs of Innocence comprises thirty-one plates in all, but their number and order varies in the twenty-three known copies of the book. 'The Little Girl Lost' and 'The Little Girl Found' were later transferred to *Songs of Experience*. As with others of his books – including *Milton* and *Jerusalem* – a final order was never absolutely determined.

The writing, engraving, printing and colouring – even the mixing of the pigments – was all Blake's work; the binding was done by Mrs Blake, who also learned to take off impressions from the plates. Some of the copies which have survived are also thought to be coloured with a rather heavy hand by Mrs Blake.

Songs of Innocence may have been planned as a book for children, but once he was involved in its making, Blake soon lost sight of any purpose but the creation of beauty. However, *The Gates of Paradise*, a book of emblems engraved in 1793, is entitled *For Children*. At the end of the eighteenth century books for children were much in evidence, most of them, like Anna Letitia Barbauld's *Hymns in Prose for Children* and Isaac Watts' *Divine and Moral Songs for Children*, having a moral and religious character. Mary Wollstonecraft translated from the German Salzmann's *Elements of Morality for the Use of Parents and Children*, a book of simple incidents from real life, with a great number of illustrations, some of which were engraved by Blake. No doubt

Mary's own *Original Stories from Real Life* (for which Blake drew
ten and engraved five illustrations) was suggested by Salzmann's
book. Mary Wollstonecraft (who worked as French editor for Blake's
friend Johnson the radical bookseller) was under the influence of
Rousseau, whose view of childhood as a law unto itself contrasted
strongly with the pedagogic habit of mind in the Age of Reason. It
must have been during his association with Mary that Blake formed
the idea of making books for children, and about childhood, which
should reflect the belief he shared with Rousseau that the unfolding
of the imagination of every creature, in freedom, is the only true
education.

In *Tiriel*, a poem illustrated with drawings but not published,
Blake had already denounced the current view of childhood –
deriving in great measure from Locke, that early forerunner of
behaviourism and brain-washing – as a passive state to be 'formed'
by 'instruction'. The poem describes with scathing indignation the
consequences of 'forming' a child according to the laws of mechanistic rationalism, imposed all from outside and regardless of the
mysterious formative laws of life itself. Tiriel, the blind parental
tyrant, is himself the product of such an education, and dies cursing
those who, by compelling him into conformity, had denied him life.
For Rousseau, every child was unique; and Blake's aphorism –
illustrated, in *The Marriage of Heaven and Hell*, by Nebuchadnezzar
compelled to eat grass – 'One Law for the Lion and Ox is Oppression', might summarise Rousseau's and Mary Wollstonecraft's views
on education as well as his own. For 'Infancy', Rousseau wrote,
'has a manner of perceiving, thinking and feeling peculiar to itself'.
Premature instruction is 'without regard to the peculiar genius of
each. For, besides the constitution common to its species, each child
at its birth possesses a peculiar temperament, which determines its
genius and character; and which it is improper either to pervert or
restrain, the business of education being only to model and bring
it to perfection. All the vices imputed to malignity of disposition
are only the effect of the bad form it has received . . . there is not
a villain upon earth, whose natural propensity, well directed, might
not have been productive of great virtues'.

So also thought Blake, who many years later said that he had
never known a bad man who had not something very good about
him. Blake's realisation, 'Every man's genius is peculiar to his individuality', is one he shared with Rousseau and Mary Wollstonecraft.

Blake was also a Platonist; he attacked Locke in his first engraved
aphorisms, *There is no Natural Religion*, precisely for his refusal to
accept Plato's view that there are innate ideas. 'Knowledge of Ideal
Beauty is Not to be Acquired. It is Born with us. Innate Ideas are

in Every Man. Born with him; they are truly Himself', wrote Blake
in about 1808 in the margins of Reynolds' *Discourses on Painting*;
and again, in his old age, he wrote in the margin of his copy of
Berkeley's *Siris*: 'the Spiritual Body or Angel as little Children
always behold the Face of the Heavenly Father'.

This, of course, goes beyond Rousseau – beyond Plato, indeed.
For the essence of Blake's Christianity was his vision of the 'God
within', 'Jesus the Imagination'. Childhood, for Blake, is the purest
essence of the spirit of life; the thing itself. The instructions of
education can add nothing to Being. 'Everything that lives is holy',
not by virtue of any added qualities, but in its essence:

> 'I have no name,
> 'I am but two days old.'
> What shall I call thee?
> 'I happy am,
> 'Joy is my name.'

Blake in these seemingly naïve lines is describing the nature of life
as he conceived it. Joy – delight – is the essence of life, and all life
seeks joy as its natural state. For him, the mechanistic view of the
universe – the popular mentality of the Enlightenment under the
guise of Deism ('natural religion'), the philosophy of Bacon, Newton
and Locke – was the enemy of life; life which is immeasurable, not
to be captured or contained within the quantitative 'laws of nature'
– a view which Bergson was later to develop in more strictly philosophic terms.

'The hours of folly are measured by the clock; but the hours of
wisdom no clock can measure.' As against the Newtonian universe,
overwhelming man's sense of his own value by awe-inspiring vistas
of space and time, Blake affirmed the holiness of life, omnipresent,
no less in the tiny than in the vast:

> To see a World in a Grain of Sand,
> And heaven in a Wild Flower,
> Hold Infinity in the palm of your hand
> And Eternity in an hour.

All Blake's most characteristic and beautiful images are of the
minute: the wild thyme and the meadowsweet – 'And none can tell
how from so small a centre comes such sweets'. 'The little winged
fly', the worm, the ant, the grasshopper and spider; the little bird –
lark or nightingale or robin redbreast; the 'moment in each day that
Satan cannot find' in which the poet's work is done; and, above all,

123

the supreme symbol of the *multum in parvule*, the Divine Child. Life is neither great nor small, and the dignity of every living essence is not relative but absolute. Childhood – innocence – was for him not a state of inexperience and ignorance, but the state of pure being.

In *Songs of Innocence* the energy and spontaneity of life runs through every line of Blake's leaping, running, flying figures, the tendrils of his 'wandering vine', symbol of the one life in all things, which is, in the world of Innocence, not a theory but a state of being. Simple as these poems may be in form, they contain a great wisdom and rest upon the firm ground of philosophy. They embody essential knowledge more enduring than the imposing structures of conceptual thought elaborated by the philosophers of the Enlightenment and their French counterparts, Voltaire, Diderot and the Encyclopedists. This is no less a miracle of imaginative insight for the fact that Blake was deeply and widely read, not only in the works of those whom he attacked, but also in the writings of Plato and Plotinus, Berkeley and the *Hermetica*, Paracelsus and Fludd, and the mystical theology of Boehme and Swedenborg.

The apparent weightlessness of Blake's figures, the ease with which they fly without the use of those cumbrous wings Baroque, and still more, Victorian angels required, arises from the realisation that life, as Blake understood it, is not subject to the forces of nature. Life – consciousness – moves freely where it wills. To leap in thought along the line of a hill, or on to a cloud, is to be there in imagination.

Already in *Songs of Innocence* Blake's figures have attained freedom from the gravitational forces which constrain material objects: the characteristic, thereafter, of all his depictions of the human form, a quality essentially Blakean, and shared by none of his contemporaries. Again, he may have been influenced in this by Early Christian art, and those angels and heavenly personages who are essentially, and not merely in name, immaterial beings occupying mental and not physical space.

In the five years between *Songs of Innocence* and *Songs of Experience* Blake produced two illuminated books of outstanding beauty: *The Book of Thel* (1789) and *The Marriage of Heaven and Hell* (1790–3). *Thel* is close in spirit to the paradisal world of *Songs of Innocence*. It consists of seven engraved plates, about six inches by four and a quarter; the larger size suggests that Blake was now more confident about his technique. The designs express, even more than those of *Songs of Innocence*, the easy grace, freedom and expressive sweetness characteristic of Blake's vision of 'Innocence'. The 'fair luminous mist' of the colour-washes Blake now began to use over the whole page seems to illuminate words and designs alike with the light of Paradise. The theme of the poem is Neoplatonic, and draws much upon Thomas Taylor's recently published paraphrased translation of Plotinus' *On the Beautiful*, and on the idea of the 'descent' of the soul into generation as described in this and other works of Taylor which appeared about this time.

The Marriage of Heaven and Hell, engraved about a year later, reflects in its fiery forms and colours the ideas of 'Hell, or Energy', no less characteristic of Blake's thought. Before the Terror and the ensuing slaughter of so many of the early liberal supporters of the French Revolution – members of the Gironde, friends of Mary Wollstonecraft and of Paine – Blake had worn the *bonnet rouge* in the streets of London. He was a Republican, and had hailed revolution first in America, then in France, as an expression of freedom, and of that spirit of life which was, for him, in whatever guise, holy. When in France the reality proved to be otherwise, Blake changed his mind about the value of political solutions. 'I am really sorry to see my Countrymen trouble themselves about Politics,' he wrote in about 1809, having seen twenty years of 'glorious revolution' and its ensuing wars. 'If Men were Wise, the Most arbitrary Princes could not hurt them; if they are not wise, the Freest Government is compell'd to be a Tyranny.' Politics seemed to him 'to be something Else besides Human Life'. He at all times hated war, believing that the arts could only flourish in peaceful States. 'Rome & Greece swept Art into their maw & destroy'd it; a Warlike State never can produce Art. It will Rob & Plunder & accumulate into one place, & Translate & Copy & Buy & Sell & Criticise, but not Make.' *Europe: a Prophecy* is an indictment of war written at a time when Blake and his friends hoped that England would not go to war with France; but later, in his 'apotheoses' of Pitt and Nelson (1809) it seems that Blake was a supporter of the national cause against Napoleon, if not in the conventional sense, at least in the prophetic region of spiritual causes. But the 'happy country' of which he called himself a citizen was the 'Kingdom not of this world'.

Meanwhile, in *The Marriage of Heaven and Hell* 'the new-born terror', Orc, the child who burns in the flames of his own energy, is hailed as the Messiah of the New Age whose prophet Blake believed himself to be. Of all Blake's books, this has perhaps the greatest power of word and of design. The literary form is no longer lyric, but aphorism and parable of visionary events experienced 'behind the veil'. 'Energy is eternal delight'; and life – no less holy in 'the new-born terror' of 'the fiery limbs, the flaming hair', than in the unhampered child on its cloud in *Songs of Innocence* – obeys the law of its innate energies. Free, life is mild and loving; impeded, it is rebellious and violent. Energy enchained, like Nebuchadnezzar, whose royal humanity was compelled into the grass-eating nature of the 'patient ox', becomes warlike and fierce. All Blake's sympathies, in this book, are with lion and devil, giant and fiery serpent of 'the nether deep'. His tyrants are kings, churches, parents, schoolmasters. 'The tygers of wrath are wiser than the horses of instruction.'

No doubt this book is an expression of Blake's mood of sympathy with the forces of revolution, seen as an expression of the irrepressible energy of life. But it is, at the same time, the fruit of his profound studies of the mystical theology of Boehme, the alchemical writings of Paracelsus, Fludd and Agrippa, and his knowledge of the Western Esoteric tradition both orthodox and heterodox. Christianity, in its popular forms at all events, has never sufficiently understood what Jung has called the ambivalence of the archetypes. No psychic energy, or mood of the soul, is merely good or merely evil; the face turned depends upon circumstances. This is a truth well understood in Mahayana Buddhism, whose deities have their peaceful and angry aspects; and also in Hinduism, where Kali and Shiva have their mild and their terrible faces; or in the ancient Greek religion; or in the Jewish mystical tradition of the Cabbalistic Tree of the Sephiroth. Boehme, perhaps more profoundly than any other Christian mystic, had understood this truth, and Blake followed him. Far beyond merely 'religious' thought, the *Marriage* is a work of prophetic vision into the nature of vital causes; 'inspired' in the sense in which we use the word of the Hebrew prophets, as Blake himself claimed. It is the 'Poetic Genius', Blake declared, that spoke through the prophets Isaiah and Ezekiel, of whom all the 'gods' of the Gentiles are tributaries; 'it was this that our great poet, King David, desired so fervently & invokes so pathetic'ly, saying by this he conquers enemies & governs kingdoms'. And here Blake's 'Jesus, the Imagination' appears for the first time in opposition to Milton's 'Messiah, or Reason': 'in the Book of Job, Milton's Messiah is call'd Satan'. Jesus, Blake concludes, 'was all virtue, and acted from impulse, not from rules'. The premiss is the same as that of *Songs of Innocence*, but more bold in its extension.

Because Blake wrote in *The Marriage of Heaven and Hell* that 'Without Contraries is no progression', it has often been assumed that the states of Innocence and Experience represent a pair of contraries like his Reason and Energy, or the peace of Heaven and the 'fires of genius'. This is not so, for 'a negation is not a contrary', he says. The state of Innocence was not, for Blake, one of ignorance,

Songs of Experience, 1789–94. Title-page

as compared with the wisdom of 'experience' so highly valued by Voltaire's Candide or Dr Johnson's Rasselas, types of the Enlightenment. The state of Innocence is that of unclouded, unhindered life; and as Blake's symbol of that state is the child, so 'aged ignorance', clipping the wings of youth, is his symbol of Experience. The title-page of *Experience* shows two weepers by a 'gothic' tomb, where the 'dead' – the spiritually dead – lie like effigies on their own tombs. Blake's 'Hell, or Energy' is one of the modes of life; 'the roaring of lions, the howling of wolves, the raging of the stormy sea, and the destructive sword, are portions of eternity, too great for the eye of man'. Experience is the antithesis of life. Life may be impeded and denied: by unrequited love as in 'The Angel' or 'Ah! Sunflower'; by childhood oppressed, as in 'Nurse's Song' and 'The Chimney

Sweeper'; by moral oppression as in 'The Garden of Love' and
'A Little Girl Lost'; or by social injustice, as in 'London'. The 'net
of religion' spread by 'aged ignorance' runs through all; and the
dark face of the human city evoked in 'London' is but the sum
of inhumanity and of the perversion and restraint of life for which
every individual is in some measure responsible:

> In every cry of every Man,
> In every Infant's cry of fear,
> In every voice, in every ban,
> The mind-forg'd manacles I hear.

It is these 'mind-forg'd manacles' (sometimes depicted as shackling
the feet of Urizen, the false god) which make thorns where there
should be roses, furtive 'whisperings' instead of childish laughter,
'tombstones where flowers should be'. Blake indicts Church and
state, parents, nurses and schoolmasters; but also, and above all, the
tortuousness of 'the Human Brain', whose reasonings confound the
simplicity of life, and which 'knits a snare' in which souls become
inextricably entangled, as in a spider's web of prohibitions and
hypocrisy. Many of the poems of *Experience* are antithetical to those
of *Innocence*; the difference between 'Infant Sorrow' and 'Infant Joy'
is that between love and the absence of love. The 'Ecchoing Green'
is a childhood world surrounded by sympathy, 'Nurse's Song' is
childhood clouded by the sick thoughts of the Nurse: an
anticipation of Henry James' *Turn of the Screw*. The 'Holy Thursday'
of *Experience* is an indictment of cold charity; the poverty of the
children is above all in the absence of love:

> And their sun does never shine,
> And their fields are bleak & bare,
> And their ways are fill'd with thorns:
> It is eternal winter there.

'The Chimney Sweeper' of *Innocence* can escape in dreams into
a heavenly country; but *Experience* reminds us that the crimes of
society against the children of the poor are none the less for that.
Nor is it only the poor who are oppressed, but the schoolboy, forced
to the joyless routine of learning; or 'A Little Boy Lost' oppressed
by the Calvinist morality which immolates souls if no longer bodies.
  The figures of *Experience* are entangled, burdened, listless or dead.
A burning jewel in that sombre setting is 'The Tyger'. In this great
poem, as in 'To Tirzah' (added about 1801), we again find Blake
seeking to rend the veil and to bring to light the meaning and the

mystery of evil. In 'To Tirzah' we find, as in *Thel*, the Neoplatonic view of 'mortal birth' as itself the greatest of evils. In 'The Tyger' there are traces of the *Hermetica*, of the mystical theology of Boehme, of the esoteric philosophy of alchemy. But the poem ends with the question unanswered: 'Did he who made the Lamb, make thee?'

9 Blake, Women, and Sexuality

Brenda S. Webster*

One eighteenth-century contemporary of Blake's described him as
an 'insane and erratic genius'.[1] In their efforts to normalise Blake
and to find shared historical and religious meanings later critics not
only shy away from the bizarre or disturbing elements of his work
but generally ignore its personal emotional components, its combat
with 'The torments of Love & Jealousy'.

In particular, Blake's attitude toward sexuality creates a variety
of problems for critics. Liberated sexuality seems a source of high
value for Blake – he links it with vision and art – but sexuality
also elicits his most hostile, negative, and regressive images. Critics
take several approaches to Blake's contradictions. Early critics like
S. Foster Damon, who sees Blake as a pure mystic, simply deny the
importance of his preoccupation with sex and fantasies of sexual
freedom. Damon urges the reader not to take seriously Blake's
apparent justification of 'illicit ways' and assures us that Blake
didn't follow his teachings himself, citing as evidence his ideal
marriage to a submissive wife.[2] Other critics are reluctant to think
about Blake's bizarre or explicit sexual illustrations and what these
imply about his personality or his attitudes toward women. They
see him as portraying degradations of erotic life only so that error
may be clarified and redemption achieved.[3]

More recently, commentators instead see Blake celebrating unre-
pressed sexuality. But here, too, the full force of Blake's sexuality
creates problems, and some critics deny its emotional implications.
Forty years after his classic book, Damon now remarks, as though it
is an emotionally neutral issue, that Blake, like Shelley, thinks incest
is innocent and 'the very root of marriage'.[4] Even such a sophisticated
critic as Diana Hume George praises Blake for articulating a non-
selfish, non-aggressive sexuality. She regards him in this respect as
freer and more advanced than Freud but does not see that Freud is

---

* From *Critical Paths: Blake and the Argument of Method*, ed. Dan Miller, Mark
Bracher and Donald Ault (Durham and London, 1987), pp. 204–24.

simply more self-aware.[5] Blake's rhetoric often serves as a cloak or defence that distracts the reader, and Blake himself, from seeing the aggressive or selfish nature of the sexual fantasies he is portraying.

Idealisation isn't the only way of dealing with Blake's emotional dynamite. Some critics do not have to mobilise defences to avoid perceiving Blake's negative attitudes. They may consciously agree with them. Before it was taboo to say such things, a male critic – I don't think it is an accident that most of the Blake critics until recently have been male – could admit satisfaction with Blake's views of women.[6] Bernard Blackstone's misogynistic remarks are embarrassing in their forthrightness but I think he has correctly caught Blake's anger at women's power and his wish that they be properly subservient. Male critics who are consciously more benign toward women may still respond to Blake's underlying fantasies without being quite aware of it. This creates a subtler kind of distortion – a not seeing what might be uncomfortable. One critic, Jean Hagstrum, misreads the line 'In Beulah every female delights to give her maiden to her husband', noting that 'maiden' means maidenhead.[7] The point of the line is that Blake's ideal female freely provides her husband with other women like Oothoon in *Visions*. At the end of his essay, Hagstrum's funny tone of mixed apology and male congratulation suggests that at some level he understands very well what Blake is talking about. He concludes that 'some modern women may have much to object to in Blake's latest thought about the relation of the sexes. But it's hard to believe that *l'homme moyen sensuel* would reject the hearty bread and full bodied wine the late Blake is offering him'.[8] Erdman, as I will show later, similarly fails to see the male sexual fantasy in *Visions*.

Women critics have parallel difficulties with Blake's sexuality. Early feminist critics generally see Blake as much more favourable to women than he actually is.[9] These writers respond positively to Blake's struggle against the patriarchal system and its paternal oppressors, which suggests that he wishes to free women to be equal partners of men. Also seductive to feminists is Blake's de-emphasis of the penis in favour of a total body sensuality, seemingly more in tune with, and more accepting of, woman's sexuality. Unfortunately, as a poet-prophet Blake is not any more interested in redefining sexuality to give a more equal place to women than as a husband he was interested in giving equal status to his wife. In his own marriage, when his wife offended his brother, he made her kneel down and beg his forgiveness, or, he told her, she would never see his face more.

In general, earlier critics ignore Blake's radical sexual ideas and fantasies; and later critics, while acknowledging them, ignore their regressive and aggressive content and Blake's guilt over them. The limitation of conventional criticism, including feminist criticism, is that it tends either to ignore these fantasies (or this fantasy world) or to recast them in terms of official theologies or ideologies and so misses the special energy of the fantasies and their unconscious origins. The power in Blake's work derives from his recognition and description of demonic forces (the eighteenth-century equivalent of unconscious drives) that influence every aspect of human relationships, but particularly sexuality.

Critics who ignore Blake's radical sexual ideas and fantasies do so partly because of a feeling that to acknowledge them would be to diminish or interfere with his religious or moral authority and return him to the status of eccentric genius. Because Blake's work embodies religious values that point to transcendence, it seems particularly offensive to relate his cosmic speculations to his fantasies or to his personal biography. One critic argues, for instance, that to accept a biographical interpretation of a major prophecy (*Milton*) would be to see Blake as 'mad Blake indeed'.[10] This feeling of incompatibility between any kind of cherished meaning and the fantasies or personal motives of the poet is one of the main blocks to understanding between psychoanalytic critics and other sorts. Conversely, if one values Blake as a prophet of sexual revolution, pointing out his guilt and conflict diminishes him as a type of Übermensch just as much as pointing out his underlying sexual fantasies diminishes his visionary claims. But to understand Blake adequately, both sides (sexuality and guilt) have to be recognised. The history of desire frozen in his images and dramatic situations has to be connected with his transcendent vision, and his conflicts of conscience with his expressions of sexuality. When this is done, we see a radically different Blake.

If we accept at least as a working assumption the importance of psychosexual issues in Blake's work, and if we are to go beyond impressionism or commonsense psychology, we need a theory of mental functioning to serve both as a framework for clarifying our responses to Blake and as a technique for exploring his psychic preoccupations and the ways in which they, paradoxically, both energise and limit his poetry.

Of the available psychologies, Freudian psychoanalysis is most productive for studying Blake. The psychoanalytic emphasis on Oedipal conflict and motives of 'Love & Jealousy' is in many ways similar to Blake's own. Freudianism is unique in its emphasis on the problems caused by man's long dependency and the psychic cost involved in the taming of his sexual and aggressive impulses. The early stages of development are crucial to Freud because of the

fantasies and modes of experience associated with them are out-
grown only imperfectly. Stress in the adult can awaken them. Blake's
diffusive narratives are given what coherence they have by a linked
series of fantasies made familiar by psychoanalysis. Particularly in
his late work, Blake's manifest emphasis begs to be described as
Freudian. In works like *Vala*, he not only deals exhaustively with
the mutual entanglements of parents and children but he literally
depicts the staples of the Freudian view of the psyche: he illustrates
acts of incest, he shows children watching adults copulate and he
presents a woman with a penis (the Freudian phallic woman) and
a man without one. It is not surprising then, that a psychoanalytic
approach can reveal aspects of Blake's attitudes toward women and
sexuality that are not available to other methods. This in turn opens
up other important related topics for investigation; for instance, his
development toward a male-centred creative world and his growing
sympathy with paternal figures makes sense as part of a reaction
against the female.

As Paul Ricoeur has argued, psychoanalysis need not be considered as the enemy of religious meaning[11] (or of other meanings);
instead it should be considered a useful tool for clarifying religious
values. Blake himself performs this kind of analysis on traditional
religious structures, values, and on the concept of an authoritarian
God (old Nobodaddy). Blake's most brilliant analysis goes into the
repressed and repressive character of Urizen. Blake acutely observes
the distortions induced by Urizen's anxiety – his need for sadistic
and total control, his terror of sexuality. This kind of insight into
the role of anxiety or suppressed sexuality is essential to evaluating
the religious vision. But Blake's insight into Urizenic values and
personality doesn't necessarily mean that he himself is free of similar
anxiety-caused distortions.

Fantasies in a text offer the literary critic a way into unconscious
preoccupations. They give him an opportunity to see elements from
the past re-experienced (much as the analyst observes the past re-
enacted in the transference). The artist replays the early patterns
of conflict and desire through character and image rather than by
projecting them onto the person of the therapist. Through creative
reorganisation similar to the reorganisation of the self that takes
place in therapy, the artist integrates fantasy material into a meaning-
ful world.[12] If integration of fantasy, dream, or childhood memories
is successful the work elaborates them in ways that illuminate their
meaning.

Though the artist is not necessarily conscious of his fantasies as
he integrates them into his larger design, he has to let them come
near enough to the surface to allow their expression without being

too threatened by them. His success may have something to do with being able to allow the fantasies to proliferate freely and then to elaborate or play with them in different textual contexts without being overcome. If he fails to balance the relative claims of his conscious design and the fantasy material (with its own logic and unity), his failure should be clear in a text that doesn't work aesthetically – is confused, dull or highly contradictory. The fantasies, instead of adding intensity and depth to the text, may be narrowed down to a single repetitive form, or if themes are being used primarily as a defence to control fantasies that are too frightening, then these fantasies may subvert or undercut the writer's conscious concerns (as in Blake's late prophecies). There are as many varieties of failure as there are of success. Analysing the fantasy content in its relation to the text helps isolate the areas in which integration has succeeded or where it has failed and unconscious motives overwhelmed the text.

In Blake perhaps more than in most writers the fantasies are not difficult to spot. The difficulty is in knowing what to do with them when we do see them. Perhaps the first task is to determine the extent of the fantasy in the body of the text and also its degree of primitiveness. (Like a disease in the body, it may change forms, move around, have different patterns in different places.) Fantasies are not such simple entities as has been assumed (Frederick Crews ironically comments on the monotony of certain standard ones[13]); they are elusive in that they perpetually shift, expressing first wish, then fear, first from one person's viewpoint, then another, changing who does what to whom with no regard for ordinary logic. A fantasy is not just an idea or wish; it reflects a totally different, archaic way of seeing and experiencing things that has its own kind of logic, expressing a wholly different way of perceiving and experiencing the world. Depending on what stage of development it derives from, it can be extremely primitive or very far removed from its archaic sources, perhaps no more than a faint verbal echo. Seeing evidence of a fantasy is only a first step. Only a full reading of the text can tell us the dimensions of the fantasy and its effect on this particular text.

For instance, in *Tiriel* a father accuses his sons of causing their mother's death. Tiriel could have made his accusation in a variety of ways. He could have said 'she died gnawed by grief'. The verb gnawed here has a nuance that Freudians would relate to the oral stage but any orality in the statement as I have formulated it is far removed from primitive fantasy; it is only a verbal echo, a half-dead metaphor. But Tiriel instead accuses his sons of devouring their parents' flesh and draining their mother dry. Later Tiriel reverses the situation and asks Pestilence to poison his sons. This is slightly less literal; he doesn't threaten to eat them as does the witch in Hansel and Gretel, but his acts still have the extreme and reversible quality characteristic of early fantasies. We don't need Freud to relate this to oral needs. Blake does it himself when he has Tiriel explain his own murderous greed as due to maternal deprivation and a harsh weaning. The point is, again, not labelling the fantasy but experiencing through it the issues that are vital in the text – questions of love, separation, and conflict. Once these issues are experienced, it is possible to see the ways in which the fantasy is given special resonance in the text. Does the fantasy enrich or limit? Is it integrated or invasive?

In order to explore these issues more fully, I am going to consider Blake's attitudes toward sexuality and women. To follow Blake's development, I divide his attitude toward women into two stages with a transition. In the first, roughly the stage of the revolutionary prophecies, he sees women (and sexuality) as a source of salvation and continually imagines his heroes liberating females from paternal tyrants. But even in the early work where he has a more positive use for women there is a strong undercurrent of hostility and fear, which is important to recognise if you want to understand his later attitudes. In mid-life during the decade-long writing of *Vala* he goes through a transitional stage during which he becomes increasingly negative toward sexuality. As he Christianises the work in rewriting, he comes to see woman as responsible for the Fall. What he is coming to think of as the 'Female Will' is blamed for war and all the world's evils. His negative images of women become ever more extreme and bizarre. The only positive images of women are totally weak females sequestered in a separate realm called Beulah. Finally, in his late Christian prophecies, *Milton* and *Jerusalem*, he suggests that the female should cease even to exist independently and become reabsorbed into the body of man where she belongs.

One of the main reasons for Blake's increasing negativity is that he isn't talking about adult love at all. Instead he constantly recreates Oedipal dramas in which his heroes experience the emotions – rage, deprivation, desire – of an adolescent or younger boy caught in dreams of competition with his father for his mother's love. In the early work you have to interpret to see this, but one need not worry about reading it dogmatically into Blake's material, because in his late work he makes it perfectly clear in the illustrations and the text – showing us, for instance, a naked adolescent first embracing his mother then chained to a rock by his jealous and fearful father.

Blake's obsession with incest has an unfortunate effect on his attitude toward women. Because he is obsessed with the overthrow of paternal rivals, he feels guilty and begins to blame women for causing trouble between fathers and sons. Another reason for Blake's increasingly negative attitude is that his demands on women as nurturers and lovers are so total – it wouldn't be unfair to call them infantile – that he can't help imagining them as being enraged and wanting revenge. So his ambivalence toward women is inherent in his harbouring these kinds of pre-Oedipal and Oedipal fantasies.

Blake's attitudes are expressed in various ways in his poems. His early poems *Thel* and *Visions of the Daughters of Albion* suggest the absolutism of his ideal of the totally giving woman and how it brings with it even in his early work a countering image of woman as murderous. For ease of understanding the layers of Blake's fantasy, I present his views of women developmentally, starting with what he expected and feared from woman as nurturer, then moving on to what he hoped from her at a later stage as sexual gratifier.

In *Thel*, an early lyric, Blake presents what at first seems simply a benign model of a good nurturing mother. In a pastoral setting, he creates fairy-tale creatures – a Lily, a Cloud, and a Clod of dirt who instruct the reluctant heroine Thel how to care for others. However, when looked at more closely what Blake is expressing is the wish for a mother's unlimited giving, even if it means her death. Both Lily and Clod give their lives in the act of nourishment. A lamb crops the Lily's blossoms; the Clod exhales her life in 'milky fondness' over the infant worm. The heroine is enjoined to think with satisfaction that at her death her own body will be food for worms. 'If thou art the food of worms. O virgin of the skies, / How great thy use. How great thy blessing'. Critics preach at Thel and criticise her for her selfishness. They do not appreciate that the prospect of being eaten by worms – death as being devoured – might be terrifying, nor do they perceive behind Blake's moral tone the implicit degradation and forced submission of the woman. The implications of the imagery are much clearer in a poem by another poet. In Andrew Marvell's famous 'To his Coy Mistress', the speaker reminds the woman he is trying to seduce that she can be as coy as she likes to him but eventually worms shall try her 'long-preserved virginity' – there the threat is plain enough.

At the end of *Thel* after describing the ideal of maternal sacrifice, Blake goes on in a coda, seemingly out of keeping with the mood of the piece, to describe the dangers of sexuality and the hatred between men and women. The language of courtly love evokes the deadly woman with 'poison' smile who will be prominent in Blake's later work. In *Tiriel*, a narrative poem written just before *Thel*, there is another such image. She is called Pestilence (and is here clearly imagined as a punishment for infant greed). She is invoked by the tyrant Tiriel to punish his sons who he says have killed their mother by greedily draining her life ('Nourishd with milk ye serpents. nourishd with mothers tears & cares /... [you] have draind her dry as this'. It is striking that the invocation of Pestilence contrasts line by line with the Lily in *Thel*. This is Tiriel's invocation of Pestilence:

> Where art thou Pestilence that bathest in fogs & standing lakes
> Rise up thy sluggish limbs. & let the loathsomest of poisons
> Drop from thy garments as thou walkest. wrapt in yellow clouds
> Here take thy seat. in this wide court. Let it be strown with dead
> And sit & smile upon these cursed sons of Tiriel
>
> (*Tir* 5:8–12:E 282)

And here is the Lily:

> Thy breath doth nourish the innocent lamb, he smells thy milky garments,
> He crops thy flowers. while thou sittest smiling in his face,
> Wiping his mild and meekin mouth from all contagious taints.
>
> (*Thel* 2:4–7:E 4)

In each line the Lily replaces Pestilence's noxious qualities with beneficent ones. Even the Lily's beauty, whiteness, and perfume are prized not for themselves but for the pleasure they give the infant lamb who smells her 'milky garments' before he crops her blossoms. Most important is the Lily's relation to the lamb as contrasted with Pestilence's to the sons. The Lily welcomes the lamb's greedy feeding with a loving smile even though it means her death. In what constitutes a final contrast between the two figures, the cropped Lily wipes the lamb's mouth of all contagious taints.

The contrasting images of Pestilence and Lily are perhaps Blake's earliest portrayal of the two types of feminine nature that became so important in his myth. We can see now that the ambivalent double image is self-perpetuating. Guilt over greed creates the punishing image of Pestilence, so Blake creates an ideal image to cancel out or compensate for imagined murderousness: his Lily reverses Pestilence's attributes. But then new guilt over the idea of devouring the mother creates the idea expressed in Thel's coda that woman is sexually threatening. In fact, Blake's efforts to create an ideally satisfying figure have to be continually renewed. The paradoxically smiling Pestilence develops in later poems into a series of wicked females whose smiles promise love but proffer death.

Going back even further in the self-perpetuating cycle of crime and punishments, Blake gives psychological reasons for the extreme greed of his characters. They feel deprived. He imagines them as so needy that they become either monstrous or depressed if the ideal mother doesn't offer herself.

Another important aspect of the ideal woman is her aspect as sexual gratifier. *Visions of the Daughters of Albion* presents a nurturing woman who unlike the Lily offers not food but total sexual gratification to the male hero who is seen as quite helpless and hopeless without her. The poem is particularly interesting to feminists because the chief woman character, Oothoon, is very strong and preaches what appears to be a doctrine of reciprocally free love to the male character. However, what is really involved is a male fantasy of having a harem of beautiful women. Oothoon in one of her final speeches offers to net girls of 'mild silver' and 'furious gold' for her lover and watch him while he enjoys them 'In lovely copulation bliss on bliss'. There is no reciprocity. Theotormon, the semi-impotent hero, is furiously jealous and rages at Oothoon abusively after she has been raped. Generosity is all on one side: hers.

Still critics persist in seeing the poem as somehow in favour of women's rights. David Erdman suggests, following Schorer, that it is a versification of Mary Wollstonecraft's *The Rights of Women*.[14] This is oddly off the mark. Blake pictures Oothoon as totally benevolent and totally available. Wollstonecraft feels that woman's first duty is to develop her mind and particularly her reason. Far from seeing woman as devoted to 'Happy, happy love', she wants to substitute equality based on reason for women's sexual character as gratifier of man.

Blake's fantasy of sexual gratification in *Visions* has another level that is vital to understanding his attitude toward women. On this level, the sexually gratifying woman is imagined as a sexually permissive mother. This is important not in order to prove a Freudian point but because Blake's attitude toward women is so saturated with his conflicting feelings toward the mother. He is interested in his female characters primarily in so far as they can be placed in triangular situations that remind him of the Oedipal triangle of mother, father, and son. In *Visions'* triangle, the heroine Oothoon is raped by an older man named Bromion while she is on her way to give herself to her young lover, Theotormon, who then spends the rest of the poem lamenting. Though she is not literally Theotormon's mother or sister, Blake suggests that this is a mother–son relationship in several ways. One of the clearest of these is his opening illustrations.

The opening illustration of Oothoon is developed from an engraving by Vien showing a procuress holding onto a small cupid by his wings. Blake adapts the figures but gives them an opposite meaning. His naked woman lifting full breasts and kissing a small male figure leaping from a flower suggests both the maternal nature and the special non-possessive quality of Oothoon's love, which combines generosity and lack of restraint. The next illustrations replace the idealised view of mother and child with sexual fantasies. The mother–son theme continues in the image of a small naked male angel standing in the lap of a woman riding a cloud horse. The sexual nature of the embrace between woman and small angel is clearly shown by the penis and testicles Blake has drawn emerging between the woman's legs where we should expect the neck and head of her cloud mount. In some versions, Blake has added a beak or bill to the penis, which seems equivalent to biting teeth in its potential to injure the maternal body.

In the illustration Blake's images of mother and child are untroubled by any hint of a rival. The fantasy is of undisputed possession of the mother. Blake's description of Oothoon raped by a paternal tyrant fits such a fantasy's assumption of the mother's resistance to the father – her loyalty to the child. However, what Theotormon struggles with in the poem is that Oothoon doesn't regret the rape. Moreover, she is aroused by it. Her arousal represents the side of parental lovemaking that the child denies because it signifies the mother's unfaithfulness to him. This idea of unfaithfulness makes emotional sense of Theotormon's extreme jealousy and his angry wish to punish Oothoon which is expressed in sexualised imagery. Blake makes Oothoon collaborate in Theotormon's ambivalent wish to punish and possess her by having her writhe naked calling on his eagles to penetrate her flesh.

Blake doesn't use just visual imagery to suggest the young boy's fantasies about his mother and sexuality. In presenting Theotormon's reaction to the rape, Blake uses imagery that evokes a young child's possible reaction to a situation that arouses impotent rage. Theotormon's first act is to surround Oothoon and Bromion with 'black jealous waters'. If the image isn't quite clear in context, it becomes clearer when we remember a previous character of Blake's, the serpent Envy, who expresses its jealousy by discharging a river of filth ('then She bore Pale desire'). Using faeces as a weapon is characteristic of very young children. Melanie Klein, for example, cites cases of children who react to observations of parental intercourse with angry soiling.[15] From Blake's imagery one might infer his own repressed memory of such a reaction, but whatever the source of his insight, as artist Blake is able to connect Theotormon's child-ishly ineffectual rage with the body imagery that best expresses it.

Blake's imagery not only evokes a young child's reactions to parental sex at a time when his only weapon is his own excrement, but he also connects this reaction with other psychological themes typical of the child's perceptions. For instance, the rape's violent sadism suggests a child's perception of intercourse. Blake depicts Theotormon as being caught in the emotions of this stage (hating the sadistic Bromion) but unable to fight back successfully, Theotormon turns his anger against himself (in one illustration he whips himself) and against Oothoon. In another illustration his eagles approach Oothoon to rip her naked body – an image of sexualised violence. Oothoon urges Theotormon to give up his anger and his masochism and enjoy her. She reminds him that she, like a mother choosing her son's wife, would gladly supply other women for his pleasure. In a series of monologues, she acts like a psychoanalyst encouraging him to dredge up his forbidden sexual desires – the forbidden 'joys of old'; here again the imagery turns to childhood as she reminds him of 'Infancy, . . . lustful, happy! nestling for delight / In laps of pleasure'. But unlike a psychoanalyst, instead of helping him give up his incestuous wishes, she urges him to act on them and free himself from his sense of failure.

What Blake seems to be doing is evoking a set of early experiences of despair and rivalry and then imagining the woman – in the past, the mother – who could by her total generosity make up for what he had suffered. When this is understood, it is easy to see how far Blake is from portraying equality between the sexes. His male characters are no more capable of mature love than a man jealously fixated on his mother is in real life.

Subsequent prophecies reinforce the interpretation of Oedipal drama in *Visions* and show what a pervasive and haunting theme it was for Blake. In the next prophecy, *America*, the hero Orc, furious about earlier deprivation, rapes his sister – committing the incest that Theotormon failed to do – while the young patriots overthrow the paternal tyrant.

In still later prophecies, we read in more detail how Orc was originally chained to a rock by his father, Los, who was furiously jealous of the boy's closeness to his mother, Enitharmon.

But when fourteen summers & winters had revolved over
Their solemn habitation Los beheld the ruddy boy
Embracing his bright mother & beheld malignant fires
In his young eyes discerning plain that Orc plotted his death
Grief rose upon his ruddy brows. a tightening girdle grew

Around his bosom like a bloody cord. . . . [He]
Calld it the chain of Jealousy.

(*FZ* 60:6–22:E 340–1)

In an illustration Blake pictures Orc as a naked adolescent embracing his mother while his father watches angrily, a red chain of jealousy around his neck. Throughout this whole series of poems Blake is depicting Oedipal dramas in which father and son are alternately dominant.

In discussing Blake's gratifying females, the Lily in *Thel* and Oothoon, it is important to realise that imagining them and their satisfaction of his most forbidden desires was uphill work against guilt. Not only are they mother figures and so taboo, but there is also guilt in imagining the death of paternal rivals. Coping with this guilt is apparently too much for Blake. Even in *America* the hero's triumph doesn't last long. The poem ends with the father god's vengeful cold mists descending on the rebels. The dangers of woman's retaliatory anger for the incestuous and greedy impulses are even more severe. In thinking himself further and further back into the experiences of childhood, Blake becomes more angry and fearful.

By the time he finishes *Vala*, a transitional work of his middle years that he worked on for over a decade, Blake's images of women have taken on a preponderantly negative tone. Though he still keeps a formal split between good and bad women, the good ones never again capture his imagination, but his fantasies about what bad women do to males get more and more violent and bizarre. *Vala* is fascinating because it shows his changing attitude toward women as well as how the change is connected with his shift from revolutionary to Christian. In its early drafts we see him giving way totally to negative fantasies: women destroy men's bodies, unweave them on their looms, drain them in sex, appropriate their penises – these are just a few of the horrors he expresses. Blake becomes increasingly certain that any attempt to satisfy basic needs for food and sex is bound to have horrible consequences. Rather than being satisfied, the characters receive a destructive version of the need itself: if they want food, they are eaten; if they want sex, they are castrated. Blake views essential needs as dangerous not only because they leave the individual vulnerable to painful deprivation, but also because they are too excessive and too mixed with aggression, thus damaging those chosen to satisfy them.

An episode at the beginning of *Vala* exemplifies the mutually destructive activities of male and female. Enion, a type of earth mother, initiates the pattern by destroying Tharmas in retaliation for his jealous possessiveness. Enion literally takes him apart. She draws out and manipulates his nerves, 'every vein & lacteal'. She then gives birth to him again by reweaving him on her loom. Her woven child soon becomes a self-glorying, righteous bully who addresses her as 'my slave' and revenges himself for her earlier treatment of him by raping her.

Tharmas's body fuses with Enion's during intercourse, creating a monstrous woman-serpent. This is a variation of an earlier fragment describing the even more bizarre mating of a woman with a penis and a man without one. Here, though, Blake seems to be suggesting that sexuality is horribly dangerous because the woman appropriates or absorbs the man's penis in intercourse. She also seems to appropriate the creativity that Blake associates with male sexuality. She acquires a poetic voice. Enion's first act after the rape is to sing. In a later revision, Blake gives her a serpent's voice whose complaints suggest that the absorbed male is protesting within her.

Having imagined himself into a corner where the male is threatened with either feminisation or death or both, Blake tries through revisions to lessen the female's power or to transfer it to the male. His most successful strategy is his concept of an outside will, Christ, directing events. This seems to be a strong internal reason for his shift from revolutionary to radical Christian. He needs Christ to help him control his imagined women and his impulses. With Christ there, retaliatory acts become a necessary if painful part of a benign pattern of redemption. Within the protection of a Christian framework, Blake is able to reintroduce his idea of the totally giving woman to counter his fears of the murderous mother. In extensive additions to *Vala* he works up the concept of a realm called Beulah, the married land, inhabited by benign females. He first introduces them right after the Enion – Tharmas episode, and their self-abnegating actions soften or deny woman's power to mutilate or kill men. Blake contrasts Enion's cruel treatment of Tharmas with an ideal state where Beulah's 'Females sleep the winter in soft silken veils / Woven by their own hands to hide them in the darksom grave / But Males immortal live renewd by female deaths'. Although the males do not actually kill these females who reportedly delight in self-immolation, this Eden seems created out of fear, not love.

Blake continues to build up his countering idea of Beulah. In *Milton*, Beulians nourish the sleeping hero feeding 'His lips with food of Eden'. In addition, in *Milton* Blake imagines the poet Los totally recreating time so that the satisfaction of basic needs will be central. Los's time is defined by satisfaction of hunger. In between each moment of time stands a daughter of Beulah 'To feed the

Sleepers on their Couches with maternal care'. This conceptualisa-
tion literally insists that there is no time in which one experiences
the maternal figure's absence. In making creation take place in the
space-time where the mother nurtures, Blake also suggests that
creativity depends on the maternal environment. Blake amplifies
his description of Beulah's loving responsiveness: 'Beulah to its
Inhabitants appears within each district / As the beloved infant
in his mothers bosom'. In his fiction of males resting in Beulah,
Blake gratifies the wish for nurture while simultaneously denying
infantile dependence. Beulah's women are correspondingly weak
and fearful of the creative and inspired males. The female world
of obedience, where they are taught how to die smiling each winter,
is carefully separated from the male world of creation – a second
realm Blake names 'Eden'. Man drops into Beulah only temporarily
for a rest cure before continuing his virile forward progress: 'thro'
/ The Bosom of the Father'. Beulah is not only the world of self-
abnegating nurture – that of Thel's Lily – but also the world of
sexual gratification. In Beulah, the female ransacks sea and land for
gratifications to the male genius who in return will clothe her in
gems. Blake lectures the recalcitrant bride of the Divine Voice in
Milton, urging her to 'give / Her maidens to her husband: delighting
in his delight / . . . As it is done in Beulah'. This is the fantasy of
the sexually generous mother-wife we saw in *Visions*. But Blake has
become much more righteous, using biblical language and thought
to bolster his ideas. He continues, '& thou O Virgin Babylon Mother
of Whoredoms / Shalt bring Jerusalem . . . / Shalt give her into the
arms of God your Lord & Husband'.

All in all, Blake's concept of Beulah, which isolates and weakens
women, doesn't really solve anything. It seems impossible for Blake
to imagine real men and women coexisting in a state of peace.
Outside of Beulah, Blake's portrayals of women's murderousness
go on. His evil women characters increasingly split off, doubling
and tripling as though he can't control their rampant proliferation.
Their acts too are increasingly horrible. In *Jerusalem*, for example,
he has them dancing in the flayed skins of their victims waving the
men's severed organs.

From this it is clear that though Blake valiantly tries to control the
fantasy of the destructive mother and give it redemptive meaning,
woman's independent presence is still threatening. In his prophecies
Milton and *Jerusalem*, he moves toward what might be called his final
solution to the woman problem. At the end of *Milton* he suggests
for the first time that if the conflict between men is to cease, woman
must stop existing. Sexual organisation, which, using a phrase from
Ezekiel, he now calls 'the Abomination of Desolation', must disappear

'Till Generation is swallowd up in Regeneration'. But although
Blake announces the end of sexual organisation, male sexuality
continues to stand as a model for the human, while the female is
either incorporated or isolated restrictively in Beulah. In *Jerusalem*
he repeats his ideas about the Beulians as gratifiers of male genius.
It is clear the female has no independent existence except as gratifier
and she must accept the male's 'Fibres of dominion'.

Finally, during the writing of *Jerusalem*, Blake begins to feel that
female sexuality can be dispensed with altogether. He considers
female sexuality inferior to the total body sensuality of the child,
for the loss of which he holds women responsible. Blake makes
Christ sanction his views by reinstating this total body sensuality.
When Christ does this, he effectively breaks the female's power
over the male.

Sexual organisation is permitted in order for Christ to be born,
but once born, his Maternal Humanity must be put off lest the
sexual generation swallow up regeneration. At *Jerusalem*'s climactic
moment, Enitharmon, who has been resisting giving up her independence, suddenly caves in under the weight of Blake's rhetoric
and announces her disappearance: 'My Looms will be no more &
I annihilate vanish for ever'. Her husband and brother Los reaches
the final insight that 'Sexes must vanish & cease / To be'.

Blake's view of male–female relationships hasn't been clear to
readers partly because it is at first to be contradicted by his enormous sensitivity to feminine traits such as tenderness and maternal
care. Blake views these traits in two ways. On the one hand, they
belong to the ideal Female and help her to care for the Male Genius;
on the other hand, the poet can incorporate and use them in creation
and in drawing close to other men. In this latter view Blake anticipates the modern recognition of bisexuality and its importance for
creativity, which arises as a dialogue between the male and female
parts of the self. But Blake did not extend the right to express traits
of the opposite sex to his females. When they do express them, they
become threatening Female Wills and, as we have seen, must be
destroyed.

Jerusalem makes it clear that Blake's obsession with sex and
women is stronger in his late prophecies than in the early ones.
But his emphasis and the structure of his defences have changed.
Sexual liberation has been replaced by forgiveness of sins. In the
early work, when he fights on the side of impulse, he is fairly conscious of his incestuous and other wishes. (This is a positive fact.
His dramatisations of the conflict between impulse and guilt or
conscience have an immediacy and power lacking in the late work.)
In his middle and late work, he fights his impulses with all his

power. He repudiates the incestuous act at the heart of his concept of liberated sex and describes it as the original sin and cause of the Fall. This seems at first a plausible solution – certainly it is a traditional one – to the problem of what to do with one's forbidden impulses, but it doesn't succeed artistically or humanly. Blake can't really transcend his incestuous wishes though he sincerely wants to. He just splits them off from his consciousness. He has to fight very hard to keep them from his awareness though they come out in various ways in the poems. This not only weakens the poetry where the avowed Christian purpose is opposed by subterranean fantasies but it is an additional reason for his misogyny. Women are now the temptresses and whores who pander to his suppressed wishes.

Notes

[Brenda Webster's essay begins from a critique of masculinist approaches to Blake, and also of some feminist ones, and advances a strong argument for the importance of psychoanalytic categories in viewing the gender content and form of Blake's texts. Considerable attention is given to *Tiriel*, following which *Visions of the Daughters of Albion* is revisited. The argument is taken further into the major Prophetic Books, thus engaging with Jean Hagstrum's essay, and culminates in a discussion of the complex ambivalences underlying Blake's textual dealings with women and sexuality. Ed.]

1. ROBERT SOUTHEY, cited in S. FOSTER DAMON, *William Blake: His Philosophy and Symbols* (Gloucester, MA, 1958), p. 246.

2. Ibid., p. 99.

3. For example, H. M. MARGOLIOUTH in his edition of *William Blake's 'Vala'* (Oxford, 1946), p. 144; or JOHN E. GRANT, 'Visions in *Vala*: A Consideration of Some Pictures in the Manuscript', in *Blake's Sublime Allegory: Essays on 'The Four Zoas', 'Milton' and 'Jerusalem'* ed. STUART CURRAN and JOSEPH A. WITTREICH, JR. (Madison, WI, 1973), p. 184.

4. DAMON, *A Blake Dictionary: The Ideas and Symbols of William Blake* (New York, 1971), p. 196. Though Damon progresses from seeing Blake as a mystic to accepting his sexuality, in both cases he idealises him.

5. DIANA HUME GEORGE, *Blake and Freud* (Ithaca: NY, 1980), p. 144.

6. See the quotation from BERNARD BLACKSTONE, *English Blake* (Hamden, CT, 1966), p. 294, cited in GEORGE, *Blake and Freud*, p. 245.

7. JEAN HAGSTRUM, 'Babylon Revisited, or The Story of Luvah and Vala'. Any doubts about the meaning of the line are cleared up by the variant in *Milton* where the female, repenting of her previous jealousy, begins 'to give/Her maidens to her husband: delighting in his delight' (M 33:17–18:E 132).

8. This passage is omitted, at the author's request, from the version in the present volume. See the original version in *Blake's Sublime Allegory*, ed. CURRAN and WITTREICH, p. 118.

9. During the time I was writing the book on which this paper is based (from 1972 to 1979), critics like CAROLYN HEILBRUN and IRENE TAYLER praised

Blake's freedom from the prison of gender while SANDRA GILBERT, SUSAN GUBAR and DIANA HUME GEORGE compared him favourably to Milton. See HEILBRUN in *Far Western Forum*, 1 (1974), 284; TAYLER, 'The Woman Scaly', *Midwestern Modern Language Association Bulletin*, 6 (1973), 87; GILBERT and GUBAR, *The Madwoman in the Attic: The Woman Writer and the Nineteenth Century Literary Imagination* (New Haven, CT, 1979), p. 200; and GEORGE, 'Is She Also the Divine Image? Feminine Form in the Art of William Blake', *Centennial Review*, 23 (1979), 129–40, 137. SUSAN FOX is a notable exception. She points out that the difference between Blake's (seemingly benign) concepts and his consistently negative images of women must connote at least some uneasiness in the author's mind. See 'The Female as Metaphor in William Blake's Poetry', *Critical Inquiry*, 3 (1977), 519. Since my book was accepted by Macmillan in 1981 several new articles have appeared that point to Blake's anti-feminism: ALICIA OSTRIKER, 'Desire Gratified and Ungratified: William Blake and Sexuality', *Blake*, 16 (1982–3); ANNE K. MELLOR, 'Blake's Portrayal of Women', *Blake*, 16 (1982–3); and MARGARET STORCH, whose psychoanalytic approach resembles mine, 'Blake and Women: Nature's Cruel Holiness', *American Imago* (1981).

10. JAMES REIGER, 'The Hem of Their Garments: The Bard's Song in *Milton*', in *Blake's Sublime Allegory*, eds CURRAN and WITTREICH, p. 260.

11. PAUL RICOEUR, *Freud and Philosophy: An Essay on Interpretation*, trans. DENIS SAVAGE (New Haven, CT, 1970).

12. See MEREDITH ANNE SKURA, *The Literary Use of the Psychoanalytic Process* (New Haven, CT, 1981), p. 216, for a description of the ways the psychoanalytic process may be seen as a model for the literary text.

13. FREDERICK CREWS, *Out of My System: Psychoanalysis, Ideology and Critical Method* (New York, 1975), p. 145.

14. DAVID V. ERDMAN, *Blake: Prophet against Empire* (New York, 1969), p. 228.

15. MELANIE KLEIN, *Love, Guilt and Reparation and Other Works 1921–1945* (New York, 1975), pp. 114, 126.

Further Reading

In some cases, essays listed below are available in more than one place; I have listed only the most recent or accessible publication.

Classic Criticism

These books, all but two published before 1970, are classics of criticism in their own right, and are essential general reading on Blake:

GERALD E. BENTLEY, JR. (ed.) *William Blake: The Critical Heritage* (London: Routledge, 1975). A collection of short criticism on Blake, from his times to our own.

HAROLD BLOOM *Blake's Apocalypse: A Study in Poetic Argument* (Garden City, NY: Doubleday, 1963).

S. FOSTER DAMON *A Blake Dictionary: The Ideas and Symbols of William Blake* (Providence, RI: Brown University Press, 1965). An essential reference text.

S. FOSTER DAMON *William Blake: his Philosophy and Symbols* (London: Constable, 1924).

DAVID V. ERDMAN *Blake: Prophet Against Empire* (2nd edn, Princeton, NJ: Princeton University Press, 1969). The most wide-ranging account of Blake's historical context and political references.

NORTHROP FRYE (ed.) *Blake: A Collection of Critical Essays* (Englewood Cliffs, NJ: Prentice-Hall, 1966).

NORTHROP FRYE *Fearful Symmetry: A Study of William Blake* (Princeton, NJ: Princeton University Press, 1947). A magnificent reading of Blake from a largely mythic perspective.

A. L. MORTON *The Everlasting Gospel: A Study in the Sources of William Blake* (London: Lawrence and Wishart, 1958). The most important early account of Blake's debt to radical Dissenting sources.

MORTON D. PALEY *Energy and the Imagination: A Study of the Development of Blake's Thought* (Oxford: Clarendon Press, 1970). A watershed book which can be seen as inaugurating modern Blake criticism.

Modern Essay Collections

The period 1970–90 has seen the publication of eight major essay collections, many arising from conferences. All contain important essays, some of which are also listed individually in later sections:

STUART CURRAN and JOSEPH A. WITTREICH (eds) *Blake's Sublime Allegory: Essays on 'The Four Zoas', 'Milton', 'Jerusalem'* (Madison, WI: University of Wisconsin Press, 1973).

DAVID V. ERDMAN and JOHN E. GRANT (eds) *Blake's Visionary Forms Dramatic* (Princeton, NJ: Princeton University Press, 1970).

10 Female Subjectivity and the Desire of Reading In(to) Blake's *Book of Thel*

GERDA S. NORVIG

My thesis in this paper is situated at the crease of a two-fold premise. The first fold is that Blake's character Thel functions within her 'book' as a figure for theory (particularly the theory of reading). The second fold is that she simultaneously refuses the assimilation of character to theory through her self-represented desire for the discovery and maintenance of her own subjectivity. As such, she herself comes to stand *for*, and stand *in*, a liminal position between theory and resistance to theory. And this is a position that the text portrays as radically gendered.[1]

The gendering is female, of course, and I call it 'radical' because at several points that liminal position is equated with root metaphors of female sexuality, even of female genitality. At the same time it is a position from which specific, socially constructed definitions of gender are themselves called into question. Yet for Blake in *The Book of Thel*, this power of interrogativity regarding ideologically determined male and female roles remains the property of a feminine perspective – a view shared by many contemporary feminist critics who claim woman's place on the margins as a privileged site of cultural critique.[2]

Such is my two-fold premise. The resultant thesis is one that I, like Thel and her motto, feel compelled to put in the quasi-liminal form of an extended question. Thus, this paper asks: If *The Book of Thel* is a book of desire, as the etymology of the Greek name 'Thel' in its title strongly suggests, whose is the desire reflected there, what is the lack on which it is based, and must an adequate reading of the text implicate us as consumers in the pathology of its inscribed epistemophilia and scoptophilia?[3]

To demonstrate how this set of thetical questions emerges from the ins and outs of Thel's liminal identity will be the burden of the ensuing discussion. I can say at this point, however, that the linkage turns on my argument about the symbiotic relationship between Thel's reading of her experience and our reading of her book. This is a symbiosis deliberately designed by Blake not as a relationship of pure reflection, but rather as one troubled by the conflicting politics of desire and identification which in the moral and philosophic discourse of the eighteenth century lay the groundwork for the practice of those patriarchal, phallogocentric systems of oppression that Blake in all his work strove to destabilise. To this degree my essay includes an implicit plea for the revision of our knee-jerk responses toward the unpalatable sexism often inscribed in Blake's texts. Like Slavoj Žižek who in *The Metastases of Enjoyment: Six Essays on Woman and Causality* (London, Verso, 1994) strives 'to "rescue" for progressive thought authors who are usually dismissed as hopeless reactionaries', I aim to uncover those elements lurking within Blake's portrait of Thel that make her an icon of resistance to sexist indoctrination. Thus instead of antithetical censure, I urge a feminist willingness to investigate Blake's treatment of gender not simply as a personal, misogynist blind-spot but rather as (also and contrarily) a liminal form of self-criticism and cultural critique.

Liminality as Hymenal Threshold and Barrier[4]

The scene illustrates but the idea, not any actual action, in a hymen (out of which flows the Dream), tainted by vice yet sacred, between desire and fulfillment, perpetration and remembrance.
—Mallarmé/Derrida/Barbara Johnson

There are a number of obvious senses in which *The Book of Thel* is a liminal text. First of all it is *about* a threshold experience, indeed about repeated threshold experiences that manifest for the protagonist both as crossings into the 'Land Unknown' (6:2) and as haltings on and at the verge of a fated/fateful/fatal 'maturity'. Thel's approach-avoidance method of proceeding through her vales (as if in a dance of veils)[5] is inscribed everywhere in the poem, but nowhere more forcefully than at the end of it when she sits on the rim of her 'hollow pit', the virgin lip of her psycho-sexual awareness, the denouement of her tragicomical 'grave plot', straddling the highs and lows – the sublime and the subliminal – of language itself. For there, reaching a climax of liminal hermeneutics, she undergoes a face-off with an utterance that enters sublimely through the ear (in an almost parodic version of the Joban passages cited by Longinus as paradigmatic of the loftiest sublime) and exits subliminally through throat and mouth in the polymorphous semiotics of her parting guttural shriek.

The orgasmic connotations of this linguistic brush with the thin line between *eros* and *thanatos* (a fate worse than death, they used to call it) are strong. Indeed that thin line is itself figured by the voice

149

from the pit as a hymenal 'curtain of flesh' (6:20) which on the (apparent) surface (*MHH* 14) functions as a lure to line and to limn the very 'bed of our [*sic*] desire' (6:20). Furthermore, in the visual text of this final plate, the same straddling is even more blatantly displayed by way of the tail-piece where we meet a naked female riding with closed thighs the snakey emblem of desire, her 'will', her bridled phallic signifier.[6] Later I shall come back to this matter of the female will and the multiplicities of its 'Litteral expression' (*M* 42:14), but for now I want to stick with the more evident instances of the barrier/threshold concept that is implied by and encoded in *The Book of Thel*.

Aside from thematising ambivalence through Thel's behaviour in the story, Blake also structures reader-response *to* her behaviour in a way that invites mutually exclusive interpretations as possible 'solutions' of the ambivalence. Any single-visioned solution puts liminality under erasure, of course, but readerly awareness of contrary interpretive solutions restores it again. How, except by a liminal reading, for example, can we negotiate such oppositional critical stances as the following: Thel is an egocentric adolescent misguidedly denying the life of mature love and spiritual openness; Thel is a disembodied, selfless soul properly resisting the prison-house of earthly existence; Thel is an innocent balking at experience; Thel has left innocence behind and seeks experience untainted with the tenets of Natural Religion; Thel has an incurable death wish; Thel has an incurable erotic curiosity. All these exegeses and more not only *can* be advanced but *have* been.[7] Yet none satisfies. And it is not simply that each one offers only a partial reading, or that all of them are 'contrarieties' at once 'equally true' (*M* 30:1/*J* 48:14) and equally untrue according to the run of indeterminacy established by an intentionally ambiguous text. Rather it is that solutions, which are fulfillments of desire, in and of themselves spell the death of desire – an aphanisis that this text as 'desiring machine' works especially hard to 'avoid.'[8] Thus in *The Book of Thel* interpretive *diss*atisfaction is courted as intensely as interpretive *sat*isfaction. In this way the reader (like the heroine who in her want-to-be shuttles endlessly between her role as desire personified and her role as a desiring subject)[9] is nudged to split him/herself – liminally – between the both/neither of contrary determinate analyses and the both/and of (ir)resolute undecideability. The Clod of Clay, in other words, cold-bedded matron of the hermeneutics of liminality that she is ('My bosom of itself is cold. and of itself is dark' [4:12], 'I ponder, and I cannot ponder; yet I live and love' [5:6]) could be advising *us* as well as Thel when she proclaims: ''tis given thee to enter / And to return; fear nothing' (5:15–16).

This invitation to continue both Thel's and the reader's interpretive journey across the liminal spaces of bodily and textual worlds is itself liminal in that its overdetermined imperative, 'fear nothing', at once assures us of safety (there's nothing to fear) and warns us of the quintessential menace of the void (the thing to be wary of is nothingness). Critics have responded to the challenge, and by fearlessly going forward in the face of the double admonition to be both sanguine and aroused, have managed to submerge the greater fear of doing and saying nothing.

Another way in which this work not only beckons across thresholds but also inscribes the liminal is that it mimics its heroine's posture by standing, sitting, lying between a vast number of intertexts, seductively drawing on them even while it simultaneously refuses adequate dialogue with them.[10] I made a personal list of twenty-five such texts – texts which bear on yet fail to penetrate *Thel*, producing readings that titillate without satisfying interpretive desire. Some of those most often cited by critics as positive or negative 'sources' are: The Old Testament (Job, Ecclesiastes, The Song of Songs), Milton's *Comus*, Darwin's *Loves of the Plants*, McPherson's *Ossian*, Thomas Taylor's translation of Porphyry's *De Antro Nympharum*, Young's *Night Thoughts*, Johnson's *Rasselas*, Spenser's *Faerie Queene*, Burke's *Philosophical Inquiry into the Origins of our Ideas of the Sublime and Beautiful*, and Swedenborg's *Divine Love and Wisdom*. But this just scratches the surface. Intriguing contextual comparisons may also be made, for instance, between *Thel* and pronouncements on identity, will, desire, utility, and modesty in Locke's and Hume's essays *Concerning Human Understanding* – or between the fictionalized teachings of moral conduct books for girls (like Mary Wollstonecraft's *Original Stories*) and the advice offered Thel by Lilly, Cloud and Clay.[11]

But attempts to base a definitive reading on any of these intertexts misses the point that Thel's book is partly about the resistance to such identification. Like the catalogue of evanescent self-likenesses that Thel rattles off in her opening lament, the very plethora of such grafted discourses ensures both their supplemental status and their function as a kind of background glossolalia or echolalia calculated to confuse rather than define.[12] The confusion of excess reference, however, bends back upon itself and becomes yet another liminal strategy in that it is not a true fusion, not a seamless stitching together. Instead, all these other veiled voices which are never fully integrated leave their traces, creating a work that is a sort of monster 'corps morcelé'.[13] This concept of the fragmented and separated body is also, of course, the one that is most pointedly thematised and most highly intoned in *Thel*, from its presence in the framing questions of the 'Motto', to its hyperbolic rationalisation in the lectures offered Thel by her interlocutors, to its gothic articulation in the litany on body parts thrown up by the voice of sorrow from the grave.

Before we leave the issue of *Thel*'s liminal intertextuality, we should perhaps note its workings in two other areas recognised by previous critics. The first of these is the matter of generic echolalia, for *The Book of Thel* flirts with a rather large array of semi-cognate literary forms. Commentators have noted, for instance, the ways in which *Thel* mimics pastoral elegy, medieval débat, Ossianic myth, graveyard laments, children's literature, folklore and fairy-tale, animal fables, Elizabethan love lyrics and so on. But again while the poem 'listens' (and even fleetingly appropriates the structural and tonal gestures of these other 'voices'), it finally lets them all pass over it in a 'mysterious tangle'[14] of potential co-minglings from which it remains virginally apart.

The second of the two final senses in which *Thel* occupies a liminal position between competing intertexts concerns its placement in Blake's own evolving canon. Usually critics speak of *Thel* (1789–90) as a 'transitional' work situated between *Songs of Innocence* (1789) and *Songs of Experience* (1794). To this observation I give a qualified nod, but I also demur on several counts. (A) To say that something is 'transitional' implies a diachronic imperative, but *The Book of Thel* interrogates precisely that compulsion to view things developmentally. Indeed the plotting of the book and all the plots in it return on themselves reflectively, so that 'progress' is pictured either as an aphanitic fading or as 'the same dull round' of recirculating energies or as a self-sacrifice that curtails personal development. There is in fact a sense in which the journey represented in this narrative is actually static, each new 'place' being only an imagined shift of position so that all the locations are one location, and the fabled vales of har/here/her are always already both here and elsewhere. This stance against incremental movement forward is, I believe, mirrored in the book's placements between other Blake texts. *Thel* may stand in the middle, but it does not face forward: neither does it face back. Since as a whole it functions as a narcissistic emblem of the plays, places, displacements of desire, its purpose is to 'seek' but not to 'know' its own 'place'.[15] (B) Furthermore, in its compositional relation to Blake's songs it may sit between *Songs of Innocence* and *Songs of Innocence and of Experience*, but that is quite different from marking the border between the states of Innocence and Experience. Rather I see *Thel* as a sort of conceptual place-holder resisting both the unitary ideals of *Songs of Innocence* (however complexly deconstructed those ideals may be in that book) and the exponentially raised dialectics of the explicit doubleness of *Songs of Innocence and of Experience.*

But *Thel* holds a critical liminal position between two other 'sets' of works from this early period of Blake's illuminated printing as well. For on the cultural critique of empiricism, natural religion and the repressive biases of hegemonic namings, *Thel* can be said to form a triptych with the *Religion* tracts (1788) on the one hand and *The Marriage of Heaven and Hell* (1790–93) on the other. And in terms of Blake's investigation of narrative itself as a screen for the socially constructed values of identification, imitation and reflection (with an emphasis on the problematics of desire and the so-called feminine virtue of sympathy), the triadic grouping of *Tiriel-Thel-Visions of the Daughters of Albion* has an interesting tale to tell.

What I am trying to suggest by all this is that *The Book of Thel* in its borderline fashion relates to texts, voices and literary conventions from outside – from the symbolic register, as it were – in the same way that it relates to its self-generated intratexts, voices and conventions: i.e. liminally, with a studied refusal to be either a black hole of influence or a repulsing structure of self-enclosed autism. Although we see this both/and, neither/nor position encoded in the actions and reactions of the character Thel, perhaps the most crucial and intriguing example of semiotic liminality within the text is its use of the trope of personification. For personification by its very nature is a liminalism that undermines the agency of the subject by making it figurative, and so questions the status of character *qua* character. Hence for Thel, subjectivity (which in this case is a part of what is being personified) is compromised even before it is sought. Inviting and refusing the assimilation of personhood to concept, concept to personhood, the trope of personification embodies the doubleness and division that *The Book of Thel* depends on. And since the thing personified in this case (desire for subjectivity) is itself dependent on doubleness and division (the splitting of self into desirer and desired) the liminalist quotient soars. To see how this works in *Thel* one must trace the links that Blake forges among the categories of gender, sexuality, identity, and projective personification.

As stated earlier, personification in *The Book of Thel* is first and foremost suggested by the generally accepted fact that Thel's name is a signifier pointing to its roots in the Greek verb 'thelow' ($\theta \acute{\epsilon} \lambda \omega$), meaning to will, to wish, to be willing, to desire. As such, she is then a figure for desire – or will (a somewhat different matter, as I will discuss below) – and so her 'book' becomes at once a book about desiring, a book about being desired, a book resulting from desire, and a desire to be a book.[16] But the name 'Thel' is also related to the Greek root 'thele', which by metonymy from the word for nipple or suckled breast (θηλή) came to mean 'female', 'belonging to the female sex' (θῆλυς).[17] That Blake was aware of these onomastics has been well established by E. B. Murray (see the previous note), and certainly the conjunction of the meanings 'female' and 'desire' in the single signifier 'Thel' points to a concern of Blake's evident in all his writings of this period, particularly the triptyched plates of the twin songs 'The Little Girl Lost' and 'The Little Girl Found' – another work about identity-figured-as-female that liminally sought but did not 'know' its place.[18]

Now if we credit Blake with the Lacanian insight that all human subjectivity as constructed in Western culture is paradigmatically based on the signifying pattern of feminine sexuality,[19] we can perhaps better understand his interest in exploring questions of identity and identification through the personification of female desire. Each term in the series, personification-subjectivity-female-desire, can be construed as depending on the idea of lack or want-to-be; and there is a perpetual augmentation of the liminality of that lack, too, in the way the concepts double for each other *as* other. Thus the divided nature of the trope of personification plays on the lack of agency in the subjectivity it partially represents. But the desire for subjectivity in the represented subject is a want-to-be that seeks fulfillment precisely *through personifying* otherness. This is certainly Thel's methodology as she projects (some say ventriloquises) subjectivity into Lilly, Cloud, Worm and Clay. Lacan puts it this way in his gloss on Freud's interpretation of the dream of the butcher's wife (a gloss that applies almost as well to the narrative of *The Book of Thel*):

> Desire is what is revealed in the space that demand creates within itself, inasmuch as the subject, in articulating the sequence of the signifiers, brings to light its lack of being by calling upon the other to make good the lack, assuming that the Other, the locus of speech, is also the locus of the insufficiency.[20]

There is finally another wrinkle in this matter of Thel as personification. For while I have been happily regarding her as a representation of female *desire*, her Greek name, as I noted earlier, may also be translated as a condensation of the English words for 'female' and for '*will*'. Generally speaking, the two words, 'will' and 'desire', were not synonyms in the discourse of eighteenth-century moral philosophy.[21] 'Desire' was thought to be a libidinal drive, but 'Will' wasn't. 'Will' simply meant intentionality or volition, and the philosophical arguments around the concept of will focused on the mechanisms by which it got translated into effective action. Blake's later formulations of The Female Will, mouthed by his mythic characters as pejoratives to describe what they see as the castrating effects of (the return of) repressed desire in women, seem influenced in part by these speculations. In *The Book of Thel*, however, the portrait of female will/female desire, like the portrait of subjectivity, does not reflect the pall of a demonic 'selfhood' but remains liminal, escaping blame or repression as it is still on the margins of its own realisation.

It *is* radically sexual, however, and that is a usage also sanctioned by tradition. For outside philosophical discourse, the word 'will', as we know from Shakespeare's sonnets (especially 57, 135 and 136), was a common slang term for 'sexual organ'.[22] It furthermore had the interesting liminal property of being a shifter term that could signify either penis or vagina; and it was the wit of this double valence, along with the coincidence of Will being Shakespeare's own name, that made the punnings on the word 'will' in the sonnets so rich. As Nelson Hilton has observed (*Literal Imagination* 256), a similar circumstance applies to Blake who represents himself autographically as 'The Author and Printer Will Blake, 1789' on the Title page of *The Book of Thel*). In light of this literally willful self-announcement on Blake's part, we are entitled to ask whether Thel, as a personification of the *Female* Will, is not meant as a figure of reversal to signify a cross-dressed, transsexual version of Will Blake who/which among other things stands in for the author's own liminal de-sire-ing desire.

If this is the case, if Blake saw Thel imaginally as his own desire in drag, who for her part experienced *her* desire as located in the discourse of the other, then it is no wonder that he forged the trope of liminality at every threshold, every barrier of signification in the text.

Epistemophilia, Scoptophilia and the Desire of Reading: Theory of Eagles, Theory of Moles

Earlier I made the claim that, besides being a personified female-will seeking her own subjectivity, Thel functioned in her book as a figure for theory. I based this on a fascination in the text with epistemophilic and scoptophilic behaviour – drives that are announced most openly in 'Thel's motto', but that persist in the narrative proper of her (mock) quest romance.[23] For Thel's want-to-be is also persistently a want-to-know; and that want-to-know, aside from appearing in the form of twenty some-odd questions, frequently manifests as a gaze of scoptophilic intensity.[24] A good example of this is Thel's 'astonish'd' viewing of the 'Worm' upon its 'dewy bed' (4:1). Here we have a seemingly first encounter with the phallic signifier, or a secondary revision of a primal scene. Or perhaps it is the significance of clitoral jouissance that is discovered to be a worm in Thel's 'dewy bed', lying as if it were 'an infant wrapped in the Lilly's leaf' (4:3).

In any case, since looking and knowing are the fundamental prerequisites for theorising, we may wish to call Thel's search for erotic and ontotheological knowledge in the poem a mirror-stage theory of reading which stimulates and predicts our own. Why a theory of reading? According to the *OED*, 'theory' derives from a Greek word signifying to behold, whence its other primary meanings: to look at, to observe, to be a spectator at a ritual event, to contemplate, to ponder, to consult an oracle. These are precisely the activities Thel as a character engages in. The oracles she consults are the Lilly, Cloud, Worm, Clay and the voice of sorrow 'breathed' (like the fabled 'mephitic' vapors at Delphi) from the pit.[25] But, as many critics have noted, while these personified objects are represented as individual speaking subjects, their pronouncements (even their presences) are clearly generated from the speech of Thel herself. So the Lilly, a 'watry weed' (1:16), manifests as an image that is a condensation of the 'lotus of the water' (1:6) and the 'watry bow' (1:8) previously invoked by Thel in her lament; the 'tender cloud' is invited into being only after Thel compares herself to a 'faint cloud' (2:11); the worm emerges at the behest of the cloud following Thel's speculation about her worm-eaten corpse, and so on. The reader thus experiences the messages of these vocalised objects of nature as oracular echos and projections of Thel's own inner 'discourse of the other'. To this degree Thel is a self-reflexive theorist, producing the very spectacle from which her speculations evolve. Indeed there are grounds for reading the whole poem after the lament (from 1:15 forward) as Thel's projected dream-life (or Desire's wish-fulfillment). In that case we would only have to assume that her yawning petition, 'Ah! gentle may I lay me down and gentle rest my head / And gentle sleep the sleep of death. and gentle hear the voice / Of him that walketh in the garden in the evening time,' is a performative immediately embodied, albeit in the overdetermined language of dreaming.[26]

If Thel does dream up her own story, which is pre-eminently a story of her liminal readings of the discourse of others, is there any Archimedean leverage-point from which *we* can launch our reading of *her*? This is the question of the motto (though whether it is also the *function* of the motto remains to be seen). The motto focuses on the problematics of reading, both by demonstration and by implied precept, and its method on each count is to engage the reader's scoptophilic and epistemophilic drives.[27] Here is the text:

> Does the eagle know what is in the pit?
> Or wilt thou go ask the mole:
> Can Wisdom be put in a silver rod?
> Or Love in a golden bowl?

Since most mottoes are *statements* that express collective ideals or recommended rules of conduct, the form of the interrogatory in this case not only asks but also raises questions. And questions want to be answered: they address the epistemophilic instinct. But because of the conventionally declarative purpose of mottoes, many readers will assume that any questions appearing there are merely rhetorical – an assumption calculated to cause epistemophilic deflation. With Thel's motto, however, *even if* the questions are judged rhetorical, the direction of the 'intended' answer is not clear (as may be attested by variant contradictory interpretations forwarded by criticism over the years). Such a lack of clarity then poses its own conundrums and returns the dissatisfied reader to a liminal position regarding the very genre of questioning: i.e. if the interrogatives in Thel's Motto may or may not be rhetorical, its questioning stance is itself questionable.

I will return to the matter of reading the motto liminally versus rhetorically in a moment. First, however, I want to look at and to ponder (i.e. to theorise) the signifying terms presented there. The three nouns of the first two lines – eagle, pit and mole – keep their ontological and referential statuses deliberately obscure (as if in a pit). Are they metaphors? if so, what is being substituted for what? Are they metonyms? If so what is being displaced from what?[28] All that *is* clear is that, taken literally, the images of eagle and mole refer to animals appropriated by common parlance as epistemological emblems: the scoptophilic seer and the blind feeler. W. J. T. Mitchell offers as an example the following apt citation from Locke: 'The ignorance and darkness that is in us no more hinders nor confines that knowledge that is in others than the blindness of the mole is an argument against the quick-sightedness of the eagle'.[29] Locke's quotation shows the binary oppositionalism that is at work in the proverbial usage of these emblems, with the eagle coming out on top, of course, as the privileged term in the privileged position. To right the balance we may turn to the *OED*'s entries on 'mole' and come away with this exemplifying citation from Dryden's translation of Virgil's *Georgics*: 'The blind laborious Mole / In winding Mazes works her [sic] hidden hole.'

Here in Dryden's verse an important clue surfaces: Blake's figures of eagle and mole may well be intentionally gendered in deliberately stereotypical ways, the eagle as (distanced, reasoned) male, the mole as (intimate, sensational) female. As it has been suggested that 'mole', like 'pussy' today, was once a popular slang word for a woman's sexual organs, Blake's play on the polarity of eagle and mole could even be seen as subliminally pornographic.[30] With that in mind, we may wish to consider the Motto's opening salvo, 'Does the Eagle know what is in the pit?' as a proper ancestor to Freud's reluctant confession of patriarchal gender perplexity in his famous query 'What does a woman want?'[31] But more germane to the issue of theories of reading is the implication that *our* eagle and mole readings of the pit-of-the-text are also gendered. Since the text is structured in such a way that it is virtually impossible for any reader to avoid either kind of reading, *The Book of Thel* (book of desire that it is) serves to challenge the social constructions of our own sexual identities.

Even without moving from motto to poem proper we can see how this forced double reading is evoked. For the question 'does the eagle know what is in the pit' is itself an 'eagle' question that demands an eagle reading. It does so, that is, insofar as it 'pits' subject and object against each other in a relation of spatial opposition mediated by the abstract verb 'know'.[32] Furthermore, the participation of the reader in the question is designed to be distant and impersonal. But the following query is a mole question requiring a mole reading: 'wilt thou go ask the mole' addresses the subject directly as 'thou' and invites an intimate approach to its grammatical object (the mole); and of course the distance between reader and question collapses like the distance between the mole and the (now unmentioned) pit since the subject, the 'thou' addressed, *is* also the reader. Additionally, as remarked in note 24 above, this molish line of the motto holds a hymenal rhetorical position in that it may be read as subsuming the previous question (wilt thou go ask the mole whether the eagle knows what is in the pit?) or it may be read as introducing (with its end-line colon) the succeeding questions about (dis)placements of Love and Wisdom. In this sense the model of mole reading we meet here is more flexible than the model of eagle reading and it sets the paradigm for the paradoxical privileging of the liminal (female) perspective in the poem as a site of critical understanding.[33] At the same time, there is a way in which the eagle-reading of the motto persists in dominating, at least insofar as it hovers, eagle-like, over the pit of the text, surveying its (female) (molish) contents from beginning (in 15 copies) to end (in 2 copies).[34]

Let me now fold this discussion back into the problem of reading the motto rhetorically versus liminally. From what I have said so far, it should be clear that I identify the choice to take the motto's questions rhetorically as an eagle-reading. A feature of the rhetorical question is that it is deemed to represent the voice not of a liminal consciousness but of a 'subject-supposed-to-know'.[35] Thus Thel's Motto, perceived as a barrage of rhetorical questions, will be read as the master text of an invisible subject containing the secret knowledge its questions pose. From this there arises a sort of competition (as in the traditional psychoanalytic situation) between the imagined subjectivity of the enunciator of the motto on the one hand and the correspondingly interpellated subjectivity of the listener/reader on the other. The result is that an epistemophilic drive to know the knower is set in motion in the listener/reader/addressee. Thus a transference occurs that looks like, talks like, walks like Thel's transferences in her projected story. This imaginary mirror relation between Thel's want-to-know and the reader's want-to-know is further complicated if one assumes that the questions-deemed-rhetorical of the motto are enunciated *by* Thel. For then the subject-supposed-to-know is identical to the one supposed-not-to-know, and another image of a fruitless, never-endingly looped cycle of desire is created to baffle the very quest for definitive knowledge that epistemophiles undertake.

Finally, when our eagle-reading tendencies view the motto rhetorically, with the notion that its riddle hides a riddler, we begin to see *The Book of Thel* as a duel of subjectivities. Then imaginary dyadic relationships over-take our reactions to the figures of the poem as well as our sense of how these figures interact. We might characterise this seduction as a fall into the register of the Lacanian imaginary; and in that case the 'Imaginary' itself (a relatively moleish state) might be one (albeit eagle-eyed) answer to the question: 'What is in the pit?'

Identification and Empathy: Thel's Feminism and Blake's Cultural Critique

> I have accustomed myself to think of others, and what they will suffer on all occasions: and this loathness to offend, or even to hurt the feelings of another, is an instantaneous spring which actuates my conduct, and makes me kindly affected to everything that breathes. (32)
>
> ... mere personal attractions ... may, it is true, for a few years, charm the superficial part of your acquaintance, whose notions

of beauty are not built on any principle of utility. Such persons
might look at you as they would glance their eyes over these
tulips, and feel for a moment the same pleasure that a view
of the variegated rays of light would convey to an uninformed
mind. The lower class of mankind, and children, are fond of
finery; gaudy, dazzling appearances catch their attention; but the
discriminating judgment of a person of sense requires besides
colour, order, proportion, grace and usefulness, to render the idea
of beauty complete. (28)

She was never in a passion, but her quiet steady displeasure
made them feel so little in their own eyes, they wished her to
smile that they might be something; for all their consequence
seemed to arise from her approbation. (26)

Continual passions weakened [Jane Fretful's]
constitution . . . instead of being a comfort to her tender though
mistaken, mother, she was her greatest torment. . . . She loved
no one but herself; and the consequence was, she never inspired
love . . . (16)

These passages, taken more or less at random from Mary
Wollstonecraft's *Original Stories from Real Life; with Conversations,
calculated to Regulate the affections, and Form the Mind to Truth and
Goodness* (first published without Blake's engravings in 1788), typify
attitudes towards the role of young females (and female wills)
promoted by the culture of the 1780s and 1790s. Even from such a
polemical feminist as Wollstonecraft was about to become, the ideals
of self-sacrifice, unremitting sympathy through identification with
others, use-value (versus beauty or pleasure) as a mark of goodness
and desirability, the repression of 'the passions' (especially anger),
and the dependence for regard on the smiling gaze of another
were the behavioral paradigms foisted upon young women. Since
at one level *The Book of Thel* includes a parody of *Original Stories*
with matron Clay taking the place of Wollstonecraft's Mrs. Mason
to direct the show, I would like to suggest that Blake represents
Thel as one who tries on, but heroically resists, all these cultural
shibboleths. Though I do not have space here to do more than hint
at this line of argument, let me aver that Thel's represented desire
for a real female subjectivity is meant to undermine the powerful
calls from her interlocutors to embrace a philosophy of repetitive
and uncreative self-sacrifice. The fact that the seductive speeches of
these interlocutors may be thought of as projected voicings of Thel's
own encodings of the culture's symbolic values makes the fight
no less real. For despite the evidence that Blake later on adopted

a revisionary form of these same Christian ideals,[36] my contention is that in *this* text he represented and endorsed a liminal view of the desiring self for the purpose of critiquing a philosophy detrimental to the energies of real women even as it served the so-called feminine values of an empirical, deistical patriarchal order. To read Locke, Hume, Burke and others on the virtues of sympathy, empathy and identification indicates the way these ideas could become weapons in a war against what we today call *difference*.

What makes Thel's and Blake's subtle disengagement from the cultural virtues of identification and empathy pertinent to my original topic – the desire of reading in (to) *The Book of Thel* – is that identification and empathy *are* also methods of reading. I have been amazed to discover how so many commentators on *Thel* are drawn by some activation of their own identifications and desire to make strong moral judgments on the character Thel. Often their critical comments are vicious, vituperative, debasing – all in the name of lamenting Thel's so-called retreat from experience evinced in her reluctance to cross-over the hymen of the grave-plot into the pit. Is this their defense against reading her as a figure for liminal desire?

Blake seems to have structured all our responses so that they will stand as potential self-critiques, as positions bent into questions that we may wish to ponder as we head back unhindered to our own liminal veils of har.

University of Colorado at Boulder.

Notes

All quotations from Blake's work are from *The Complete Poetry and Prose of William Blake*, ed. DAVID V. ERDMAN (New York: Anchor, 1982). Abbreviations used: M (*Milton, A Poem*), MHH (*The Marriage of Heaven and Hell*), J (*Jerusalem*).

1. For other discussions of the figure/character split, see MARJORIE LEVINSON'S '"The Book of Thel" by William Blake: A Critical Reading,' *ELH* 47 (1980): 287–303 and TILOTTAMA RAJAN's *The Supplement of Reading* (Ithaca: Cornell University Press, 1990) pp. 238–43.

2. The discussion of this idea in feminist theory is too widespread to need specific citation. An interesting essay on marginality and 'oppositional consciousness', however, appears in a special issue of *Genders* on theorising nationality, sex, and race. See CHELA SANDOVAL, 'Oppositional Consciousness,' *Genders* 10 (1991): pp. 1–24. Proof of the currency of the notion of liminality as a site of feminist critique can be established by the fact that it has already become the subject of satire in at least one popular novel – see A. S. BYATT's *Possession: A Romance* (New York: Vintage, 1991) p. 61.

3. FREUD introduces these terms in his essay on the Rat Man. He is discussing the regression from acting to thinking that in his observation typifies

obsessional neurotics and relates this move to 'an early development and premature repression of the sexual instinct [*Trieb*] of looking and knowing (the scoptophilic and epistemophilic instincts)' (SIGMUND FREUD, *Three Case Histories* [New York: Collier, 1963] p. 98).

4. EDWARD LARRISSY, in his taut introductory book on Blake, draws attention to the applicability of Derrida's discussion of the hymen to *Thel*. See LARRISSY, *William Blake* (Oxford: Blackwell, 1985) p. 125. Derrida uses the hymen trope in his reading of Mallarmé. See JACQUES DERRIDA, *Dissemination*, trans. BARBARA JOHNSON (Chicago: University of Chicago Press, 1981) pp. 173–285.

5. See NELSON HILTON on vales/veils in *Literal Imagination: Blake's Vision of Words* (Berkeley & Los Angeles: University of California Press, 1983) pp. 127–46.

6. One critic has detected a scatalogical pun present in the idea that the phallic serpent pictured here is 'inserted' as a 'tail piece.' Certainly Blake could play such games, and perhaps he *is* doing so in this colophonic inscription, underscoring it by engraving 'The End' beneath the mound of earth on which the serpent writhes.

7. Rather than provide a comprehensive list of the various interpretations that fall into these divided camps, I direct the reader to the competent overviews of both DONALD PEARCE, 'Natural Religion and the Plight of Thel,' *Blake Studies* 8 (1978): pp. 23–35, and NANCY BOGEN, *The Book of Thel: A Facsimile and A Critical Text* (Providence: Brown University Press, 1971). For a partial discussion of the trends of more recent readings, see BRIAN WILKIE's *Blake's Thel and Oothoon* English Language Monograph Series #48 (Victoria, B.C.: University of Victoria Press, 1990).

8. On 'aphanisis' see JACQUES LACAN, *The Four Fundamental Concepts of Psycho-Analysis* trans. ALAN SHERIDAN (New York: Norton, 1981) 216–29; on 'desiring machines' see GILLIAN DELEUZE and FELIX GUATTARI, *Anti-Oedipus: Capitalism and Schizophrenia* (Minneapolis: University of Minnesota Press, 1983) *passim*; on 'avoid' see NELSON HILTON 241.

9. On the neologism 'want-to-be' as a term for the idea of lack (Lacan's own translation of his original *manque-á-être*) see JACQUES LACAN, both *Ecrits: A Selection*, trans. ALAN SHERIDAN (New York: Norton, 1977) and *The Four Fundamental Concepts passim*; on personification as a trope of liminality see STEVEN KNAPP, *Personification and the Sublime: Milton to Coleridge* (Cambridge: Harvard University Press, 1985) 66–97; and on taking Thel as figure for desire see LEVINSON.

10. The many odd standing, sitting, lying posturings in *Thel*, both pictorial and verbal, seem significant given the fact that this is a text interested in the placements and displacements of desire. Each position, furthermore, carries with it a libidinal connotation as when the lilly is imagined by Thel to be sitting in the face of the cunnilinguating lamb (2:6–7). The rhetoric of violence that is masked by such terms as 'mild' and 'meekin' in this otherwise violently rhetorical description of sacrifice/oral sex is par for the course in *Thel* and meets its release only at the end through the voice of sorrow's martial metaphors. See LEVINSON and RAJAN for further comments on this strain of Thelian imagery.

11. Wollstonecraft's *Original Stories from Real Life* (1788; London: Henry Frowde, 1906) are full of *Thel*ian echoes, with the ideal behaviour advocated for the most part directly contravening Thel's. For example, Mrs. Mason, (the

deliberate equivalent of *Thel*'s Matron Clay, also named after a house-building term) lectures her unruly charges about how as a child she 'always made it my study and delight to feed all the dumb family that surrounded our house; and when I could be of use to any one of them I was happy. This employment humanized my heart, while, like wax, it took every impression; and Providence has since made me an instrument of good – I have been useful to my fellow creatures' (Wollstonecraft 8). These sentiments and the virtues they extoll are the ones Thel overhears, the ones she herself lacks. Since Blake's negative take on Mrs. Mason is fairly well established, there is a strong likelihood that the pronouncements of similar ideologies made by Lilly, Cloud and Clay in *Thel* are meant not as visionary truths but rather as parodic echoings of the tenets of such educators as Mrs. Mason. A similar point about the cultural critique implied by Thel's resistance to the parodic voices of the dominant ideology was made some fifteen years ago by DONALD PEARCE in his essay 'Natural Religion and the Plight of Thel' to which I owe a powerful debt.

The pertinent references in Hume and Locke are readily available in the indices and extended table of contents of these works.

12. See LARRISSY 36, on Blake's 'grafts' – a term taken from Derrida's 'Economimesis,' *Diacritics* 11 (1981): 3. On the term echolalia, see STEVEN KNAPP 89.

13. See LACAN's *Ecrits* and *The Four Fundamental Concepts passim*, for the invention of the term 'corps morcelé' to describe the imago of the fragmented body. ELLIE RAGLAND SULLIVAN, in *Jacques Lacan and the Philosophy of Psychoanalysis* (Urbana & Chicago: University of Illinois Press, 1987) (*passim*) explains its relation to identification and the formation of subjectivity in the mirror stage of personal development.

14. See HILTON's 'An Original Story,' *Unnam'd Forms: Blake and Textuality*, ed. NELSON HILTON & THOMAS VOGLER (Berkeley & Los Angeles: University of California Press, 1986) p. 69.

15. 'Knowing one's place', of course, is often promoted as desirable by ideological prescription intoned from the hegemonic center in order to keep women (and other disenfranchised groups) powerless on the margins.

16. Blake generally (not just in *Thel*) chooses a liminal use of the genitive so that it performs as both possessive and partitive. But in *Thel* that usage is particularly resonant because Thel's drive for subjectivity is conditioned by her own persistent worries *about* partitivity as well as possession.

17. See MURRAY, 'Thel, *Thelyphthora*, and the Daughters of Albion,' *SiR* 20 (1981): pp. 275–97. Here, as Murray explains, the root 'thel' means 'female' and the title of the treatise Murray studies as a case of influence on Blake is *Thelyphthora; or A Treatise on Female Ruin in its Causes, Effects, Consequences, Prevention, and Remedy*. On the Greek thele (θηλή) deriving from the word for breast, note the prevalence of milky-fondnesses appearing in *Thel*. (The milk of this text, of course, is part of a more extended imagery of feeding in which woman's nurturing role consumes her identity.) A final Greek verb with the root sound of 'thel' (θηλέω) means to flourish, abound, bloom – the very activity that Thel associates with aphanisis.

18. In an unpublished essay, 'The Movable Text: Blake's U-topic Imagination in *Songs of Innocence and of Experience*,' I discuss the themes of lack and liminality in 'The Little Girl Lost/Found.' Lyca has much in common with Thel, not the least of which is the personifying pun on her name as one who is ever 'like-a' likeness of another, i.e. not a substance, hence in a state

163

of perpetual aphanisis (she sleeps throughout most of the two songs). Her reliance on identification and displacements as readings of her desire, and the collapse of most of the places and times named in her journey into each other, as in a dream, mirror similar happenings in *Thel*.

19. See CYNTHIA CHASE's 'Desire and Identification in Lacan and Kristeva,' *Feminism and Psychoanalysis*, ed. RICHARD FELDSTEIN and JUDITH ROOF (Ithaca: Cornell University Press, 1989) pp. 65–83. Chase is actually drawing from CATHERINE CLÉMENT's *The Lives and Legends of Jacques Lacan*, trans. ARTHUR GOLDHAMMER (New York: Columbia University Press, 1983). Clément, she says, took Lacan's claim that desire finds its signifier in the phallus 'as evidence that Lacan draws his model of subjectivity from feminine sexuality.' The basis for this contention is that in Lacan's psychoanalytic theory, subjectivity grows from consciousness of a lack, and lack-of-the-phallus is taken to be the signature of feminine sexuality.

20. *Ecrits* 261. The quotation is from Chapter 7, 'The Direction of the Treatment and the Principles of its Power,' but here it is translated afresh from the French by ARTHUR GOLDHAMMER in his translation of CLÉMENT's *Lives and Legends* 131.

21. HUME, LOCKE, and ROUSSEAU all take up the question of the will (for Rousseau it is a political idea: the 'general will'). Note Blake's differentiation between will and desire in his annotations to SWEDENBORG's *Divine Love and Wisdom* (1788) where he names 'Will, Desire, Love, Rage, Envy, & all other Affections' as natural, but singles out will as 'pernicious to others or selfish' and calls it 'always Evil'. See ERDMAN 602. In this negative response by Blake to Swedenborg's analogy between human will and divine love, he characterises 'will' as the reverse of liminal: it is a hindering of the discourse of the other. But *Thel*, I am arguing, critiques that position.

22. See ERIC PARTRIDGE's *Shakespeare's Bawdy*, 3rd edn (London: Routledge & Kegan Paul, 1968) pp. 218–19.

23. The problematic ambiguity of the genitive in the phrase 'Thel's Motto' complicates interpretation here as well as in the title of the poem. Thus we are left to ponder whether the motto belongs to Thel because (a) it is spoken by Thel about herself (her énonciation and her énoncé), (b) it is addressed to her as a riddle by an unknown narrator, (c) it is introduced by the printer & author Will Blake to comment on her dilemmas, her desires, her fate, or (d) it is the litany of its own thelian desiring which will meet its match at the end of the poem when the pit-that-the Eagle-does/doesn't-know-the-contents-of has become a grave entombing the implied, subliminal speaking subject generic to all mottoes.

24. I have counted the questions in the motto and in the text and come up with different numbers at different times. The problem is that often questions are liminally folded into each other and it is difficult to say whether the resultant mix is to be read as one question or two or even three. For example, in the motto when the opener asks, 'Does the eagle know what is in the pit?' we seem to have a single question, yet it is divisible into two equal enigmas: (1) does the eagle know? and (2) what is in the pit? The next line is no clearer in *its* singleness. Is 'Or wilt thou go ask the mole:' to be read as a separate inquiry, an appendage to line one, or the introduction to the additional queries of lines 3 and 4? In other words, the syntax permits any of the following construals:

1. Will we ask the mole what's in the pit?
2. Will we ask the mole whether the eagle knows what's in the pit?

3. Will we ask the mole whether Wisdom can be put in a silver rod. Love in a golden bowl?

25. Before the oracle at Delphi belonged to Apollo, it purportedly belonged to Gaia, the goddess Earth, of whom the Matron Clay is surely an 'original derivation' (Blake's *All Religions Are One*, Principle 6). As to the method of oracle-consultation, my positivist encyclopaedia entry doubts that the ancient 'tale of intoxicating mephitic vapours' has sufficient authority or scientific probability to be credited as factual.

26. The curious insistence on the word 'gentle' here (made the more echoic by Blake's re-engraving an originally etched 'gently' in line 13 to read as the fourth iteration of 'gentle') carries with it a subtle, sotto-voce reverberation of the word 'genital' to suggest the libidinal underpinnings of this desire for 'the sleep of death'. Whether or not a reader hears the gentle/genital rhyme, however, the 'sleep of death' may be understood as a conventional euphemism for sexual fulfillment.
   I have called this whole envoi to Thel's lament 'yawning' because of its precedent 'Ah!' – a primitive semiotic vocalisation that imitates a yawn and, like other breathy sighs/signs of this order that fly over the ground of *The Book of Thel* (5:15), disturbs the decorous discourse of the text's often hyperbolic dialogue.

27. The question as a rhetorical form is itself a lure to the addicted epistemophile, stirring up the want-to-know in the reader. And its mark, the '?' of its end-stop punctuation, tempts the scoptophile. Blake seems to pander to that scoptophilic interest by seeding the designs of many of the plates with visual echoes of the shape of the question mark. See, for example, on the title page alone, the curve of the stem of the flower on the right side of the plate, and the hint of inverted question-marks in the loop of Thel's willow tree, the tip of shepherd's crook, and the upper curve of the letter 'f' in the word 'of' of the title.

28. See Robert Essick, *William Blake and The Language of Adam* (Oxford: Clarendon, 1989) p. 126, for a brief discussion of the problematics of signification in these and the other terms of the motto.

29. In *Blake's Composite Art* (Princeton: Princeton University Press, 1978) p. 85.

30. Marie-Louis von Franz discusses the mole as a figure for female genitals in *Problems of the Feminine in Fairytales* (New York: Spring Publications, 1972) p. 39.

31. See Freud's letter to Marie Bonaparte, cited by Ernest Jones in *The Life and Work of Sigmund Freud* (New York: Basic Books, 1955) 2:421.

32. Of course 'knowing' is an abstract concept only if we blind ourselves (molelike?) to the so-called biblical sense of the verb 'to know' as a synonym for intimate sexual relations.

33. A noticeable shift of syntactical structuring moves through the questions of the motto as well, with the interrogative 'does he' (present tense, male subject) shifting to 'wilt thou' (future tense, moveably gendered subject) and then to two 'can it's (optative mode, arguably gendered subjects – is Wisdom male and Love female as the attributes rod and bowl suggest? Or are these abstract qualities of Wisdom and Love to be thought of as personified in the reverse gendering roles as are the Greek Sophia/Wisdom and Eros/Love?).

34. Another eagle/mole/pit formula may be applied to the relationship of motto to text versus a reading of the motto taken in and of itself. Thus we

might say that motto:text = eagle:pit, but motto:motto = mole:pit. Readings of the motto often depend on how 'eaglishly' an interpreter wants to see its contents as conditioning the meaning of the rest of the text.

35. See LACAN's *Four Fundamental Concepts*, chapter 18.

36. Some of the Christian ideals revisioned that I am thinking of are those that denounce 'selfhood' and embrace 'self-annihilation'.

11 Who Didn't Kill Blake's Fly: Moral Law and the Rule of Grammar in 'Songs of Experience'*

Michael Simpson

There is some critical consensus that Blake's 'The Fly' has an ironic sting in its tail. A rough sampling of the criticism indicates a large range of such irony: Pagliaro's reading finds a merely conditional 'visionary defeat' for the poem's narrator; Bloom reads a more destructive critique of the pious consolations of an orthodox Christianity; and Wagenknecht proposes a nihilistic final stanza that critically parodies syllogistic reasoning by demonstrating its effects as a heap of bodies at the end of the poem.[1] But I shall argue instead that it is we who are in danger in any encounter with the poem and that this danger originates not in the poem but in ourselves. I shall also propose, however, that the grammar of the poem, along with its formal identity as part of a chapbook, can enable us to recognise our destructive and ultimately self-destructive complicity in the text. It is in my emphasis on the agency of a reader, invoked by the poem, that the difference between my argument and the previous criticism consists.

I

There is, perhaps expectedly, more critical agreement about the poem's plot than there is about the consequences and significance of its 'events': the fly always gets to die, and in the rest of the poem it is understood that the narrator's attempt to identify with his victim is variously complicated according to the degree of irony thus read into it. It is, however, this very stability, constituted by a critical

* I thank Norman Bryson for the chance remark that first engaged me with this poem; Timothy Webb for some healthy scepticism along the way; Peter de Bolla for an invitation to present this reading at his seminar on practical criticism at King's College, Cambridge; Andrew Cooper for inspiration and a very helpful critique of the piece; the anonymous readers for *Style* for some sharp commentary; and Barbara Goff for discussing the poem and this piece in excruciating detail. Such eternity in this grain of sand.

consensus about the plot, that I shall challenge by the version of reader-response criticism that follows. While virtually all critics of the poem have stabilised its plot by declining to consider their own agency in this project, I shall develop the notion of 'affective stylistics', formulated by Stanley Fish, to reflect on both my own reading agency and on that of a critical consensus concerned to deny, or at least to ignore, its own complicity in the drama of this poem. My working notion of an affective stylistics will, however, differ from Fish's version by sidestepping the fairly received objection that Fish's reader never learns from his or her own experience. Jolted into self-recrimination by a disruption of its syntactic expectations, Fish's reader then approaches the next sentence, and then the next, and so on, without any suspicion that the moral lesson of the preceding sentence is about to be taught again. Since I focus here on a single lyric rather than the large narratives that Fish analyses, I do not face the problem of an incredibly sustained credulity. But even if my reading practice were applied to the whole corpus of Blake's *Songs*, the problem would still not occur, both because this collection is considerably shorter than, say, *Paradise Lost* and because each lyric, unlike each sentence in Milton's epic, presents a different dramatic situation. Differently situated in each poem, my reader is taught a lesson that is contextually distinct. Since this lesson, staged chiefly by the genre of the chapbook, entails an exercise in reading just as much as it enjoins the exertion of moral discrimination, Blake's *Songs* seems proleptically to invite a version of such criticism.

Despite the supposed stability of this poem's plot, the death of the fly and hence the narrator's culpability for it are highly contingent upon how we read the first stanza. What the narrator admits is that he has 'brushed away' the fly's 'summer's play'.[2] Either this admission is a soothing circumlocution for an act of destruction or it is an innocent account of how the narrator merely repelled, accidentally or otherwise, the fly's activity. To convict the narrator on the basis of his self-incrimination, we must first undergo a little jury selection. Virtually all the critics of this poem have established the murder by supplying the body themselves. But did they really get it from the text when the text itself does not definitively state that a death in fact occurred? In order to answer this question about whether the narrator or the reader is the dominant agent in this first stanza, we must, since the extent of the narrator's malefaction is suddenly at issue here, decide how much agency the narrator and the fly possess relative to one another.

However implausible the following scenario within a code of realism, the syntax of the first stanza allows 'Thy summer's play' to be either object or subject of the verb 'has brushed', and 'My thoughtless hand' to be subject or object respectively. Depending on how we resolve the syntax, the narrator kills or repels the fly, or, inversely, the fly's impulsive activity successfully resists the encroaching hand. Whether the narrator or the fly is read as the subject of the verb, the sequence of the sentence, in both its variants, involves an inversion of the conventional word order of prose, so that no objection to the fly as subject can rest on an assumption about word order. Given that there is here no 'normal' word order, because the poem is signalling its identity as poetry through the trope of syntactic inversion, we have no way to determine which of the two readings is more or less probable. Even if we suppose that the sequence 'Little dog, your ready tooth the mailman's boot has damaged' would tend to be conventionally resolved so that the mailman's boot would be the subject of the sentence, and if we further suppose that this convention of prose syntax might govern the construing of Blake's stanza, installing the 'mailman's boot' and the 'thoughtless hand' as subject would nonetheless be only the most probable syntax in a range of plausible resolutions we might entertain until the sentence was read to its conclusion. That all critics who have written on the poem seem to understand the 'thoughtless hand' as subject does not necessarily deny that there are no other possibilities that might finally be over-ridden at the end of the stanza.[3]

Conditioning my alternative reading of the stanza are numerous instances within the scope of Blake's notoriously versatile syntax of such possible fluctuations of subject and object. In 'The Sick Rose', for example, which is another 'Song of Experience', the rose may be sick because its life is being destroyed by the worm's 'dark secret love' or because this 'dark secret love' is being destroyed by the rose's 'life'.

> O Rose thou art sick.
> The invisible worm.
> That flies in the night
> In the howling storm:
>
> Has found out thy bed
> Of crimson joy:
> And his dark secret love
> Does thy life destroy.
>
> (23)[4]

The factor that specifically allows 'his dark secret love' to be read as the object of 'destroy' and 'thy life' as the subject, is the rhetorical figure of syntactic inversion called 'anastrophe'.

What I am emphasising in this focus on the possible transpositions of subject and object is how the plots of these brief lyrics can be easily and totally transformed and how considerable responsibility thus devolves onto a reader who can be seen to read among opposed options. What happens *to* the text determines what happens *in* the text (this continuity is incidentally signalled by the punning title of the poem, for it names an item within the text as well as the text itself). Despite the poem's apparent invocation of a reading subject, however, this subject will not be here elaborated into the familiar and less than sophisticated concept of the naive reader who, by recognising his or her errors, is progressively educated to become a sophisticated reader. The reading subject I characterise will be such that we would be ingenuous to describe it as either naive or sophisticated. Invoked in the first instance by the polarised interpretive choices that the poem seems to offer, my reader is only as determinate as the choice that it finally makes within this dilemma. Since such a reader is figured by the dilemma only before it is resolved, the text itself provides no indication of which choice this reader must make, or, indeed, whether it must finally make a choice at all. This figured reader could choose either way, or might choose, agnostically, not to choose. It further confounds any effort to characterise and so judge this reader that it is already characterised as a particularly complex persona by the generic identification of Blake's *Songs* as a children's chapbook. Projecting both an adult and infant reading persona, Blake's *Songs* denies a conveniently unitary figure that might thus be anticipated and judged. Since the poem refuses to delineate this reader, even as it vigorously constitutes it, and the chapbook models two readers simultaneously, the only readers of the poem available for characterisation are those critics who have grappled with it on record. As part of my account of the uncertain reading position provided by the poem, I must in due course consider how other critics have tried to occupy it.

Helping to drive the prevailing interpretation of the poem, in which the fly dies and the narrator identifies with it, are some earlier literary texts that seem to be cited as prototypes by this account of the poem. Whether or not Blake is assumed to have been familiar with these texts, they are certainly available to be cited by the criticism of Blake's poem. One of these texts is William Oldys's lyric 'On a Fly Drinking from his Cup':

> Busy, curious, thirsty fly!
> Drink with me, and drink as I:
> Freely welcome to my cup,

Couldst thou sip, and sip it up:
Make the most of life you may,
Life is short and wears away.

Just alike, both mine and thine,
Hasten quick to their decline:
Thine's a summer, mine no more,
Though repeated to three-score.
Three-score summers, when they're gone,
Will appear as short as one.

Oldys's lyric impinges specifically on Blake's text by rehearsing a plot in which the fly dies and thus becomes a determining or legitimating factor in later criticism of 'The Fly'. By advancing the following simile, the blind Gloucester in *King Lear* similarly establishes the death of a fly and one's consequent identification with it that later criticism of Blake's poem will quote specifically in the context of this passage.

As flies to wanton boys, are we to th'Gods;
They kill us for their sport.

(2.1.36–37)

In their reading of Blake, Hirsch and Bloom both refer to this passage.

To quote this excerpt from *King Lear* as part of an account of Blake's poem is, of course, to presume that the fly dies. If, however, the fly is presumed to survive, an equally compelling literary antecedent might be invoked to corroborate this reading. In Chapman's *Iliad*, as the Greeks hesitate in their mission to recover Patroclus's body, Menelaus is said to have a special relation with Pallas:

... The king's so royall will
Minerva joy'd to heare, since she did all the gods outgo
In his remembrance. For which grace she kindly did bestow
Strength on his shoulders and did fill his knees as liberally
With swiftnesse, breathing in his breast the courage of a flie
Which loves to bite so and doth beare man's bloud so much
 good will
That still (though beaten from a man) she flies upon him still:
With such a courage Pallas fild the blacke parts neare his hart.[5]

(17.485–92)

Unlike the Shakespearean 'flies,' and for that matter Donne's' 'flea', which also meets an unceremonious end, the Homeric fly is an epic emblem of action, 'courage', and sheer survival. So resourceful is this Homeric fly that Pope, in his edition of the *Iliad*, denies that it can be a fly by effectively mis-translating the Greek word μυια, as 'hornet'.

II

So much for the small swarm of literary flies that may have conditioned, and in some cases have certainly not conditioned, the criticism of the poem's first stanza. Much of the criticism discussing 'The Fly' has read darker, more ironic options in the narrator's apparent identification with the fly than did, for example, E. D. Hirsch, who effectively congratulated the narrator for his visionary sympathy (236–41).[6] Although Hirsch's reading also subscribes to the unnecessary assumption that the narrator has killed the fly, I want to suggest that the text can offer either the guilty narrator of critical consensus or the extenuated, even exonerated narrator of Hirsch, depending on whether we identify ourselves as unimpeachably righteous judges or as judges whose integrity can be reclaimed only by a self-impeachment for fabricating the evidence on which the judgement of the narrator was first based. Any repercussions that the latter reading might have for the former will merely disturb the moral distance that earlier criticism thinks that it can stabilise between itself and the narrator. Whether condemning the narrator from a vantage of moralistic superiority or approving of him from the perspective of a Humean sympathy, the criticism has assumed a distance between itself and the text. This distance is, however, as fictional, or otherwise, as the fly's death, because it depends on the assumption that there is a standpoint from which this death can be confidently predicated. Once the poem's grammar is seen to be at issue, this death and its judicial consequences become just as uncertain as this grammar.

If there are crucial differences between the narrator and the fly, they are constituted, ironically, by the narrator's efforts to urge an identity between the two in order to override differences that otherwise would not be an issue. It is by staging a comparison that the narrator triggers contrasts that threaten to displace the initial comparisons between the two figures. The second stanza canvasses the possibility of this identity, and the next stanza can be read to provide the conditions for it. Apparently connecting the narrator with the fly is the dancing, drinking, and singing that is manifested not only as the thoughtlessness that impels the narrator to destroy, or dismiss, the fly, but also as the fly's 'play' that enables the

narrator to despatch it. Dancing, drinking, and singing here collapse
thoughtlessness, 'play', and blindness into an overall unity. The
identification with the victim that this unity entails conveniently
obviates any question about whether the fly's fate at the hands of
the narrator was deliberate or accidental. Whether the narrator's
hand was 'thoughtless' in the sense of oblivious or whether it committed a deliberate but unreflective act are questions finessed by the
supposed identification on the ground of a common impetuosity. If,
however, this identification is questioned, either by the narrator or
by the reader alone, this discrimination between different degrees
of the narrator's motivation is considerably enhanced.

There is a similarly importunate effort to identify with an insect,
first alive and then dead, in Donne's 'The Flea'. This poem entails a
manipulative narrator who is about the usual business of seduction.
He tries to achieve this goal by a synecdoche identifying the narrator
and his potential lover within those 'living walls of jet' that com-
prise a promiscuously blood-sucking flea. Since their bloods have
already been mingled, the narrator asks, why not go the whole
way? The related doctrines of incarnation, crucifixion, and com-
munion, with which Donne's narrator dices, seem to stand behind
Blake's poem too. It is these related doctrines that 'The Fly' might
be seen to resist as it interrogates the terms of the supposed identification between narrator and fly. All of these doctrines are predicated on a separation between God and Man that an act of sacrifice
closes. Just as 'The Fly' itself seems to disrupt this formulation,
so other works by Blake, such as the first stanza of 'The Human
Abstract', deny both this separation and the necessity of sacrifice.

The fourth and fifth stanzas can be understood to continue the
attempted identification between the narrator and the fly on further
grounds. Correlating 'thought' and its absence with 'life' and 'death',
and then suggesting that his happiness, as a fly, is already secure,
the narrator may be arguing that just as he assures a continued life
to the absent fly by thinking about it in the poem, so also is he
supplying a perpetuity for himself by thinking of himself and the
fly in a poem the reader will read commemoratively. Not only does
the reader 'think' of the narrator as the narrator 'thinks' of the fly,
but the narrator and the fly are also ultimately suggested as parallel
and thus similar objects of thought for the reader. Characteristic
of amatory verse, such as Shakespeare's sonnets 15, 18, and 19, the
convention whereby the lyric 'I' immortalises a privileged addressee
is deployed here to suggest the intimacy of an identity between
narrator and fly. What contradicts the predication of a total identity
in the lines 'Then am I/A happy fly' is the fact that narrator and
fly are constituted as parallel objects of the reader's thought by an

initial hierarchy that the narrator constructs and that allows no place for the fly's thought. It is the commemorative thought of the narrator alone that initiates a process of resurrection then underwritten by the reader.

The last two stanzas of 'The Fly' and especially the relations between them, have been generally acknowledged as the most enigmatic portions of the poem.[7] Another reading of these stanzas might be just as plausible as the one advanced above: the fourth stanza could be a speculation that 'life' may consist only in an awareness of itself, thus precluding any awareness of its absence, while the fifth stanza could be drawing the inference that death is not to be dreaded because it is merely the absence of 'thought' about both itself and everything else. If thought is what constitutes a subject in relation to itself as object, the 'want' of thought will cancel both subject and object, so that oblivion will be its own consolation. The rhetorical project of these stanzas seems once again to be to urge the narrator's identification with the fly, since he is shown in the process of endorsing its apparent nonchalance about death. And yet again, this identification is highly resistible: only if the subjects 'thought' and 'want of thought' and their predicates 'life' and 'death' are read as applicable to both narrator and fly is this identification at all possible. If, on the other hand, we suppose that these subjects and predicates are not all generally applicable to narrator and fly and that it is specifically the narrator's thought or want of it that determines life and death, specifically for the fly, then the alleged identity of the two figures is denied by the uni-lateral characteristic of the narrator's 'thought' about the fly. There is a similar denial of identity if we assume instead that it is the narrator's 'thought' that assigns 'life', 'want of thought', and 'death' to the fly. The fourth stanza will support at least three permutations of how these subjects and predicates can be correlated with the fly and the narrator.

What is perhaps most resistant in all of this to my claim of identification is not merely the power that accrues to the narrator's thought in two of the permutations above, but that it is the narrator alone who forms these propositions about 'thought' and indeed about everything else in the poem. By appearing as the only discurs-ive subject in the poem, the narrator enacts the unilateral thought that can be read in the fourth stanza. David Wagenknecht, however, suggests a provocative complication of this notion:

> But The Fly is unique among the Songs in that it is etched in two columns, the first three stanzas in one column and the two-stanza rejoinder to the right, the typographical form suggesting a dialogue

with two speakers and perhaps implying 'two laws.' In fact we can see the last two stanzas as constituting a 'reply' ... to the first three, the reply of the fly addressed in the first stanza. We assume that the speaker of the final two stanzas is in fact an interlocutionary fiction of the speaker of the first, a fiction resulting from his successful identification with the fly in stanza 2.

(109)

Although Wagenknecht countenances the possibility of a second speaker, he concludes nonetheless that this persona is only a projection of the narrator. Wagenknecht assumes that this speaker is an interlocutionary fiction because he has already presupposed that the fly has been destroyed by the narrator. If we accept his presupposition, we intensify the unilateral component of the narrator's identification with the fly, and the identity itself is thereby falsified, because all the predications about this identity are made in the absence of the fly, which cannot therefore assent to, challenge, or propose alternatives to this identification. How can there ever be an intimate similarity between these figures when its articulation depends on one of them, and only one of them, being dead?

III

Although I shall go on to argue that the poem can be read to ask this same question of itself, so far I have operated mainly within the parameters of a critical consensus that supposes this question to be asked only by the reader. The narrator is enabled, or made, to avoid ever acknowledging this question because he has already conflated all the attributes of himself and the fly so that they become conditions of an identification: he glosses the impulsiveness of the 'thoughtless hand', the exuberance of the 'summer's play', and the oblivion of 'death' all as a common innocence. To accept this conflation, as do the narrator and critics such as Hirsch and D. C. Gillham (218–19), is to repeat the act of destruction that the poem is trying to rationalise. That this rationalisation is such a repetition becomes the extremity of the narrator's crime. While the narrator claims that the cause of the fly's destruction is the impulsiveness that identifies him with it, he also maintains that this identity justifies that destruction by allowing the narrator himself to compensate for the fly's absence. Cause, justification, and reparation are alleged to be identical. Their identity, however, depends crucially on the identification of the narrator with the fly, which is in turn disrupted by the unilateral component in those gestures of explanation, justification, and compensation. Each of these two logical circuits needs the other to validate itself, but when they intersect, both of these circuits are radically broken.

If the 'thoughtless hand' is read as the hand of the writer or engraver, the complicity of the poem with the destructive act that it claims to investigate could even be registered in the first stanza. The obliteration, or dismissal, of the fly would thus be caused by and partly contemporaneous with the acts of writing and engraving, because the fly would be despatched not before but during the writing. This incriminating proximity of the writing hand to the fly's fate, however, is once again a function of how we construe the relevant lines. Our very attribution to the writing hand of an extreme power over life and death is itself figured, by the starkly alternative reading of the first stanza, as a mere attribution that originates in the more awesome power of the reader. If this reader is to be characterised by features other than the power of choice, which is the property with which the poem itself figures this persona, it is the poem's genre that must supply these elusive details. Signing itself as an instance of the chapbook and hence as a form of morally edifying literature, *Songs of Innocence and of Experience* projects a reader who must be induced by exemplary and cautionary tales to make moral discriminations between those tales. Since the chapbook was a means, in a culture with few books, of teaching literacy as well as moral judgement, the reader it supposes and consequently figures is a persona to whom considerable work is assigned.[8]

So much labour is in fact required of this reader, who must do the work of actually becoming a reader, that the text implies the presence of another, more competent reader who might mediate, on the one hand, between the competence assumed and demanded by the text, and, on the other, the lack of such competence it also assumes of its illiterate or semi-literate addressee. 'The Fly', in common with the other poems in the collection, implies an adult reader who must assist a juvenile subject to modulate from non-literacy to the condition of literacy. Explicitly invoking such an adult reader to help her or his junior counterpart is the preface to John Newbery's *A Little Pretty Pocket-Book*, published in 1767. Inscribed at the outset 'TO THE PARENTS, GUARDIANS, AND NURSES IN GREAT-BRITAIN and IRELAND', this text features a preface that effectively instructs this adult audience how to use the succeeding text, comprising simple fables and morals.

Would you have a *Wise* Son, teach him to reason early. Let him read, and make him understand what he reads. No Sentence should be passed over without a strict Examination of the Truth of it; and though this may be thought hard at first, and seem to retard the Boy in his Progress, yet a little Practice will make it familiar, and a Method of Reasoning will be acquired, which will be of use to him all his Life after.

(58)

It is just such a practice of not passing over any sentence without 'a strict Examination of the Truth of it' that 'The Fly' is here being said to invite.

A modification of this scenario of reading, in which the juvenile reader is assisted by an adult, is proposed by Maria Edgeworth's *Harry and Lucy Concluded; being the Last Part of Early Lessons.* Repeating a proposal featured in other examples of children's literature written by the Edgeworths and that seems thereby to be elevated into a principle, the 'PREFACE; ADDRESSED TO PARENTS' makes this recommendation:

Much that would be tiresome and insufferable to young people if offered by preceptors in a didactic tone, will be eagerly accepted when suggested in conversation, especially in conversations between themselves. . . . The great preceptor, standing on the top of the ladder of learning, can hardly stretch his hand down to the poor urchin at the bottom looking up to him in despair; but an intermediate companion, who is only a few steps above, can assist him with a helping hand, can show him where to put his foot safely; and now urging, now encouraging, can draw him up to any height within his own attainment.

(11–13)

This hierarchy of pedagogy, plotted on a vertical axis, is especially pertinent to the tableau depicted in the poem's illustrated plate where the nurse bends down towards the small child, apparently in order to elevate his arms, and the older child aims upwards in an effort to elevate the descending projectile. Whether by means of the bipolar hierarchy characterised in Newbery's preface or by means of the more mediated stratification typical of the Edgeworths' prefaces, children's chapbooks of the eighteenth century invoke a dual audience. Even if we read Blake's poem as a parody of these structural conventions of the chapbook rather than as simply instantiating them, the text still implies a bipartite audience. It is not that Blake's *Songs* in general and this poem in particular invoke these readers literally, but rather that they figure such reading positions symbolically. By identifying itself as a version of the chapbook Blake's *Songs* structurally projects these reading positions.

That these poems formally address themselves both to a juvenile persona and to an adult figure is indicated not only by their often patronising tone and the simplicity of their vocabulary, which might in any case be purely ironic elements of the text, but also in that earlier instances of the chapbook explicitly target children as a substantial component of their audience. So many pieces of popular literature throughout the eighteenth century and earlier address themselves to children, at least rhetorically, that they seem to compose a fairly stable genre. William Sloane's *Checklist* catalogues 261 such publications, excluding primers designed specifically for use in schools, between 1557 and 1710. The most influential texts of this kind published after 1710 include William Ronksley's *The Child's Week's Work* of 1712, Isaac Watts's *Divine and Moral Songs for Children*, appearing in 1715, and Charles Wesley's *Hymns for Children* of 1763. Significant instances of this genre that appear more immediately before Blake's *Songs* and that might consequently be read as its direct antecedents include the Edgeworths' *Practical Education: The History of Harry and Lucy*, first published in 1780, Mrs Barbauld's *Lessons for Children from Two to Three Years Old* of 1780, and her *Hymns in Prose for Children* of 1781, Thomas Day's *The History of Sandford and Merton: A Work Intended for the Use of Children*, and the prolific John Newbery's *The History of Tommy Playlove* and *Jacky Lovebook: wherein is shown the Superiority of Virtue over Vice*, both published initially in 1783. Since many of these works incorporate a preface evidently addressed to adult readers, along with a text that seems specifically targeted on children, the eventuality of co-reading seems to be structurally implied by this form. Even if Blake's *Songs*, and especially 'Songs of Experience', is, as I have started to suggest, a parody of the children's chapbook, ironising its pieties and certitudes by complicating the moral that it is supposed to communicate unproblematically, this parody nonetheless employs the device of team reading that is a feature of the form being satirised. The parody is, therefore, an intimate one. Moreover, such a parody may emphasise this dual readership, because it works by implying both a literal and an ironic reading of the text that might each be correlated with the innocent and more experienced readers invoked by the text's generic identity.

IV

Having followed, in the earlier discussion of the poem, the main contours of the criticism focused on 'The Fly', and having allowed my own account of the poem to emerge largely by contrast and by implication, I must explain how the poem's invocation of a reader constitutes a poem that is different from the poem produced by a criticism perceiving no consistent invocation of the reader. I suggest that to factor a reading persona into a discussion of 'The Fly' is to construct a relation between reader and narrator that can in turn reconstruct the specific relation between narrator and fly that critical consensus has begun to stabilise, but has done so destructively. Insofar as the poem invokes an active and self-conscious reader, any predications made about the poem's narrator will be seen by the predicating reader to reflect on him- or herself. This version of the poem contrasts with certain other critical accounts of it by transferring to the reader any irony that the poem would otherwise be seen to direct at the narrator. Any moral judgements directed by this reader at the narrator will, in the context of a chapbook that works to teach moral discrimination, tend to return as questions about the reader's own ethics in making that moral judgement. Having merely hinted at an alternative narrator who might be constituted by a practice of reading more conscious of its own risks than either Hirsch's congratulation of the narrator or Wagenknecht's indictment, I will now supplement those hints with a fuller characterisation that offers a more direct statement of the alternative than this narrator poses.

Whether we read the first stanza so that the fly dies or whether we read the fly deflecting, or at least escaping, the thoughtless hand, the remaining stanzas can provide a narrator who postulates an identification with an actual or potential victim only to question it. The second stanza comprises two questions. These often seem to be understood as merely rhetorical, and as thereby affirmative of their interrogatives, but they might also be something other than rhetorical.

> Am not I
> A fly like thee?
> Or art not thou
> A man like me?

If we assume that the fly survives, then the second-person address in these two questions has a real destination denied if we make the opposite assumption that the fly is dead. To read this stanza so that it is composed of actual questions is to invite ourselves to ask the question of whether they imply a positive answer, as a rhetorical question would, whether they beg a negative response, or whether their motivation is neutral. The relation between the two questions can also be an issue, since the word 'Or' (which relates or dislocates these questions) could mean 'or to put the same thing another way', but could also mean 'or should I formulate this first question in another way?' The second question might be a simple repetition of the first one or it might be an interrogation of it.[9] Depending on whether we read the word 'Or' as such a reinforcement or as a questioning of the process of asking these questions, the narrator appears as either assertive or reflective.

How the narrator appears in the third stanza is determined largely by how the drama of the first stanza has been configured. If the fly is presumed to die, the narrator's notion that he resembles it by dancing, drinking, and singing is palpably spurious, since this is exactly what the fly cannot now do. If, however, the fly is allowed to survive and even win the encounter, the narrator's attempt to identify with it becomes an ennobling personification instead of an effort at self-justification by replacing the victim. Assuming a destroyed fly correlates the phrase 'dance,/And drink, & sing' with the ironic 'dance & sing' of the victimised child in 'The Chimney-Sweeper', while assuming a victorious fly identifies the above phrase with the words 'drink, & sing' as they form part of the positive proposals made by the juvenile narrator in 'The Little Vagabond'. Not only the internal relations of 'The Fly', but also its external relations to other poems in the sequence are at stake in how the poem is construed.

The narrator of the fourth stanza can be manifested, on the one hand, as a callous, and probably empiricist, philosopher who traffics in such abstract categories as 'thought' and 'want of thought', or, on the other hand, as a narrator who carefully anatomises a specific act by allocating the property of 'thought' to his own role and 'want of thought' to the lot of the fly. And the narrator's recognition of a difference, which is also an inequality, in the whole transaction is foregrounded if we read the condition introduced by 'If' as extending only as far as 'breath' but excluding 'want of thought', so that the stanza comprises not two parallel conditional clauses, but two separate clauses representing 'thought' as the narrator's luxurious option and 'want of thought' as the fly's probable fate within that luxury. In this reading, the second clause would effectively be a parenthesis between the conditional clause and the main clause that opens the next stanza.

However we construe the fourth stanza, the narrator of the final stanza is either confident of the proposition that he deduces from the premises of that penultimate stanza, whether they be mutually universal or alleged to be applicable to narrator and fly respectively, or he is vulnerably unsure of what conclusion to draw. If we try to reconstruct a hypothetical reading experience of this stanza, we might suppose that the inversion of subject and verb in the line 'Then am I' signals the introduction of a question and that the alternative condition staged by the word 'or' then compounds this signal by posing a binary opposition within which the narrator is fluctuating, perhaps interrogatively. Only at the end of the sentence, which does not feature a question mark, can this hypothetical reading exclude the eventuality of a question by resolving the syntax into the equally available, but ultimately more probable, format of an indicative statement. Resolving any momentary alternatives in the sentence into this inevitable indicative format again involves a recourse to the literary trope of anastrophe that allowed the thoughtless hand to brush away the fly and that now enables 'am I/A happy fly' to mean 'I am a happy fly'. The difference between these inversions in the first and final stanzas is that anastrophe insists on its profile as a stylistic form conditioning the grammar far less in the first stanza than it does in the last. It seems that we have less choice about grammar at the end of the poem. What we can recognise, nonetheless, in this final stanza is a momentary manifestation of that more benign and diffident narrator that we can understand the poem as a whole to provide – or at least not to deny. Rather than immediately concluding that his happiness is as independent of his own survival as it is of the fly's, and so proving his case by appearing so insensitive as to be dead, the narrator appears instead, at least for a moment, as one who questions the oblivion of that thoughtlessness which identifies this oblivion with death itself.

Although the poem can be said to provide, at different junctures, thoroughly different narrators who can thus be fashioned into coherent alternatives, there is no necessity that these characters be so rigorously polarised throughout. While the narrator who kills the fly and the one who does not may be mutually exclusive, the destructive narrator is not incompatible with the one who then doubts his or her identification with the victim even as she or he proposes it. The opposed alternatives in the grammar that I have been suggesting need not be correlated to distill a perfect narrator on the one hand and a highly imperfect one on the other, because a narrative of moral progress, or degeneration, can be interpolated to allow less consistent narrators to emerge. While my own reading, much more than even Hirsch's, invests in the extreme of the virtuous narrator, much of the criticism follows the more promiscuous trajectory, described above, to find a changing narrator. Pagliaro (pp. 78–9), for instance, finds a speaker who knows more about what s/he is saying at the beginning of the poem than she or he does at the end; Wagenknecht (p. 109), on the other hand, reads the final two stanzas as more sagacious than the preceding three because they are the speaker's version of what the fly might say to him.

What compels my reading to commit itself to the extreme of the virtuous narrator, even as it claims to be able to account grammatically for other trajectories, is that none of these readings acknowledges its implication in a grammar that will accommodate a range of options that stops, or starts, with this extreme. Also enjoining a commitment to this extreme reading is its implication that to read otherwise, once this specific choice is constituted, is, first, to participate in the fly's destruction by arranging the grammar so that the narrator kills it and, second, to repeat the crime by assassinating the narrator's character in the same grammatical arrangement. Once we acknowledge an alternative to this grammar, to read otherwise is also to abandon a narrator whom we have abetted in destruction and are now in turn destroying. But we may find at least one obvious objection to the construction of a diplomatic narrator: such diplomacy might be no more than a self-idealisation performed by the reader. We behold what we would like to think we are. What answers this objection is that the alternative, ventured by Wagenknecht and company, produces a self-idealisation of the reader that is similar, but actually more reprehensible because contingent on a denigration of the narrator.

The same gestures whereby we deny the reader's agency in the text can be seen in how criticism has treated the illustrated plate of 'The Fly', and specifically in its account of the relations between text and illustration. Although Wagenknecht usefully observes that 'The Fly is unique among the Songs in that it is etched in two columns' and that the second column is the fly's fictional 'rejoinder', he does not consider that this typographical departure might allow us to read the poem from left to right and then downwards instead of downwards and then across the page.[10] This is an arrangement that would yield the following sequence:

> Little Fly
> Thy summer's play,
> My thoughtless hand
> Has brush'd away.
>
> If thought is life
> And strength & breath:
> And the want
> Of thought is death;
>
> Am not I
> A fly like thee?

Or art not thou
A man like me?

Then am I
A happy fly,
If I live,
Or if I die.

For I dance,
And drink & sing:
Till some blind hand
Shall brush my wing.

Precluding and hence overriding the possibility of this sequence
is the typographical and logical convention in Blake criticism that
insists on a reproduction of the relevant plate accompanied by a
full quotation within the critical text of what thereby becomes the
lyric. Subject to principles of publishing economics as they allow
only short 'lyrics' to be quoted in full, this convention is especially
powerful in criticism of *Songs of Innocence and of Experience*; indeed,
Wagenknecht and Pagliaro both rely on this convention.

The imperative that drives this process of abstracting 'a poem'
from Blake's texts is the institutional necessity of casting them as
fundamentally literary. Despite the Urizenic implications of this
process, which recent work on the ideological possibilities of Blake's
printing process serves to emphasise, much criticism, including to a
large extent this essay, continues to take its cues about the ideology
of the graphic text from the linguistic text.[11] What accordingly
licenses the customary vertical reading of 'The Fly' is the purely
linguistic version of its text featured in the 'Notebook' and more
closely resembling the familiar poem produced by a vertical reading
than it does the horizontal sequence just presented. But only if we
ignore the intertext of revisionary codes and graphic protocols
separating as well as conjoining the 'Notebook' and the *Songs
of Experience* can we allow the text of the 'Notebook' to authorise
the precise typography of 'The Fly' in the *Songs*. To allow the
'Notebook' to write the *Songs* themselves, by arguing that the
'draft' in the 'Notebook' is more similar to the accepted version
of the poem in the *Songs* than it is to the horizontal version of the
poem, is also to ignore the considerable differences that still obtain
between the draft and the accepted version of the 'finished' poem.

In a sense, this vertical reading is more sensitive to the graphic
text than is the suggested horizontal reading. To read vertically may
well be to confer a literary authority on the 'Notebook', but it is
also to accommodate that authority to the exigencies of the graphic

image by supposing that the sequence of the lyric is determined, or at least indicated, by the boughs of the two trees as they separate the stanzas horizontally, but allow a space for vertical access between them. There are, however, other plates in *Songs of Experience* in which the branches of trees intervene between stanzas without punctuating the reading sequence so stringently. In 'The Tyger', for instance, branches figure on a horizontal axis without apparently arresting the reading. Understanding 'The Fly' as though its sequence is signaled arboreally presupposes a particular relation between linguistic and graphic text whereby the former is harmoniously framed by the latter; the lyric effectively doubles as the foliage of the trees.[12] Although this graphic profile of the linguistic text is sanctioned by the conventional pun on 'leaves', since the term refers to both foliage and pages, there is a signal alternative. Instead of figuring as blooms or leaves and so forming a composite with the graphics, the lyric of 'The Fly' might be seen as a displaced skywriting hovering around those graphics with a spatial uncertainty matching the logical indeterminacy of its relation to them.

The significance of a horizontal reading of 'The Fly' is that it stages the space between stanzas as a place for the reader-in-the-text who must arbitrate the lyric's sequence. That the stanzas themselves do not lexically resist either of these formal possibilities consolidates the power and responsibility of this reader. The main difference a horizontal configuration of the lyric produces within its plot is a more tentative identification between narrator and fly than that proposed by a vertical reading. While this usually-supposed vertical arrangement asks the questions

> Am not I
> A fly like thee?
> Or art not thou
> A man like me?

immediately after the contact between the fly and the thoughtless hand, the horizontal format prefaces these questions with hypothetical conditions that thus seem to limit the assertiveness of the questions and their implication of an identity. If one of these readings is any more plausible than the other, it seems to me that the horizontal sequence produces a lyric that avoids the problematic transition from the stanza beginning 'If thought is life' to the one beginning 'Then am I/A happy fly' that many critics consider the most difficult part of the poem.[13]

What licenses the whole focus throughout this essay on matters of grammar is, as already implied, the genre of the chapbook. Like

earlier instances of this genre, Blake's *Songs* seems to offer itself as
an occasion for the development of reading competence at the same
time as it works to inculcate morals. How the *Songs* in turn differs
from, say, Isaac Watts's *Divine Songs* or Mrs Barbauld's *Hymns in
Prose for Children* is not by proposing morals more heterodox than
those of these earlier works, but by providing a grammar that
reflects back conventional moral judgements so that they become
questions about the first person ethics of delivering such moral
pronouncements. Since 'The Fly', specifically, supplies a grammar
that can accommodate a presumption of the narrator's innocence,
as well as a presumption of his guilt, any judgement that does not
recognise its grounding on a mere presumption, whichever way
the judgement may ultimately incline, is more destructive than the
act that it evaluates. To presume that the narrator is unequivocally
innocent is more destructive than the narrator's action, not only
because the narrator is, in this scenario, innocent, but also because
this scenario is based on an aggressive suppression of any equivo-
cation about this innocence. To presume that the narrator is guilty,
however, is more destructive than the guilty action itself because
it is a presumption that claims to be predicated on a position of
knowledge even as it ignores any contra-indications in the grammar.
Although an inclination towards either presumption is thus potentially damaging, I have weighted my reading of the poem towards
an assumption of innocence because previous critical accounts have
inclined towards the opposing premise.

It is not only the poem's grammar that provides a critical perspective on efforts to read it. The format of the children's chapbook
also offers a standpoint beyond the text that allows this very standpoint to be observed as it collapses into the poem. By projecting for
itself two readers, a child and an adult, the chapbook allows for a
reading persona able to observe itself because it is composed of two
parts. In this image of a reading persona, just as an adult oversees
the difficulties a child might be expected to encounter in construing
the text and interpreting the moral, so any difficulties that this adult
might confront in this moral grammar are monitored by the child.
Each of these reading positions seems to watch the other becoming
absorbed into the text. While projected by the genre of the children's
chapbook, this scenario of mutual scrutiny is also depicted in the
graphic in the intersecting gazes of the woman and child. Since to
read the poem is also to watch oneself reading, because of the mutual
monitoring implied by the chapbook's pedagogy, whereby child
and adult observe one another's reading practices, the educational
process can become a two-way street in which experience is not
only taught to the child by the adult, but innocence is reciprocally

conveyed to the adult by the child. Enabled to watch ourselves reading the poem, we need not gain our experience of the text at a cost borne by the fly and the narrator. Subject to an invigilation from the perspective of innocence, the reading experience can avoid guilt by allowing the fly to survive and by consequently exonerating the narrator.

Whether this adult reader of Blake's *Songs* is understood as an agent mediating between a real chapbook and a juvenile narrator or as the ultimate destination of a chapbook that is childless because a parody of the genre, these are questions that do not affect the *Songs'* figuring of a dual readership. Either way, this text affords a critical perspective on how it is read by implying, parodically or otherwise, this dual audience. It is, moreover, this inherent faculty of self-monitoring that prevents such a model of reading from immediately resembling those other critical readings, castigated above, that seek to empower themselves over the text. None of my argument is to imply, of course, that the poem cannot be read, as it has tended to be, so that a costly experience, rather than innocence, is what the narrator and reader exchange between themselves. My own reading is not concerned to disqualify other readings, but rather to indicate their cost. Just as the art of lying seems to be taught in both directions, from adult to child and vice versa, in Wordsworth's 'Anecdote for Fathers', so the exchanges between reader and narrator in 'The Fly' could, as other criticism of the poem has shown, be a traffic in mutually destructive and self-destructive experience. Once the question 'Whodunit?' is posed about events in 'The Fly', however, the versatile grammar of the poem and the self-monitoring reading persona offered by the form of the chapbook answer this question with another: 'Who *didn't?*'

Notes

1. See HAROLD PAGLIARO (pp. 77–81), HAROLD BLOOM (pp. 19–20), and DAVID WAGENKNECHT (106–10).

2. William Blake, *The Complete Poetry and Prose of William Blake* (23). All subsequent quotations from Blake's works will be taken from this edition, and the references to that edition will be found in this text.

3. STANLEY GARDNER (pp. 128–29) insists that the poem must be read at least twice, as a matter of empirical necessity, in order to be apprehended at all.

4. This poem, with its own syntactic versatility, immediately precedes 'The Fly' in the sequence of *Songs of Experience* in at least some of the copies that Blake produced.

5. The evidence for Blake's possession of a copy of *Chapman's Homer*, and for which existing copy is the likeliest candidate, is weighed by ROBERT N. ESSICK, 'William Blake's copy of Chapman's Homer'.

6. ANNE KOSTELANETZ MELLOR effectively endorses Hirsch's reading. See especially 334.

7. See especially Hirsch's castigation of Blake (pp. 204–41).

8. Of all the criticism devoted to *Songs of Innocence and of Experience* it is ZACHARY LEADER's that makes the strongest case for these texts as versions, often parodic, of the chapbook. See especially Leader's historical account of children's literature (pp. 1–36).

9. Essick also reads a distinction between these two questions (*William Blake* pp. 128–29).

10. The *Book of Urizen* is another text, exceptionally among Blake's works, that exploits the format of dual columns.

11. STEPHEN LEO CARR's argument would probably gloss the construction of a largely literary Blake as an effort to deny Blake's project of difference which is prosecuted by the incessant variations among copies of the printed plates. According to Carr, the graphical aspects of Blake's texts and the printing process by which they are produced, multiply these differences massively. The contrast between engraving, as practiced by Blake, and letterpress printing is outlined by MORRIS EAVES (pp. 186–90).

12. It is this general presupposition of a harmony between text and design that W. J. T. MITCHELL resists (pp. 57–81). This is a resistance to which I happily subscribe.

13. See JOHN E. GRANT (p. 42). The difficulties that JEAN HAGSTRUM (p. 380) locates in the poem's final stanza seem actually to devolve onto the relations between this stanza and the penultimate one.

Works Cited

BLAKE, WILLIAM *The Complete Poetry and Prose of William Blake* Rev. edn Ed. David V. Erdman (Berkeley: University of California Press, 1982).

BLOOM, HAROLD Introduction, *William Blake's Songs of Innocence and of Experience* Ed. Harold Bloom (New York: Chelsea House, 1987).

CARR, STEPHEN LEO 'Illuminated Printing: Toward a Logic of Difference' *Unnam'd Forms: Blake and Textuality* Ed. Nelson Hilton and Thomas A. Vogler (Berkeley: University of California Press, 1986).

Chapman's Homer: The Iliad, the Odyssey and the Lesser Homerica Ed. Allardyce Nicoll. vol. 1. Bollingen Ser. XLI (New York: Pantheon, 1956).

DONNE, JOHN *Poetical Works* Ed. Herbert J. C. Grierson. 1971 (Oxford: Oxford University Press, 1977).

EAVES, MORRIS *The Counter-arts Conspiracy: Art and Industry in the Age of Blake* (Ithaca: Cornell University Press, 1992).

EDGEWORTH, MARIA *Harry and Lucy Concluded; being the Last Part of Early Lessons,* vol. 1. 2nd edn (London: Printed for R. Hunter *et al.,* 1827).

ESSICK, ROBERT N. *William Blake and the Language of Adam* (Oxford: Clarendon Press, 1989).

—— 'William Blake's copy of Chapman's Homer' *English Language Notes* 27.3 (1990): pp. 27–33.

William Blake

GARDNER, STANLEY *Blake's 'Innocence and Experience' Retraced* (London: Athlone: St Martin's, 1986).

GILLHAM, D. C. *Blake's Contrary States: The 'Songs of Innocence and of Experience' as Dramatic Poems* (Cambridge: Cambridge University Press, 1966).

GRANT, JOHN E. 'Interpreting Blake's "The Fly"'. *Blake: a Collection of Critical Essays*, Ed. Northrop Frye (Englewood Cliffs: Prentice-Hall, 1966).

HAGSTRUM, JEAN 'The Fly'. *William Blake: Essays for S. Foster Damon*, Ed. Alvin H. Rosenfeld (Providence: Brown University Press, 1969).

HIRSCH, E. D., JR *Innocence and Experience: An Introduction to Blake* (New Haven: Yale University Press, 1964).

HOMER *The Iliad* Trans. Alexander Pope (London: George Bell and Sons, 1881).

LEADER, ZACHARY *Reading Blake's Songs* (Boston: Routledge and Kegan Paul, 1981).

MELLOR, ANNE KOSTELANETZ *Blake's Human Form Divine* (Berkeley: University of California Press, 1974).

MITCHELL, W. J. T. 'Blake's Composite Art'. *Blake's Visionary Forms Dramatic* Ed. David V. Erdman and John E. Grant (Princeton: Princeton University Press, 1970).

NEWBERY, JOHN *A Little Pretty Pocket-Book* Facs. with an intro. and bib. by M. F. Thwaite (London: Oxford University Press, 1966).

OLDYS, WILLIAM 'On a Fly Drinking From His Cup'. *The Oxford Anthology of English Poetry*. vol. 1. Ed. John Wain (Oxford: Oxford University Press, 1990) p. 525.

PAGLIARO, HAROLD *Selfhood and Redemption in Blake's 'Songs'* (University Park: Pennsylvania State University Press, 1987).

SHAKESPEARE, WILLIAM *King Lear* Ed. Kenneth Muir. 1964 (London: Methuen, 1978).

SLOANE, WILLIAM *Children's Books in England and America in the Seventeenth Century: A History and Checklist* (New York: Columbia University Press, 1955).

WAGENKNECHT, DAVID *Blake's Night: William Blake and the Idea of Pastoral.* (Cambridge: The Bellknap Press of Harvard University Press, 1973).

WAIN, JOHN Ed. *The Oxford Anthology of English Poetry*. vol. 1 (Oxford: Oxford University Press, 1990).

12   Blake's *Songs of Innocence and Experience*

MATT SIMPSON

Few people read *Songs of Innocence and Experience* in ways the poet intended. Most encounters with the poems, one may safely assume, will be through reading anthologised selections in black-on-white print. Anthologies revere the individual poem, sell uniqueness: in disengaging poems from their primary contexts (and here I particularly mean poems that were intended to belong together, not just symbiotically but as it were ecologically, in clusters or sequences) they may be said to be selling dismemberments: readers are denied the experience of knowing how a whole (cluster, sequence) can prove to be considerably greater than the sum of its parts. One thing Blake is clearly demanding is that we experience *Songs of Innocence and Experience* in a three-dimensional way and know them – in the manner in which they energise and activate one another – as something, not just intellectually challenging, but rich and strange, vigorously alive at the point of reading – in a word, as visionary.

E. P. Thompson talks wisely of 'that universe of Blakean symbolism in which we must turn from one poem to another for cumulative elucidation', warning us that in the process we 'must be prepared for seventeen types of ambiguity'.[1] Of course we all know that elucidating Blake has risks attached to it, principally of turning the commentator into one of those 'ghastly, obscene knowers' that Lawrence in his essay on Poe accused Blake himself of being: scholarly code-breakers found to be wearing yet another one of the masks of Urizen. Thompson again:

> There was . . . an incandescence in his art in which incompatible traditions met – tried to marry – argued as contraries – were held in a polarised tension. If one may be wrong to look for a coherent intellectual system, there are certainly constellations of related attitudes and images – connected insights – but the moment when we attempt a rational exegesis we are imposing bounds on these insights.

The most common and most serious form of amputation is the practice of ignoring the pictorial contexts Blake provided for the poems. In some instances – if we only know poems from black-on-white sources – illustration may come as a surprise, may even contradict meanings we have in our memory banks. A case in point may be the illustration to *The Tyger* which shows nothing cosmically fiercesome but rather a cuddly nursery-wallpaper creature (couldn't Blake draw tigers? or is there something else here to puzzle the will?). Or, again, take the poem *Infant Joy* (to be considered in detail later) in which two voices are heard speaking. With no knowledge of Blake's engraving we might assume that the voices are those of parent and child, whereas the picture gives us a third figure (that of a fairy/angel) much more likely in the context to be the voice answering the child. Likewise *Infant Sorrow*, as soliloquy, might lead us to expect a single-figure illustration, whereas what Blake gives us is an angry-faced woman attempting to lift a child dodging away from her extended arms.

A dimension that will always be missing is one that almost goes without saying, namely the musical settings Blake is reported to have composed for his songs, so that they were literally songs and not as we see them *Songs*. In other words, they belong to the voice as well as to the page, as the work of composers like Vaughan Williams and Britten who have made Blake settings can testify – though it may be considered that such settings, as beautiful as they undoubtedly are, claim Blake's words for high or polite art as opposed to the popular tradition they spring out of. Grierson's 'a good song, even if set to no music and read in silence, still sings and dances in the reader's brain'[2] is a modern consolation and a hope. Nurmi tells us Blake's

> . . . composition of poetry during the early period was accompanied, evidently, by musical composition in the form of melodies to which he is said to have sung his songs – which as a contemporary J. T. Smith said were 'sometimes most singularly beautiful and were noted down by musical professors'. Whether he actually composed music for all of his songs simultaneously with writing the words, as an early biographical sketch (by Cunningham) suggests, his lyrics are singable, as is shown by the very large number of musical settings of them by contemporary composers.[3]

The pity of course is that the *Songs* are no longer singable in Blake's settings. What one wouldn't give for the jottings of those 'musical professors'. Or, like Ginsberg, to be visited in a vision by Blake and have the songs sung to one.

So we are condemned to partial readings. Even if some readings are less partial than others, partiality leads us into a variety of traps, many of which (some grow in the human brain) are self-constructed or constructed according to fashion. For example, conventional wisdom in our sceptical, iconoclastic age will say that *Songs of Experience* are 'greater', 'profounder' than *Songs of Innocence* – or, put the other way round, that *Songs of Innocence* are 'slighter' (naive, simplistic) and that some negative experience in Blake's life – perhaps the such-a-flower of Mary Wollstonecraft . . . Thompson suggests that it's Blake 'renewing his earlier interest in Behmenist (and perhaps Muggletonian) thought' – made him produce a more 'disillusioned' (less deceived) and 'deeper' poetry. Numbers of readers would doubtless go along with Margaret Bottrall when she describes the *Songs of Innocence and Experience* as being 'utterly free from literary affectation and from moral attitudinising'[4] and as acting 'on us with the immediacy of a scent or a melody', but there are those who would perhaps feel that such words apply to *Songs of Innocence* merely. What they need reminding of is 'the universe of Blakean symbolism' (Thompson) and that

> By publishing the two sets of songs together, Blake tried to make it impossible for anyone to react sentimentally to either set. Whoever wished to babble over the natural sweetness and happiness of childhood would be reminded by Songs of Experience that childhood was by no means sweet and that happiness was against Nature . . . On the other hand, social reformers who might wish to use the Songs of Experience to beat Church and State would be reminded by Songs of Innocence that human perfection never arises from material well-being, but only from spiritual strength.[5]

(As a gloss on the 'against Nature' of the above extract, let us remind ourselves of Blake on Wordsworth: 'I see in Wordsworth the Natural Man rising up against the Spiritual Man Continually, & then he is No Poet, but a Heathen Philosopher at Enmity against all true Poetry or Inspiration . . . Natural Objects did & now do weaken, deaden and obliterate Imagination in Me. Wordsworth must know that what he writes Valuable is not to be found in Nature.')

It is now generally accepted that the poems of Innocence and those of Experience have such a structurally unified force, explicitly stating an intention to show 'two contrary states of the human soul', the consequence of which is that our commitment to a view that Joy is 'just as' 'profound' as Sorrow becomes an imperative, a *sine qua non*: it is this that provides us with the possibilities for that three-dimensional reading I mentioned at the start: but, more than that,

191

it is concerned (in Thompson's words) with 'an unrealised potential, an alternative nature, within man: a nature masked by circumstance, repressed by the Moral Law, concealed by Mystery and self-defeated by the other nature of "self-love"'. *The Clod and the Pebble* with its beautiful and fearful symmetry insists that we weigh the selfless love (of Innocence) and the selfish love (of Experience) in equal scales in a poem that, like so many of the others, lives in a stasis or perfect tension between opposites. In the end, of course, what is being weighed in the poems is the degree of innocence/experience each one of us individually is marked with or can lay claim to – in other words, where exactly we come in the scale that runs in a continuous line from innocence to experience. A test of this may be to try reading *A Laughing Song* out loud and confronting the question of how one approaches and renders 'ha, ha, he!' And while we are at it, let's ask whether you can/cannot call a poem like this 'profound'. Or whether the children in *Infant Joy* and *Infant Sorrow* aren't – in the archetypal sense – the same child.

Did he who made the Lamb make thee?

Though rendered in the language and imagery of pastoral, Innocence does not inhabit an idyllic country. It is born into, and has to exist in, the postlapsarian world of Experience, a world which is continually at pains to corrupt and exploit it. Its vulnerability requires it to be watched over by protectors, a whole range of whom we find at work in the poems. In *Infant Joy* the fairy baptismally names the child and confers blessings ('Bless relaxes') on it; a mother holds the child (as does a mother in the illustration to *Spring*) on her lap. However, the blessing 'Sweet Joy befall thee!' is as much subjunctive in mood as it is imperative and the intention to 'sing the while', with its unequivocal indication of duration, alerts us to the fact that beneath surface solicitudes a sub-text of anxiety is to be read. Though Innocence is a state of soul belonging to eternity, it is, in the temporal and sensual world, in need of protectors and redeemers. Blake, I repeat, is no sentimentalist. Innocence is not to be automatically equated with babyhood nor the time of chronometers ('The hours of folly are measur'd by the clock; but of wisdom no clock can measure'): *Infant Sorrow* allows for the possibility of entering this life without trailing clouds of glory. In this particular poem we are awesome witnesses of a child directly entering the world of Experience at the point of birth and recognising in doing so that its world is associated with pain, sorrow, resentment. In among the realities of fallen things Innocence is corruptible; it is

also redeemable ('The death of Jesus set me free'), for 'except ye
be as one of these, my little ones, ye shall not enter the kingdom of
Heaven'. Then and only then, when all the contraries are reconciled,
will 'the lion lie down with the lamb and a little child shall lead
them' and so journeying beyond the marriage of Heaven and Hell
we are able to enter an inspired state of full light. From Innocence
to Experience is part of the process, for 'without Contraries is no
progression': the fourfold vision requires the reconciling of body,
reason, emotion and spirit.

> Now I a fourfold vision see
> And a fourfold vision is given to me.
> 'Tis fourfold in my supreme delight
> And threefold in soft Beulah's night
> And twofold Always. May God us keep
> From Single vision & Newton's sleep.[6]

What *Songs of Innocence and Experience* in conjunction make possible is the dialectics from which the Energy of Eternal Delight is
released. But until then, Innocence needs to be watched over and
guided, not by regulations, but by wisdom and prophecy and
by selfless ('The most sublime act is to set another before you')
protector figures: angels, fairies, stars, the moon, shepherds, fathers
(though fathers come off badly in this role more often than not),
mothers, nurses, the chimney sweeper that consoles Tom Dacre,
the little black boy who, innocent of the irony, has him offering
to protect and comfort his white (slave-owning?) brother, the glow-
worm guiding the lost emmet back to her fretting family – in fact
all those who, through selfless love and the spontaneous exercise
of mercy, pity, peace, are truly Christ-like in their joys and desires
('Jesus was all virtue, and acted from impulse, not from rules').
It is such figures whose joy not only impregnates but amplifies
until all nature is gathered up in an act of universal rejoicing: hills
echo, green fields laugh, dimpling streams run laughing by and
'Exuberance is Beauty'.

But night must fall and the tiger-spirit of predatoriness be loosed
upon the universe. If Innocence is associated with pastoral then that
may be said to be its glimpse of eternity, a glimpse which poems
hold in perfect stasis. The world of Experience is the empire of
predators and exploiters, a place where the soul may lose itself
among tangled ways, beset by doubts, perplexities, obscured and
mystified by clouds of reason; where it may be perverted, regi-
mented, restrained, regulated by the Thou-Shalt-Nots of the Moral

William Blake

Law of an institutionalised system ruled over by the many clones
of Urizen; where Albion is 'chartered' by aged ignorance (but
where the New Jerusalem may be built . . . Thompson mentions 'the
millenarian effervescence in London throughout the 1790s and into
the next decade'); where the horses of instruction, Dame Lurch,
priests in black gowns, an envious and bilious nurse, beadles, wise
guardians of the poor, mothers and fathers who neglect, curse, sell
their children into servitude, the king himself, all prowl the dark
night of the world's soul. The hand that brushes away the fly, the
maiden queen who *uses* her virginity to resist her angel, the invisible
worm that invades the sexual heart of the rose, thorns, threatening
horns, the pebble warbling in meters of selfish love, harlots, rose
trees turning away – all create, build a Hell in Heaven's despite,
all inhabit Urizen's realm of secrecy, cruelty, jealousy and terror:
the human brain where snares are knit and manacles forged.

> He who binds to himself a joy,
> Does the winged life destroy;
> But he who kisses the joy as it flies
> Lives in eternity's sun rise.

The figures inhabiting the *Songs of Experience* tend to cling to the
earth in attitudes of sorrow – huddling, kneeling, stooping or, as
in *A Poison Tree*, lying flat on the ground. In *Songs of Innocence* the
figures are normally upright or seated, with children dancing or at
rest in the laps of their mothers; a sense of sharing, of community
is usually emphasised or implied. In *Infant Joy* mother, child and
fairy are raised up off the ground in the cup of a deep red flower,
the petals of which curl and swirl like flames (clearly not infernal).
In the left-hand side of the flower the mother, dressed in lime-
green,[7] holding a naked child is seated and the flame-like blood-red
petals arch protectively over their heads, while on the right-hand
side stands the fairy, dressed in yellow, facing them with the petals
behind leaping up in a flaming aspiration heavenwards. In addition,
the plant circling the words of the poem has, bottom right, a bud
that droops towards the earth as if trying to resist its gravitational
pull. The illustration is a potent fusion of stillness (the figures look
beatific) and fierce energy in the upward swirling dance of the
flower. But it is obvious too that Blake wants us to understand that,
because it exists in the world of time, Innocence is no absolute state:
it is rather poised at the start of life's journey; and in the tension
that's also there between flower and drooping bud to see failure,
shame, sorrow adumbrated.

194

In *Infant Sorrow*, instead of openness to sky, we find enclosed space, a claustrophobic bedroom containing yet further enclosed space – a curtained bed of conception/birth heavily draped in sickly green. A grim-faced mob-capped woman, in a full blood-red gown that seems to flow downwards into the carpet – a carpet that has an ironic suggestion of flowers – holds out her arms to a naked child that squirms, on its own separate bed, away from her. A refusal is depicted. The child holds up its arms as if begging heaven's assistance but the room is curtained, carpeted, ceilinged and windowless so that the child's supplication looks as though it has nowhere to go. Again, the figures are caught in a stasis but there is a disjunction between the child's words (the poem) and what is going on in the picture: there is a deliberate paralleling of planes of meaning rather than a harmonising.

Songs of Innocence tend on the whole to be *dynamic* – in the sense that active communication takes place (paradoxically it does not always have to be spoken); different voices are registered; often (though not always) inverted commas are used; people speak and listen: the shepherd hears the lambs' innocent calls, the ewes' tender replies; parents are heard communicating their wisdoms (in equations that obey a poetic rather than ratiocinative logic); and children (as in *The Little Black Boy* or *The Lamb*) cannot contain their enthusiasm, can't wait to share ('Little Lamb I'll tell thee/Little Lamb I'll tell thee') with those around them. In this way joy is broadcast, amplified, so that all the hills echo. In some of the poems a public voice, often tinged with ironies, is heard in a rhetoric that requires no answer; and sometimes a prophetic voice calls to those who would listen.

In *Songs of Experience* we are frequently involved in monologue or soliloquy: dynamic communication is replaced by thought-out statement-making. In *Infant Sorrow* we hear a cerebral click of cogs as the child's *brain* formulates its tactical decision:

> I thought best
> To sulk. . . . .

Likewise, in *A Poison Tree*, repressed emotion (wrath) leads to a hothouse cultivation of wiles and guile: the foe, himself infected by deceit, sees the apple:

> And he *knew* that it was mine.

The Clod and the Pebble sing their opposing songs in tandem but alone (i.e. not communicating with each other); and there is deliberateness in the Pebble's warbling of metres meet (polished and polite literature) when compared with the simple 'sang' of the Clod. The 'Introduction' to *Songs of Innocence* is artlessly spontaneous in its piping/singing and its unpolished repetitions and dynamic communication is taking place between child and piper . . . though we cannot fail to note that the water has to be stained if the poems are to be written down and exist in the fallen world. At the beginning of 'Songs of Experience' however Bardic Voice and the eventual Answer to its summons are significantly split into discrete (schizophrenic?) poems, into, as it were, a 'communication' of refusal and defeat.

In other poems in *Songs of Experience* two voices are sometimes heard, as in *A Little Boy Lost* or *The Chimney Sweeper*, but there is no apparent interaction; and there are others in which their subjects (as in *The Sick Rose*, *The Fly*, *The Tyger*) are apostrophised but given no voice ('the tongue stuck in my jaw') with which to reply. *The Tyger* is a prime example not only of this (what would the tyger say by way of answer?) but also of a poem of stasis, one that may be said to exist in the moment of recognition only, the timeless moment in time when the eyes of the hunted and hunter meet (who is hunting whom?), the instant of eternity between *pounce* and *shot*; it is also the stasis of question where no answer can be given. 'Opposition is true Friendship'.

Of *Infant Joy*'s fifty words, forty-six are monosyllables. The poem is 'artlessly' constructed of repeated words and phrases, entirely child-like (Innocent) in character and, aside from the subtext of anxiety mentioned earlier, the reader is involved in an exuberance ('Exuberance is Beauty', 'Energy is Eternal Delight') of 'happy'/'Joy'/'sweet'/ 'pretty' and in the Zen-like 'logic' of Joy = happiness = child = child's name = universal rejoicing. The same 'logic' occurs in 'The Lamb':

> He is called by thy name,
> For he calls himself a Lamb.
> He is meek, & he is mild;
> He became a little child.
> I, a child, & thou a lamb,
> We are called by his name.

or in *The Little Black Boy*:

> Thus did my mother say, and kissed me;
> And thus I say to little English boy:
> When I from black and he from white cloud free,
> And round the tent of God like lambs we joy,

I'll shade him from the heat, till he can bear
To lean in joy upon our father's knee;
And then I'll stand and stroke his silver hair,
And be like him, and he will then love me.

Thus in visionary dialectics an alternative mode of thinking/
perceiving is brought into action; the mindscape is different from
that in which Baconian/Newtonian/Lockean reason operates. As
Peter Marshall has said 'Blake was convinced that their mechanical
philosophy made the cardinal error of separating the perceiving
mind from the object of perception, the observer from the observed'.[8]
It is no surprise to see Blake entering as an influence into poetry at
the time of the Beats. And it is not difficult, in subsequent reactions
– and I refer to political swings to the Right here – to see Urizen as
having regained most of the ground.

In contrast to 'Infant Joy', 'Infant Sorrow' is a *knowing* poem.
It expresses a wilful consciousness in the I-thought-best of its solil-
oquist, in the intentionality of 'sulk' and 'leapt', and in the knowing-
ness of its allusiveness both biblical and classical (the suggestiveness
of 'swaddling bands' is obvious; 'bound and weary', among other
things, brings both Prometheus and Adam – Adam lay ybounden –
to mind). The poem is a powerful manifesto, as meticulously worded
as most manifestoes are, of a delinquency ready to take on the
world and turning its own weaknesses – helplessness, nakedness,
piping loud – into awesome weapons. In Frye's words, 'a little
bundle of anarchic will, whose desires take no account of either
the social or the natural order'.[9] Or Bowra's, who wrote of this
poem that it 'shows that even in the beginnings of childhood there
is the spirit of unrest and revolt . . . At the start of its existence the
human creature feels itself a prisoner and, after its first efforts to
resist, angrily gives up the struggle'.[10] Yes, that is, of course, if we
divorce it from the other human potential declared in *Infant Joy* and
if we read the poem as suggesting an end in resignation and defeat.
If there is any submission here it is merely a tactical one:

> I thought best
> To sulk upon my mother's breast.

'Sulk' is a potent (largely the result of one of the most stupendous
enjambements in English poetry) and danger-filled word; the child
is wilfully, craftily biding its time (cf. the 'sing a while' of *Infant
Joy*), just ticking away like a time bomb. The drooping bud of
'Infant Joy' is breeding a whole colony of invisible worms.

I talked earlier of Blake's demand that we read his poems three-dimensionally, which statement I then had to countradict by saying that we are all condemned to the experience of partial reading, with some readings being less (or more) partial than others; I further suggested that an ability to read Blake aright (impossible . . . but, as Eliot says, 'For us there is only the trying') was a measure of where we are on the Innocence/Experience scale (Blake's evangelical purpose is to make us do exactly that and, beyond that, to liberate the 'unrealised potential, an alternative nature, within man'). There are times when we are – like Blake with the tyger – stuck with questions, having to realise that the greater wisdom lies with them. Blake may not know what the tyger is, nor who made it; but he can register his perception that something is awesomely *there* prowling (even to the point of being a prophecy of nuclear power) the universe – the truth of the poem lying in this recognition and so, in this sense, falling in line with Lowell's dictum that 'a poem is an event and not the record of an event'.

Of course it is not fruitless to ask what, in that perfect miniature, *The Sick Rose*, the rose represents, nor what its sickness consists in, what the worm represents, why it is invisible, what the relationship is between worm and rose, worm and howling night, etc. As Thompson tells us, Blakean symbolism is a whole universe of meanings ('One thought fills immensity'). The rose is the sum total of all the meanings we can ascribe to it, even meanings that are contradictory, from England to royalty to something infected with venereal disease to anything subject to mortality to a real-life actual rose-is-a-rose-is-a-rose, and on. . . . As an event, we experience the poem through its formal and rhythmical energies as well as through our apprehension of 'meanings' – the latter serviced by, among other things, the accumulation of meanings that we have stored in our memory banks from readings of the other poems. I want to read the opening line of 'The Sick Rose' as containing five heavy stresses, as if an incontrovertible statement of truth is being declared in the Bardic/prophetic mode: five monosyllables followed by a three-word line with two stresses, so that line two has suddenly speeded up, the invisible worm has started on its secret, deadly-earnest mission. We don't see the worm but we hear the swish of its wings as it speeds on through the next two lines, its unstoppably onward movement guaranteed by the regular pulse of stresses in '*inv*isible', '*flies*' '*howl*ing'. Then comes that extraordinary gap between verses that tells us that the worm has landed, arrived on target – the moment of alighting preceded by a momentous silence – by re-establishing the five heavy stresses of line one and also the Bardic intonation. In the two stresses of the line that follows

Of *crim*son *joy*

penetration has been effected; and in the last two lines the poisons begin the process of infiltration into the substance of the rose. The way that the stress falls on 'love' in line seven is masterly . . . a totally shocking word unexpected after 'dark' and 'secret', one that requires a startling reevaluation of our assumptions and expectations. The poem is a love poem! The relationship of rose to worm is one of love! ('Opposition is true Friendship'). Does love destroy then? Is the relationship, say, between Othello and Iago 'truer' than Othello's relationship with Desdemona? Are worm and rose necessary to each other's existence? Aren't we all involved in a test to destruction?

> The crow wish'd everything was black, the owl that everything was white.
>
> Without contraries is no progression. Attraction and Repulsion, Reason and Energy, Love and Hate, are necessary to Human Existence.
>
> From these contraries spring what the religious call Good and Evil. Good is the passive that obeys Reason. Evil is the active springing from Energy.
>
> Good is Heaven. Evil is Hell.

So Blake wrote famously in *The Marriage of Heaven and Hell*. And in *The Clod and the Pebble* we find Heaven and Hell held in a perfect either-or counterpoise: the selfless love of the Clod 'builds a Heaven in Hell's despair' while the selfish love of the Pebble 'builds a Hell in Heaven's despite'. This is fearful symmetry; this is the stasis of the traveller transfixed by a signpost . . . one at which History itself is – eternally – poised.

A tombstone, resting flat on the ground in an old Liverpool churchyard, carries the following inscription:

> Stranger, passing by,
> Pause awhile and think
> That I am in Eternity
> And you are on the brink.

As we take our quick step back from that self-righteous Victorian piety we might just perhaps let these lines from 'Auguries of Innocence' flick through our minds:

> He who mocks the infant's faith
> Shall be mocked in Age and Death.
> He who shall teach the child to doubt
> The rotting grave shall ne'er get out.
> He who respects the infant's faith
> Triumphs over Hell and Death.

Notes

1. E. P. THOMPSON *Witness Against the Beast William Blake and the Moral Law* (Cambridge: 1993).

2. H. J. C. GRIERSON *Lyric Poetry from Blake to Hardy*, 1928 quoted in *Vision and Verse in William Blake* see below.

3. MARTIN K. NURMI *William Blake* (Hutchinson, 1975).

4. MARGARET BOTTRALL Introduction to *Songs of Innocence and Experience Casebook Series* (Macmillan, 1969).

5. ALICIA OSTRIKER *Vision and Verse in William Blake* (University of Wisconsin, 1965).

6. See JOHN BEER's *Blake's Humanism* (Manchester: 1968) which gives the following account of Blake's four levels of vision:

   (i) State of Darkness (Ulro) in which unilluminated Reason alone holds sway.
   (ii) State of Fire – energy freely exercised – creative artist or lover – later called Generation. Symbol – the destructive sun.
   (iii) State of Light (paradise) – Beulah (= married). Here Heaven and Hell are 'married'. The sexual lover can give a brief revelation of the eternal light that belongs to the state of full vision. Symbol – the moon.
   (iv) The state of full Light and Vision which reconciles all the others. Recaptured rarely by the genius in his moments of full inspiration.

7. I am using the illustrations to be found in *William Blake Songs of Innocence and Experience* introduction by Sir Geoffrey Keynes in association with the Trianon Press Oxford 1990.

8. PETER MARSHALL *William Blake Visionary Anarchist* (Freedom Press, 1988).

9. NORTHROP FRYE *Blake's Treatment of Archetypes* in *English Romantic Poets – Modern Essays in Criticism* ed. M. H. ABRAMS (Oxford: 1975).

10. C. M. BOWRA *Songs of Innocence and Experience* in *Songs of Innocence and Experience Casebook Series* ed. MARGARET BOTTRALL (Macmillan, 1969).

Notes on Authors

JOHN BARRELL is Professor of English at the University of York and the author of several books, including *The Idea of Landscape and the Sense of Place, 1730–1840: An Approach to the Poetry of John Clare* (1972); *The Dark Side of the Landscape* (1980) and *The Political Theory of Painting From Reynolds to Hazlitt* (1986).

STEWART CREHAN is an American academic who has written widely on the Romantic period. His study *Blake in Context* was published in 1984.

DAVID ERDMAN is among the best-known of all Blake scholars. His classic work *Prophet Against Empire* has been continuously in print since its first appearance in 1954. He is also author of *A Concordance to the Writings of William Blake* (1967) and, with John E. Grant has edited *Blake's Visionary Forms Dramatic* (1970).

JOHN LUCAS is Research Professor of English at The Nottingham Trent University. Among his many books are studies of Dickens, Elizabeth Gaskell, Arnold Bennett and John Clare. In 1990 he published *England and Englishness: Ideas of Nationhood in English Poetry, 1688–1900*. He is the author of five volumes of poetry, most recently *One for the Piano* (1977).

SUSAN MATTHEWS is a lecturer in English at Roehampton Institute. She is the author of a number of articles on eighteenth-century and Romantic literature and is completing a full-length study of Blake.

JOHN MEE is author of *Dangerous Enthusiasm: William Blake and the Culture of Radicalism in the 1790s* (1992). After spending some years as a lecturer in the Department of English at the Australian National University he has now resumed academic life in England.

GERDA S. NORVIG teaches in the Department of English and Women's Studies at the University of Colorado. Her book *Dark Figures in the Desired Country: Blake's Illustrations to 'The Pilgrim's Progress'* was published in 1993. She is also the author of a number of articles on writers, including Blake.

KATHLEEN RAINE is a distinguished poet who has also made a lifetime's study of Blake. Among her books are *Blake and London* (1960); *Blake and Tradition* (1979) and *Blake and the New Age* (1979).

MATT SIMPSON lectures in the English Department at Liverpool Hope University College. He has published several important collections of poetry, including *An Elegy for the Galosherman: New and Selected Poems* (1990) and *Catching Up With History* (1995). *Cutting The Clouds Towards* is forthcoming.

MICHAEL SIMPSON is a visiting scholar in the Department of English at the University of Texas in Austin. He is the author of *Political Exhibition and Prohibition in the Dramas of Byron and Shelley*.

E. P. THOMPSON, who died in 1993, was and remains one of the twentieth-century's greatest social historians and writers. His works include *William Morris* (first published 1955, re-published in a revised edition as *William Morris:*

William Blake

Romantic to Revolutionary (1977)); *The Making of the English Working Class* (1963); *Whigs and Hunters* (1975); *Customs in Common* (1991) and *Witness Against the Beast: William Blake and the Moral Law* 1993. He is also author of a satire *The Skyros Papers* (1988) and, published posthumously, *Beyond the Frontier: The Politics of a Failed Mission, Bulgaria 1944* (1996), about the shameful killing of his brother, which was made possible by the collusion of Churchill's government with the gathering Cold War forces in Eastern Europe.

BRENDA S. WEBSTER is a freelance writer, critic and translator. She is the author of two critical works: *Yeats: A Psychoanalytic Study* (1972) and *Blake's Prophetic Psychology* (1983). In 1994 she published her first novel, *Sins of the Mothers*.

Further Reading

What might be called 'The Blake Industry', employing so many hands thirty years ago, has in recent years slowed down. There have been fewer books on him recently and those critics who have wished to apply some of the more fashionable theoretical approaches to his work have tended to confine themselves to essays. For this reason, I list below a number of collections in which what seem to me some of the more significant essay contributions have made their appearance.

Marxist Criticism (Including New Historicist Works)

This approach to Blake continues to thrive. Among the more important recent books are:

BUTLER, MARILYN *Romantics, Rebels and Reactionaries: English Literature and its Background, 1760–1830* (Oxford: Oxford University Press, 1981).

BUTLER, MARILYN (ed.) *Burke, Paine, Godwin and the Revolution Controversy* (Cambridge: Cambridge University Press, 1984). (Butler isn't strictly speaking a Marxist literary historian but she has always shown herself remarkably hospitable to Marxist approaches.)

GLEN, HEATHER *Vision and Disenchantment* (Cambridge: Cambridge University Press, 1980).

HALL, MARY *Materialism and the Myths of Blake* (London: Routledge, 1980).

LUCAS, JOHN *England and Englishness: Ideas of Nationhood in English Poetry, 1688–1900* (London: Chatto & Windus, 1990).

LUCAS, JOHN (ed.) *Writing and Radicalism* (London: Longman, 1996).

MCGANN, JEROME *Social Values and Poetic Acts: The Historical Judgement of Literary Work* (Cambridge, Mass: Yale University Press, 1988).

MEE, JOHN *Dangerous Enthusiasm: William Blake and the Culture of Radicalism in the 1790s* (Oxford: Oxford University Press, 1992).

PUNTER, DAVID *Blake, Hegel and Dialectic* (Amsterdam: Free Press, 1982).

THOMPSON, E. P. *Witness Against the Beast: William Blake and the Moral Law* (London: Merlin Press, 1993).

London in the Later Eighteenth Century

This subject is important enough to deserve a section to itself.

ALTICK, RICHARD *The Shows of London* (London: Yale, 1978). (While not exclusively about the relevant period, Altick's book has an invaluable section on the later eighteenth century.)

ERDMAN, DAVID *Blake: Prophet Against Empire* (Princeton: Princeton University Press, 1954). (I list Erdman here because he has such important things to say about London as well as Blake's 'London': but he could almost as easily have been included in the previous section.)

MCCALMAN, IAIN *Radical Underworld: Prophets, Revolutionaries and Pornographers in London, 1795–1840* (Cambridge: Cambridge University Press, 1988).

PALEY, MORTON D. *The Continuing City: William Blake's Jerusalem* (Oxford: Oxford University Press, 1983).
WORRALL, DAVID *Radical Culture: Discourse, Resistance and Surveillance, 1790–1820* (Hassocks: Harvester/Wheatsheaf, 1992).

Blake and Art Criticism

BARRELL, JOHN *The Political Theory of Painting from Reynolds to Hazlitt* (London: Yale, 1986).
BINDMAN, DAVID *Blake as Artist* (Oxford: Clarendon Press, 1977).
BINDMAN, DAVID *William Blake: His Art and Times* (London: Oxford University Press, 1982).
EAVES, MORRIS *William Blake's Theory of Art* (Princeton: Princeton University Press, 1982).
ESSICK, ROBERT N. *William Blake, Printmaker* (Princeton: Princeton University Press, 1980).
MITCHELL, W. J. T. *Blake's Composite Art: A Study of the Illuminated Poetry* (Princeton: Princeton University Press, 1978).
RAINE, KATHLEEN *William Blake* (London: Thames & Hudson, 1970).

Feminism and Psychoanalytic Criticism

This is trickier, partly because, as I have already noted, most of the work on Blake which relies on these approaches is confined to articles, while other, fuller, works, tend to indulge or endorse the image of 'mad' Blake. I list below some of the books and collections which seem at once interesting and persuasive.

ACKROYD, PETER *Blake* (London: Sinclair-Stevenson, 1995). A biography which, *inter alia*, makes intelligent use of psychoanalytic writings on Blake.
BLOOM, HAROLD (ed.) *The Marriage of Heaven and Hell* (New York: Chelsea House, 1987). (This contains several essays which develop either a feminist or psychoanalytic approach to Blake's work.)
FOX, D. 'The Female as Metaphor in William Blake's Poetry' in *Critical Enquiry*, no. 3. 1977, pp. 507–19.
PUNTER, DAVID (ed.) *William Blake: New Casebook Series* (London: Macmillan, 1992). As with Bloom's collection, this also contains essays which develop psychoanalytic or feminist perspectives on Blake.
WEBSTER, BRENDA S. *Blake's Prophetic Psychology* (Stanford: Stanford University Press, 1983).

Language and Deconstruction and Reader-Response Theory

To the Bloom and Punter collections listed above may be added the following:

COPLEY, S. and WHALE, J. *Beyond Romanticism: New Approaches to Texts and Contexts 1780–1832* (London: Routledge, 1992). Susan Matthew's essay is to be found in this collection.
CURRAN, S. *The Cambridge Companion to British Romanticism* (Cambridge: Cambridge University Press, 1993).
LARRISSEY, E. *William Blake, Re-Reading Literature* (Oxford: Blackwell, 1985).

Index

Note: some longer titles have been abbreviated, for ease of reference; the entry 'Blake's works' shows literary and artistic works in one sequence.